Money Secrets
the Pros Don't Want
You to Know

Money Secrets the Pros Don't Want You to Know

Stephanie Gallagher

American Management Association

New York · Atlanta · Boston · Kansas City · San Francisco · Washington, D.C.
Brussels · Tokyo · Toronto · Mexico City

This publication is designed to provide accurate and authoritative information in regard to the subject matter covered. It is sold with the understanding that the publisher is not engaged in rendering legal, accounting, or other professional service. If legal advice or other expert assistance is required, the services of a competent professional person should be sought.

Library of Congress Cataloging-in-Publication Data
Gallagher, Stephanie.
    Money secrets the pros don't want you to know / Stephanie Gallagher.
    p. cm.
    ISBN 0-8144-7893-X
    1. Finance, Personal. I. Title.
    HG179.G264   1995
    322.024—dc20   94-41741
                                                CIP

Printing number

10 9 8 7 6 5 4 3 2

Contents

Preface

Some things you'd just rather not know. Like what your teenage daughter is really doing when she stays out until 1 A.M. or how sausage is made. But when it comes to your money, it's different. You want to know exactly what's going on.

That's why I wrote this book. I know too many people who have been taken advantage of by bankers, realtors, car dealers, insurance agents, financial planners, lawyers, stockbrokers, and the IRS. And the sad fact is it could have been prevented. All they needed was just a little understanding of how things work, how the insiders manage their own money.

The fact of the matter is *you* are the best person to manage your own finances. You just need to know what the pros know. Now I'm not advocating that you go out and take the Certified Financial Planning course. Believe me, I've done that, and I can tell you that *Fundamentals of Risk and Insurance* is *not* good beach reading.

What's more, financial courses are way too theoretical. You'll get a wonderful analysis of geometric versus value-weighted stock index averages, but you won't learn a thing about how to pick stocks that will make you money.

For the best advice on everything from salary negotiations to estate planning, you need to know the secrets of the people who work in the business, the insiders who can help you separate the claims from the crock. In my work as a reporter for the banking industry and later an executive editor of investment and personal finance newsletters, I've had the opportunity to meet, interview, and study the tricks of the trade from some of the most knowledgeable bankers, brokers, investment advisors, mutual fund managers, insurance agents, real estate professionals, tax attorneys, and estate planning specialists in the business.

I've quizzed them on everything from the cheapest way to borrow money to the best ways to invest for retirement, and the answers are all right here. Even better, you don't have to be a pro to understand it.

You see, for all their years of experience and all their degrees and designations, these experts know that it doesn't take a Ph.D. in economics to manage your money intelligently. All it takes is an understanding of a few key facts, smart ways to use those facts, and the courage to do it yourself.

I can give you the facts. They're all right here in this book. You'll have to supply the courage yourself. Just remember, it's *your* money and *your* future we're talking about, and there's no one better qualified to take control of it than you.

STEPHANIE GALLAGHER
October 1994

Acknowledgments

I'd like to thank the following people without whom this book would not have been possible:

Claire Taylor, who said, "Why don't you write a book?"
So I did.

Margaret Russell, who said, "Be persistent."
So I was.

Jackie Simenauer, who said, "You're savvy. You're bright. I'm going to get you a contract for your book."
And she did.

Mary Schell, who said, "Why don't you try ..." and invariably a great idea followed.

Joanne Irving, who said, "You can do it."
She was right.

My mother, who said, "Tell them your mother said to buy it."
So I am.

My father, who said, "What if . . . ?" enough times that I learned anything was possible—even working through government red tape until you're blue in the face, so a Green Beret could come home from Vietnam to see his paraplegic sister one last time.

Mark Skousen, who has had more influence on my thinking about freedom and economics than he'll ever know.

Jay Schabacker, who went along with my ideas more times than I can count and whom I never thanked for it.

Dick Young, who taught me the incredibly powerful value of consistency.

Richard Stanton-Jones, Bob King, and *Tom Phillips*, who have made sure that I've never been without a challenge and who have encouraged me to spread my wings farther than I ever thought possible.

Tony Vlamis, my editor, who is proving every day that it is possible to have the passion of an entrepreneur and still succeed in corporate America and whose authors are eternally grateful for that fact.

And, of course, my wonderful husband, *Mark*, who always believed this book would happen—even when I didn't.

1
The Easy Road to Financial Freedom

There was a time when a fool and his money were soon parted,
but now it happens to everybody.

—ADLAI STEVENSON

Let me tell you a secret: Financial freedom doesn't come from making a lot of money. Anybody can make money. Donald Trump made money—a lot of money, in fact. But that still didn't prevent him from ending up in bankruptcy court for his prized Taj Mahal casino. And while he managed to escape filing for personal bankruptcy, he came dangerously close.

Wayne Newton wasn't so lucky. He did have to file for personal bankruptcy, despite having earned millions. Willie Nelson faced similar humiliation. The top country singer was reduced to putting his most prized possessions on the auction block to pay off the IRS.

The truth is it doesn't matter how much money you make. Millionaires go bankrupt every day. The problem isn't what they earn, it's what they do with what they've got.

Financial pros know that earning a lot of money is no guarantee of financial freedom. In fact, all too often, the wealthy find themselves in the same dire financial straits as the middle class: mountainous credit card debt, not enough money to pay the bills, a crushing tax burden, a meager retirement savings.

The solution: Be smart with what you have.

Secret #1
The One Financial Goal Everyone Should Have

Each of us has different goals—to buy a home, retire early, travel around the world—but there is one goal every one of us should have: a way to handle financial emergencies. The smartest technique? Create a liquid reserve equal to six months of your living expenses.

I know, six months' living expenses is a lot to save. But it's important. If something were to happen to you or your spouse, if you were to lose your job or someone in your family became seriously ill, how would you handle it? Most people would be broke within 90 days. Insurance is an important tool, but it won't cover everything. When things get tough, you'll need cash on hand.

How to save it? I say shove all your bills aside and start writing your own name on the "payable to" line. I'm serious. Every time you get paid, take out your checkbook and write a check to yourself. Consider it an obligation, a bill, just like your mortgage or car loan. Deposit it into a separate savings account or money market fund for emergencies. That way, you won't be tempted to touch it if things get tight one month.

Even better, pay yourself automatically. Simply decide where you want to put the money—in a savings account, money market account, mutual fund, or whatever (see Chap. 7 for suggestions). Then tell the financial institution or mutual fund company that you want to set up an automatic investment plan. Under these plans, the financial institution automatically deducts the amount you specify from your bank account or paycheck and puts it into your savings account.

You can set up the plan so that the money is withdrawn every week, every paycheck, every month, even every quarter. And many financial institutions allow you to invest as little as $25 or $50 a month. The beauty of this approach is that you don't have to make the decision every month whether you want to save or not. It forces you to do it because you have no choice! You have to act to stop saving—not to start.

It's the same technique those record companies use to get you to buy CDs and tapes. You sign up for six free CDs, then every month, a new CD is sent to you. If you want it, fine, but if you don't you have to send it back. If you've ever been a member of one of these clubs, you know what a hassle it is to send the CD back. Most of the time, you just end up keeping it. The goal of an automatic investment plan is to make it that hard to avoid saving.

Secret #2
How to Control Your Expenditures
Without a Budget

Do you often seem to end up with extra month after the money is gone? Are your friends, roommates, parents, or spouse pressuring you to stick to a budget? Well, I have just three little words for you: *Never say budget.*

How can I say this? Because like diets, budgets don't work. You start with good intentions. You set up a strict regimen, limiting yourself to only what's good for you, only what you absolutely need. But cravings inevitably sneak up on you, and soon you find yourself overwhelmed by a desire to eat those chocolate chip cookies or to buy that cashmere sweater. Suddenly, your diet or budget is out of whack, and you decide to forget the whole thing.

Sound familiar? Not to worry. You aren't alone. Budgets don't work because budgets are the opposite of financial freedom. They require a commitment to a way of life that depends on self-denial.

So how do you manage your money without a budget? By creating a spending plan that's livable for you. People who succeed at dieting don't deprive themselves of what they really want. It's the same with money. As JoAnn Skousen, co-author of *High Finance on a Low Budget* (Dearborn, 1993) puts it, choose to spend on what you really want, and you'll succeed in the long run.

Start by figuring out where the money is going now. How much are you really spending on entertainment? How much do you spend on vacations? Is that where you really want the money to go? If so, fine; you don't need to change a thing. But if you have a goal you're trying to reach, say buying a home, and you can't make it on what you're saving now, this will give you an opportunity to look at how you might do things differently.

Take a month and write down everything you spend. Every time you pull out your wallet, write a check, or use a credit card, jot down what you're buying and how much it costs. Remember, you're not projecting what you will or should spend, rather, you are simply recording what you *do* spend.

At the end of the month, bunch your expenses into categories such as rent, car payment, student loan, gas, insurance, utilities (telephone, water, cable, electric, gas), medical, gifts, clothes, etc. You can be as detailed or as general as you wish, but make sure you include categories for entertainment and pocket money.

Now look at your expenditures. How much do you spend on eating out? What about clothes? Impulse purchases? In my experience, most people are shocked when they see just where the money goes. When my husband and I were first married, we did this exercise and we were stunned to find out that we spent *over $400 a month* just on eating out. I didn't (and still don't) like to cook, so we ate out every weekend, as well as lunches during the week. And we typically went out for dinner at least one night during the week too.

I had no intention of staying home and cooking every night—cooking during the week was bad enough! But we were trying to save for a new home, and I just couldn't get it out of my head how much more we could be socking away if we ate out less. Finally, we decided to brown bag it to work at least three days a week. We stopped eating dinner out during the week altogether, and we decided that we'd only eat two meals out over the weekend (as opposed to three or four). Did we stop eating out entirely? Absolutely not. But we did manage to save an extra $200 a month with our new plan. And a year later, we bought our new home.

This strategy can work for you too. The key is to look at what you are spending. Then decide if that's where you really want the money to go. You'll have to make some adjustments, but don't deprive yourself of things you really want. If you do, you'll just end up wanting them more. So keep track of your expenditures, but if you decide to make some changes in your spending habits, give yourself enough leeway so you can still succeed in reaching your goals.

Secret #3
How to Live Debt-Free

There is nothing like the feeling of not owing anybody anything. Having a car that's paid off, no balances on your credit cards, and no personal loans—now that's financial freedom!

And the opposite is financial slavery. If you have large balances on your credit cards, an outstanding home equity loan or a huge balance on your car loan, your paycheck is essentially owned by the lender before it's owned by you! If you die, your lender gets paid first!

Now I'm not saying all debt is bad. Some loans, mortgages especially, can actually be more beneficial to you than paying cash. But other loans are outrageously expensive, loaded with profit for the lender. These are the debts I want you to pay off as soon as possible.

Start with credit cards. There is no good reason to owe money on your credit cards. The interest is often exorbitant (often 10 to 15 percentage points above the prime lending rate), and it isn't even tax-deductible. If you can, switch your balances to a card with a lower interest rate (see Secret #66) and pay if off as fast as possible. Don't charge anything new until your outstanding balance is down to zero.

Next, look at your remaining loans. If you have a large balance on your car or student loan, find out what kind of loan it is. Many car loans are installment loans with add-on interest, which means you'll owe the same amount of interest whether you pay it off early or not. If you have a loan like this, *don't pay it off.*

Similarly, if you have a very low interest rate loan or an older loan where you've already paid most of the interest and your remaining payments are mostly principal, don't pay those off either. Loans from your retirement plan and older mortgages would likely fall into these categories.

Finally, if the interest on your loan is tax-deductible, like a mortgage or home equity loan, it may not be in your best interest to pay if off early. It depends on how old the loan is, whether you'd rather have a tax deduction or less debt, and how long you plan to stay in your home. (See Secrets #31 and #32 for more about the advantages and disadvantages of prepaying your mortgage.)

The nice thing about paying down debt is that you not only gain the freedom of having more of your money to yourself, but you also guarantee a solid return on your investment. Think of it this way: Say you have $500 and you can choose between investing it in a stock mutual fund that *may* earn 10 percent, or paying off the balance on a credit card with a 15 percent interest rate. Paying off the credit card allows you to *lock-in* a 15 percent return. With the mutual fund, you hope for a 10 percent return. Now, which is a better use for your money?

Secret #4
A Simple Technique to Make the Money Come in Faster

Achieving financial freedom is more than paying off debt. It's also sound cash management. Your objective: to make the money come in as fast as possible. The smartest way to do that is with direct deposit of your paycheck.

Just about every employer, including the federal government, offers this wonderful service. Direct deposit allows your paycheck to be electronically deposited into your bank account on pay day.

A lot of people are uncomfortable with the idea of an employer having "access" to their bank accounts electronically. There's really no need to worry. Your employer doesn't have any more access than when you were being paid by check—it's just that with direct deposit, the transaction is handled via computers rather than paper.

But the benefits to *you* are significant: You gain use of your money immediately, rather than having to wait the two-to-five days it takes for a check to clear. Plus you don't have to actually physically deposit a check, which means no waiting in long teller lines, no 50-yard dash to get inside the door before the bank closes, no lunch hours spent in bank lobbies. And even if you're not at work the day you get paid, your check still gets deposited.

Direct deposit is a safe, quick, convenient, and smart way to manage your cash. Take advantage of it!

➤ **Inside Tip:** Social Security and many pension plans also offer direct deposit. Call your fund administrator or Social Security and sign up today!

Secret #5
How to Find a Financial Advisor You Can Trust

Have you come into a lump sum inheritance or pension plan payout recently? Are you a new parent and in need of a plan to fund your child's college education? Have your recently gotten married or divorced and need to develop a plan for managing your money? These are just some of the situations that may warrant the help of a financial advisor.

Financial planners can help you with a broad range of money management issues, from budgeting to estate planning, investment advice to insurance buying. Still, you can't expect a financial planner to be an expert in every area of money management. Try to identify the key areas you're interested in, say tax preparation or investment advice. Then make sure you find a planner whose areas of expertise match your needs.

You'll also want to be sure your planner is certified. Anyone can call themselves a financial planner—and many do. Look for the Certified Financial Planner (CFP) designation to ensure your planner has tested competently in basic areas of taxation, retirement planning, investing, insurance, and estate planning.

Be sure to ask the planner about her education and experience too. Try to find someone with at least three years of experience doing what you're interested in. So if, for example, you're looking primarily for investment advice and your planner has spent 15 years selling insurance, you'd better look elsewhere.

Once you've found someone you like, ask for references. Good planners will be happy to furnish you with names and numbers of satisfied clients. If yours won't, go elsewhere. It may indicate the planner has something to hide.

Finally, ask how the planner is compensated. It's important that you word the question that way, rather than, "How much do you charge?" You want to hear that the planner is fully compensated by the client (that's you). The technical term is a "fee-only planner."

If the planner says she is "fee-and-commission" or "commission-only," forget it. It's not that commission-based planners aren't competent; it's just that making recommendations in your best interest doesn't put meat on their tables. They know that when they recommend certain products, they get a commission. Now how objective do you think their advice is?

I want you to have someone whose driving force is to satisfy you. A certified, fee-only planner is the only one who can possibly fall into that category.

Secret #6
The Two Worst Places to Go for Financial Advice

If there's one thing I hate, it's salespeople pretending to be advisors. As a general rule, stockbrokers and insurance agents fall into this category. It's not that there aren't some very good stockbrokers and insurance agents out there—in fact, I've had the privilege of meeting several. But remember, stockbrokers and insurance agents earn their living in one way and one way only: by *selling* you something. Despite their impressive titles and expert command of technical language, they are still salespeople, just like the shoe salesman at Macy's. No more, no less.

And being salespeople, it is their job to try to sell you as much as possible. That's why your insurance agent is going to push whole life over term insurance. That's why your stockbroker is going to have a "hot tip" for you that's the same as his "hot tip" for every one of his other clients. That's why both of them will call you without invitation.

That doesn't mean that there aren't some very knowledgeable brokers and insurance agents out there. But the good ones are few and far between. If you've found one, terrific. If not, find your financial advice elsewhere and use your stockbroker and insurance agent for what they were originally designed to do: Execute *your* decisions.

2

Finding Your Castle in the Sky—At a Price Your Pocketbook Will Love

In the 1980s, we had a real estate boom. If you were in the market for a house then, the motto was, "Buy anything you can get your hands on. You'll make 20 percent in two years." Ah, those were the days. Unfortunately, they're long gone. Today, the best—in fact, the only—smart reason to buy a house is to live in it.

Yes, there are people who are experts at finding bargain properties, fixing them up, and selling them for a mint. Yes, you can get great deals by buying foreclosed property or property held by the Resolution Trust Corporation. Yes, there is the possibility that you could buy in an area just before a boom. But it is far more likely that that seemingly ideal fixer-upper is more trouble than it's worth. And after several years and several thousand dollars your "sure thing" investment won't have quite the luster it did when you bought it.

If your only reason for buying a house is as an investment, don't do it. Read Chap. 7 instead. You'll learn ways to get more for your investment dollar and save yourself a lot of heartache too. But if you want to buy a home to live in, read on …

Secret #7
How to Figure Out How Much House
You Can Afford

Figuring out how much home you can afford needn't be a mystery. All you need to do is divide your gross salary by 12. Then multiply by 0.28. That's the total amount you can afford to pay in principal, interest, taxes, and insurance. You may be able to stretch it more if you don't have a lot of other debt. Lenders like to see no more than 36 percent of your gross monthly income go to total debt, including your mortgage.

So if, for example, you make $50,000 a year, using the 28 percent guideline, you'd be able to afford a $1,166 mortgage payment. But say the only outstanding debt you have is a $250 car payment. You may be able to afford as much as a $1,250 mortgage payment, since that would bring your total debt to 36 percent of your income.

When you use FHA or VA financing, your "ratios" can be even higher. FHA financing will allow you to borrow up to 29 percent of your income, and you'll only have to put 5 percent down on the home. VA financing is even more liberal, allowing you to borrow up to 41 percent of your gross monthly income and requiring no money down. Also, many lenders will let you borrow more if you're buying an energy efficient house. The reasoning is simple: Your utility bills will be cheaper, allowing you to put more of your monthly income toward your mortgage.

➤ **Potential Trap:** Even though you may qualify for a higher mortgage, I'd still recommend borrowing no more than 30 to 32 percent of your gross monthly income. Otherwise, you could risk being "house poor." It's a 30-year trap that could cost thousands of dollars to get out of. Don't fall into it.

Secret #8
The Smartest Move You Can Make Before
You Go House-Hunting

Before you even scan the ads in the Sunday real estate section or set foot in a realtor's office, visit a mortgage lender and get prequalified for a loan. Not only will this allow you to get an idea of how much you can afford to borrow, but it will also give you a clearer picture of what your closing costs will be. And most importantly, it will give you leverage with the sellers.

Think of it this way: The sellers' main goal is to get rid of their house as soon as possible. They know that once they get an offer, they'll have to take their house off the market. They'll have to wait for you to get a loan approved, for an inspection (if you request it), and for any other contingencies you put into the contract to be removed. If you can speed that waiting process by coming in with a preapproved loan, you're a much more attractive buyer to them. That way, they can rest assured that at least you can afford the house.

Use this advantage to the fullest. When you make your offer, mention that you're preapproved for a mortgage and ask for a concession at the same time. The concession need not be on price. It could be a request for the sellers to do some repairs, settle on a certain date, or leave some furniture. Whatever your request, don't wait. Even a few minutes delay will allow the sellers to forget the benefit they're getting from having you as a buyer with a preapproved loan.

Secret #9
What First-Time Buyers Have That Other Buyers Don't

If you're a first-time buyer, you have a significant, and often overlooked, advantage that other buyers don't have: You can offer the seller a contract without a contingency requiring that your home be sold before you buy the new home.

This is a big advantage to sellers because it means they'll be able to settle as early as they want. Otherwise, they'd have to wait for the buyers to sell their home, which could take months, even years! What's worse, the buyers may not even be able to sell their home, which means the sellers would have had their home off the market for all that time with nothing to show for it.

When you make your offer, be sure to mention that you're renting (or living with your folks or whatever) and that you can settle within 30 to 60 days—if that's possible. If you're getting an

FHA loan, better allow 90 days. Then ask for whatever concessions you want. As I mentioned in Secret #8, it's best to ask for what you want right away. That way, the sellers can correlate the benefit you're giving them with the tradeoff you're asking for.

Secret #10
Your Down Payment May Not Be Your Biggest
Expense and What You Can Do About It

If I've heard it once, I've heard it a dozen times. The home-buyer's lament. "Oh, if only I could get together the money for a down payment, I could buy a home." It's a sad refrain, but unfortunately, not true. In many cases, in fact, you can buy a home with as little as 5 or 3 percent down.

That doesn't mean, however, that you won't need to come up with some serious cash at closing. Indeed, closing costs, those nasty little fees charged by the lender for things like credit checks and transfer taxes, can add up to as much as 6 to 8 percent of the mortgage. That's $6,000 to $8,000 cash on a $100,000 loan in addition to your down payment! Doesn't it make sense, then, to learn a few tricks for cutting closing costs?

First, assume everything is negotiable. Go over every line item with the mortgage lender and ask if each one can be reduced or simply waived. For example, some lenders will charge $100 or more for a document preparation fee. This is absurd. All document preparation means is that someone types up the forms. This is a cost of doing business for the lender and the tens of thousands of dollars you're paying in interest ought to cover it. The same goes for the application fee, attorney's fees (the bank's—not yours), and credit check. You can get your own copy of your credit report free (see Secret #81) and offer that to the bank. If they want something more, they ought to pay for it themselves.

Second, see if there is a cheaper way to pay for some of the closing costs. Title insurance, for example, is a must for any homeowner. But that doesn't mean you have to buy new title insurance. Ask the sellers if they have a title insurance policy that can be transferred to you. It could save you several hundred dollars. Also, be sure that you're buying title insurance for yourself as well as the lender. Most lenders require you buy lender's title insurance, which protects the bank's interest in the property. But if you don't have an owner's policy, you'll be left out in the cold should some distant cousin of a previous dead owner come back to claim her "inheritance."

Finally, try to avoid paying private mortgage insurance (PMI). If your down payment is less than 20 percent, the lender will require you to carry PMI, which can cost upwards of $1,000 at closing, plus a monthly premium. To avoid this, try one of these ways to come up with the 20 percent:

1. Borrow from a relative, friend, or your retirement plan.
2. Ask the owner to carry back a small, second mortgage (10 percent or whatever the difference is between what you can put down and 20 percent).
3. Get a cheaper mortgage, either an adjustable rate mortgage (ARM) or a two-step, and add the extra money the fixed rate loan would have cost you to your mortgage payment every month (making sure that the bank credits it to your principal). You'll still need PMI when you get the loan, but you'll build up equity faster, and once you have 20 percent equity in your home, you can ask the lender to drop the PMI.

Secret #11
Cut Your Costs by Borrowing From a Wholesaler

With borrowing costs on the rise, a new breed of mortgage lender has been born: the wholesaler. As in other businesses, wholesalers cut their costs by doing a high volume of business and cutting out the middlemen.

For example, Kennett Square, Pennsylvania-based InfoTrust (610/444-3333) is able to shave about three-eighths of a percentage point in interest off of its loans by giving borrowers wholesale, rather than retail rates. InfoTrust has 11 mortgage money suppliers who are linked through a computer network that can instantly size up the creditworthiness of buyers. By only lending to top-quality buyers, the lenders reduce their costs and pass on that savings to customers.

Another company, Bethesda, Maryland-based Wholesale Mortgage Centers, charges a flat $595 origination fee, regardless of loan size and gives wholesale rates too. How do they do it? No loan officers, low overhead, and a high volume.

Although the number of wholesale mortgage lenders is rather small right now, I look for the trend to spread as lenders look for ways to bring in borrowers who've been forced out of the market by rising interest rates.

Secret #12
Why You Should Never Trust
Your Real Estate Agent—
Even When You're the Seller

You hired her. You disclosed your income, savings, financial goals, and housing dreams with her. She even knows your kids' names and your dog's sleeping schedule. She's your real estate agent.

And despite the fact that she knows practically everything there is to know about your finances, I don't want you to trust her. She doesn't work for you. She works for the sellers. They're the ones paying her commission. And because of that, she's duty-bound to disclose to them any knowledge she has about your financial situation, negotiating strategy, or needs. That's why you should never, I repeat, never discuss your negotiating strategy with your agent. Never tell her how much you like the home. Never say what your bottom line price is. In fact, never discuss your finances with her unless you have to. The less the agent knows about you the better.

Of course, you can go the nontraditional route and hire a "buyer's broker" to represent you. But be careful: Most buyer's brokers these days are still paid by the sellers (see Secret #19). And if you aren't paying the buyer's broker yourself, I'd still treat the broker as you would any other real estate agent.

Now what if you're the seller? You can relax because the agent will do whatever is in your best interest, right? Wrong. Agents will plot strategy with you, give you suggestions for making your home more marketable, and try to work the deal to your advantage. However, they are still salespeople. As such, their goal is to sell the home, first and foremost.

Take this example. Say you've listed your home for $188,000. The buyer offers $182,000 and the agent talks the buyer into $185,000. You still don't want to budge. You're looking for full price and don't want to give in until you get it. But your agent keeps insisting how tough the market is and how hard it will be to find a buyer to pay full price. You reluctantly agree. Now look at what's happened. You've lost $3,000 in profit. And your agent has too, right? Nope. Your agent would've made $11,280 if you had sold the house for $188,000. She made $11,100 for selling it at $185,000. A $3,000 difference to you was only a $180 difference to her. It was even less ($90) if she had to split the commission with another agent.

Whether you're the buyer or the seller, don't be fooled into thinking the real estate agent works for you. *You* are the only one who has your best interests at heart. As long as you remember that, you'll be able to use real estate agents to your best advantage—not theirs.

Secrets #13–14
Two Ways to Save on Real Estate Commissions

If you want to save on real estate commissions, but don't want to go through the hassle of doing everything from advertising to writing contracts yourself, consider one of these options:

Secret #13
Use a Discount Broker

Discount brokerage services run the gamut, from bare bones agencies that just give you a "For Sale" sign to quasi-full service agencies that will help you set the price, advertise, prepare the contract, and even help the buyers locate financing.

One of the best deals around is offered by WHY USA (WHY stands for We Help You), an Arizona-based franchise that charges sellers a flat $990 fee, half to be paid up front, the other half at settlement. The fee covers six months of marketing, an appraisal, newspaper ads, and signs. WHY USA agents will also assist you in preparing the contract and will even represent you at settlement. Look in the yellow pages under Real Estate Discount Brokers for a WHY USA agency near you.

Secret #14
Offer to Use the Same Agent When You Buy

If you don't want to do any of the selling work yourself, but still want to find a way to cut the 6 percent commission, offer the realtor this deal: Tell her that you'll list your home with her and uses her to represent you when you buy your new home if she cuts her commission down to 4 or 5 percent. It'll be tough to get a realtor to go for 4 percent, because essentially, she'd really only be making 1 percent (she would have to give 3 percent to the agent who finds the buyer). But if the agent knows your new house will be more expensive, the 3 percent she'll get there may be enough to offset the 1 to 2 percent loss of commission on your old home.

Secrets #15–17
Three Smart Ways to Market Your Home
So It Sells *Fast*

Buying a home is an emotional decision. You want prospective buyers to imagine themselves living the life of their dreams when they tour your home. And you want to make it easy for them to evaluate the home to see if it meets their needs and if they can afford it. The following secrets will help you create an environment that is so inviting a prospective buyer will have no choice but to offer you a contract!

Secret #15
Presentation Is Everything

Before you put your home on the market, visit several model homes in your area of comparable size and price. Notice how they're decorated. Do they have wine glasses on a table by the fireplace to create a feeling of romance and luxury? Do they have bright colors and children's toys in a playroom to create the sense that a vibrant, fun-loving family lives there? Or maybe they're trying to appeal to high-powered career couples with an elegant cherry desk in an office and business magazines on the coffee tables.

Think about the kinds of people who might buy your home and

try to create a similar experience for them with your furniture. You don't have to go overboard—maybe it's just putting fresh flowers and guest towels in the powder room. Or rearranging the furniture so the rooms appear bigger or putting vanilla-scented oil on the lamps so the house smells like freshly-baked cookies. The point is you want prospective buyers to be able to imagine themselves living in your home and showing it to their friends and family with pride.

Secret #16
Real Numbers Make All the Difference

Once you've gotten prospective buyers to fall in love with your home, you have to make it easy for them to figure out their costs. Have a local lender draw up a sheet calculating monthly mortgage payments at various interest rates and with various down payments. Be sure to include your real estate taxes and an estimate of homeowner's insurance and homeowner's or condominium association fees. Print the lender's address and phone number on top of the sheet, so buyers can call for more information.

You may also want to include information about average utility bills, so buyers can get an idea of how your heating and electric costs compare to what they're spending now.

Secret #17
Souvenirs Give Buyers Something to
Remember Your Home By

When buyers go house-hunting, they typically see five to ten houses in a single day. To make yours stand out, give them something to take home with them that will remind them of your home. It need not be fancy, just a sheet of paper with a flattering picture of your home on the front and maybe a floor plan on the back (don't forget room measurements). Include useful information about nearby schools, places of worship, day care centers, transportation, pools, tennis courts, and other amenities that are part of the homeowner's association facilities or are located nearby.

If you're stumped as to what to include and how to present it, visit a new development in your area. See what the builders/developers there are giving prospective buyers and borrow their ideas. If it works for them, it ought to work for you too, right?

Secret #18
How to Price Your Home Effectively
Without a Real Estate Agent

Experts agree that the key to selling a home yourself is to price it effectively. If you price it too high, you could lose a lot of potential buyers who won't even consider it. If you price it too low, well, obviously, you lose potential profit. The question is how do you know what price is right? Enter Inpho Inc.

This Massachusetts-based company offers the Home Sales Line, a telephone service that lets you get detailed sales price information on homes in about 30 markets around the country. The service costs $5 to $6 (depending on where you live) for a five-minute search and allows you to look for home sales by street, specific address, or price range (the service is helpful when you're buying too). You get the address, sale price, and sale date for each home. Information dates back to 1989, and in some cases, you can even find out what the seller paid for the home. Call Inpho Inc. at 617/868-7050 for details.

Secret #19
How to Use and Find a Buyer's Broker

Buyer's brokers. They're the latest rage in home buying, and no wonder. Since traditional real estate agents work for the sellers, it only makes sense that buyers would want to hire someone who truly represents them. The problem is some buyer's brokers are still getting paid by the sellers.

Despite the new title, these buyer's brokers are still compensated by earning a commission from the seller. How then, I ask, is this person working for you? What could possibly be his incentive for getting you a better price on the home or warning you about potential pitfalls in the home?

Other buyer's brokers are paid by the buyers, usually an hourly fee, a flat fee, or a percentage of the purchase price. This arrangement is certainly preferable to the former, but it still has risks. For example, the broker may not be exclusively a buyer's broker. He may be working for you as a buyer's broker, but he may also have other traditional real estate listings. I'd avoid this kind of arrangement. It's too tempting for your broker to show you properties that he is also listing.

Buyer's brokers do provide a worthwhile service, but I'd only use one if you pay a flat or hourly fee. That way, you'll have an expert negotiator on your side, and you'll know he's working for you. You'll also have access to other homes not normally listed in the multiple listing services, including Fizzbos (For Sale By Owner homes). And theoretically, if the buyer's broker takes no commission, he ought to be able to get you a better deal on the purchase price, simply because the sellers are saving at least 3 percent.

If you're interested, ask your local Board of Realtors for referrals. Or contact the Buyer Broker Registry (800/729-5147) for help in finding a buyer's broker.

Secret #20
The Most Important Question to
Ask About a House—
It Could Save You Thousands

It's amazing how easy it is to have a win-win real estate negotiation, yet surprisingly few transactions are. The reason? Most buyers and sellers don't tell each other what they want. It's a simple enough idea, yet it's all too often ignored, as buyers and sellers set up all sorts of convoluted games of cat and mouse in vain efforts to get the best of each other. If buyers and sellers would just say what they really want, more often than not, they'd be able to give it to each other.

Case in point: I know a woman who was selling her house and planning to move to Florida to retire. She found a buyer, but the buyer could only come up with a 10 percent down payment. The buyer was also looking at a smaller house, and although she liked the bigger house better, if she bought the smaller house, she could put 20 percent down and avoid paying for private mortgage insurance (PMI).

Since the seller was planning to use the proceeds from the home in order to live, her main concern was income. But the buyer's main concern was avoiding having to pay for private mortgage insurance.

By having the seller carry back 10 percent of the purchase price, the buyer was able to get what she wanted (avoid buying private mortgage insurance) and was still able to pay the seller back at a higher interest rate than she could get at the bank. Now that's a true win-win situation!

Focusing on external issues like how low can you get the seller to go or what can you get the seller to throw in aren't important. What is important are your needs and the seller's needs.

➤ **Inside Tip:** The most important question to ask a seller is "Why are you selling?" Only after you know the answer to this will you be able to figure out what the sellers' needs are and how they compare with your own. Maybe they're being transferred and settling soon is more important to them than anything else. Maybe they want to start their own business and are planning to use the equity from the home to finance it.

If you listen carefully, you'll learn the sellers' true needs. And if you're creative, you'll often find they don't clash with your own. Then you can go to work finding a solution that benefits both of you.

Secret #21
The Negotiation Starts the Minute
You Set Foot in the Home

Most people think the negotiation starts when you make an offer, write a contract, or sit down at a table to hammer out disagreements. But in reality, the negotiation starts the minute you set foot in the home.

Use this time to your advantage. Think of it as an opportunity to gain information you'll be able to use later when the real "negotiation" has begun.

For example, as you're touring the house, pose casual questions like, "Have you considered a lease-purchase plan?" or "Have you thought about carrying back part of the financing?" to gauge how receptive the sellers are to creative financing.

Ask about the sellers' plans, how long they've lived in the home and where they're planning to move. Try to find out which issues are most important to them, while letting them know what your needs are.

Be sure to use language that encourages them to say "yes." For example: "How could you sweeten the deal with closing costs?" In this way, you're putting them in a position of convincing you to accept your idea as opposed to asking them for your concession outright.

A word of caution: I would not use this strategy on major issues like price. To sellers, price is everything, and as soon as you bring up the issue, you've put them on guard. Use it instead for gaining information, helping them understand your needs, and bringing up something they may not have considered such as throwing in some furniture, paying for repairs, or settling at a time that's convenient for you.

Secret #22
Two Things to Consider When Choosing a Mortgage

Once you've found the home of your dreams, the next step is figuring out how to pay for it. Today, mortgages come in almost as many flavors as Baskin Robbins ice cream, but choosing between them is no picnic. The good news is that there are really only two key points you need to consider in selecting a mortgage: (1) how long you plan to own the home and (2) what your tolerance for uncertainty is.

First, how long do you plan to own the home? Say you're buying a condominium, and you only plan to live in it for three years. Without a doubt, your best bet would be an adjustable rate mortgage (ARM).

Here's why: Interest rates on ARMs do just what the name says, they adjust (unlike fixed rate mortgages, which maintain the same interest rate for the length of the loan). Generally starting at about two percentage points lower than a fixed rate mortgage, a typical ARM will adjust no more than two points per year and no more than six points over the life of your loan. (ARMs do differ from lender to lender, so check with several lenders in your area for the specific rules on their ARMs.)

So say you wanted to borrow $125,000 and you could either get a fixed rate mortgage at 8 percent or an ARM starting at 6 per-

cent and adjusting up to 2 percent per year with a 6 percent cap.
Even if the ARM went up the full 2 percent per year, you'd still
end up paying *less* in total than you would with the fixed rate
mortgage:

	Fixed rate	Adjustable rate
Payment first year:	$917.21 (8%)	$749.44 (6%)
Payment second year:	$917.21 (8%)	$913.57 (8%)
Payment third year:	$917.21 (8%)	$1,086.32 (10%)
Total payments:	$33,019.56	$32,991.96

You'll notice that the ARM payment in the second year is
lower than the fixed rate payment in the second year, even
though both are at an 8 percent rate. That's because the ARM is
recalculated each year based on the number of payments left on
the loan and your remaining loan balance. So the second year's
rate is 8 percent for 348 payments (not the full 360 payments of
the fixed rate loan) on a loan balance of $123,465 (not the original
$125,000).

What if you know you won't stay 30 years, but you can't be
sure you'll sell in three years? Consider a two-step mortgage. These
mortgages offer a fixed rate for the first five or seven years that is
anywhere between 1/2 to 2 percent lower than the current market
rate for a fixed rate mortgage. After the fifth or seventh year, you
pay a fee, and the mortgage adjusts to the market rate. *I do not recommend the two-step unless you are absolutely certain that you will not
be in the home after the adjustment*—it is too risky (see Secret #25 to
find out why).

And even if you know you'll sell before the two-step were to
adjust, you still may want to go with a conventional, 30-year fixed
rate mortgage. The point is you must evaluate your own risk tolerance. If you can't stand the thought of watching your mortgage
payment go up every year, don't do it! You must be comfortable
with your decision.

Try this exercise to see if you can handle the uncertainty of an
ARM. Figure out what a 2 percent higher mortgage payment
would be, and ask yourself, could I handle that today? What about
a 6 percent higher payment? If the answer is "no" to either question, go for a fixed rate mortgage.

Secret #23
Five Questions to Ask When You're Shopping for a Mortgage

Once you've decided on the kind of mortgage you want, compare rates and terms from three to five lenders to find the best one. If you are a member of a credit union or are eligible to join, start there. Credit unions typically offer very competitive rates.

When you call around, there are really only five questions you need to ask:

1. What are your current rates for conventional financing? You'll typically get a list of options like, 9⅛ with no points, 8fl with 2 points, 8fi with 3 points, etc. Forget about whether or not you want to pay points for the moment. What you need now is simply a basis for comparison, and the best way to get it is to ask for the annual percentage rate (APR). The APR gives you the total cost of the loan, including points and finance charges. This way, you'll be comparing apples to apples when you get quotes from different lenders.

2. Can I lock in the rate? If so, for how long and what will it cost? Most lenders will charge anywhere from nothing to a percentage of the loan to lock in a rate. If you think rates are heading up, it's best to lock in as soon as possible. But be sure you can go to settlement within the lock-in period. If there's any chance that you won't be able to settle before the lock in expires, wait to lock in until you know you can settle within the lock-in period.

3. What other fees and closing costs do you charge? Be sure to ask specifically about private mortgage insurance (PMI) if you're planning to put down less than 20 percent and escrow money (lenders often hold money in escrow for payment of real estate taxes, mortgage insurance, homeowner's insurance, etc.).

4. What are the income requirements for this loan if I put down 20, 10, or 5 percent? The lender will typically quote you a ratio, like 28-35. That means no more than 28 percent of your gross monthly income can go toward your mortgage payment and no more than 35 percent of your gross monthly income can go toward total debt, including your mortgage payment.

5. Do you have any special deals now? The mortgage industry is constantly devising new and unusual ways to make loans more accessible to customers. These deals run the gamut from lender-sponsored programs, like shop 'n' lock, which allows you to lock in an interest rate while you're shopping for a home, to state and federal government programs that offer relaxed down payment requirements, closing cost help, and more lenient borrowing terms. These deals can be huge money-savers, so be sure to ask. You'd be surprised what's out there.

Secret #24
What to Look for in an ARM

Adjustable Rate Mortgages (ARMs) come in literally hundreds of different varieties, depending on the adjustment intervals, index used, adjustment margin, periodic and lifetime caps, convertibility, assumability, and prepayment penalities, to name a few. If you're interested in an ARM, look for the following features:

- *An initial interest rate of 2 to 4 percent lower than conventional 30-year fixed rate mortgages.*
- *Adjustment periods no shorter than every year and potentially as long as every 10 years.* You can get longer-term ARMs that adjust only once every three, five, or ten years. You can also get ARMs that have initial rates that last three, five, or seven years and then adjust every year after that. I find these longer-term ARMs especially attractive, since they keep your monthly payments much more stable than the traditional ARM.
- *An interest rate that adjusts based on the 11th District Cost of Funds Index.* All ARMs use some sort of index to base the adjustment on. Lenders take the current rate of the index and add a margin of 2.25 to 3 percent to come up with the rate you'll pay. It makes sense, then, that you'd want your loan to be based on the index least likely to rise dramatically. My choice: the 11th District Cost of Funds Index. This index is widely believed to be one of the most stable available for ARMs.
- *Rate caps of 2 percent or less for every adjustment and 6 percent or less over the life of the loan.* Rate caps are designed to cushion the blow of rising interest rates. You want to be sure that each time the loan adjusts, whether every year, three years, or longer, your rate is no more than 2 percent higher than your current rate. You also

want to be sure that you are protected from exorbitant interest rate increases over many years, hence the 6 percent cap for the life of the loan. That means if you have an initial interest rate of 6 percent, no matter how high interest rates go, you'll pay no more than 12 percent.

- *No payment caps.* A seemingly attractive feature, payment caps are really a potential time bomb for borrowers. They ensure that your monthly payment remains below a certain amount. The catch is if the interest you should be paying exceeds the cap, it is added on at the end of the loan. This is called *negative amortization*, and it means that you're not really paying off your loan. You're actually increasing the loan with every lower-than-market-rate payment you make. Avoid loans that have payment caps at all costs.

- *No prepayment penalty.*

- *A convertibility feature that charges you only if you convert.* The convertibility feature allows you to convert your ARM to a fixed rate mortgage at some point in the future, a useful tool to have. But it's important that you aren't paying for this privilege up front. Some lenders will charge you a higher interest rate on the ARM if it has a convertibility feature. I don't like this arrangement because you lose some of the benefit of getting a lower interest rate with an ARM and you may never even convert! Opt instead for a loan that charges you a fee *at the time you convert the loan.* This way, you'll be able to compare rates and terms more freely, without having to factor in what you've already paid in higher interest on the ARM.

Finally, ask if the loan is assumable. It's a nice feature to have, but certainly not worth passing up an attractive ARM for. If you can get an ARM with these features, go for it, whether the loan is assumable or not.

Secret #25
The Hidden Surprise of Some
Two-Step Mortgages

Most two-step mortgages adjust to the current market rate after an initial period, usually five to seven years, of an introductory below-market rate. The problem is some two-step mortgages are not really 30-year mortgages. They are five- or seven-year mortgages with bailout provisions for the lender.

These come in several varieties. One provision allows the lender to review your creditworthiness at the time of the adjustment. If the lender deems it unsatisfactory, you'll have to refinance or pay the rest of the mortgage in single lump sum (a balloon payment). Another nasty provision allows the lender to force you to refinance or pay off the loan if interest rates are significantly higher (usually 5 or 6 percent) than your initial rate.

I would avoid two-step mortgages with these kinds of provisions. The easiest way to ensure you have a two-step mortgage that's really good for 30 years is to make sure it is backed by the Federal National Mortgage Association (Fannie Mae). Fannie Mae requires that the two-step loans it backs are 30-year loan commitments.

Secret #26
The Truth About FHA Mortgages

Contrary to popular belief, FHA mortgages do not have income requirements and are not for first-time home buyers only. The only qualifications are that the loan amount not exceed a specified amount set by the government, currently $151,725 (the limit is based on local housing costs and will be lower in areas where housing costs are lower).

Of course, you still have to qualify for the loan, but FHA allows borrowers to borrow up to 29 percent of gross monthly income for principal, interest, taxes, and insurance and up to 41 percent for total monthly debt (including the mortgage payment). If the home meets certain standards for energy efficiency, the qualifications are even more liberal: 31 percent of gross income for the mortgage payment and 43 percent of total debt.

In addition to these liberal qualifications, FHA mortgages allow you to put down as little as 3 percent, and you can wrap your closing costs into the loan. Also, FHA loans are assumable to qualified buyers who plan to live in the home, a feature that can enhance the resale value of your home.

However, FHA loans do generally take longer to process (thanks to all the paperwork required by the government) and the rates may be higher than current market rates for conventional loans in your area. And FHA loans have hefty mortgage insurance requirements, requiring both an up-front fee of 2.25 percent and an annual premium of 0.50 percent.

Before you commit to an FHA loan, shop around. It's a great way to get a low-down-payment loan with liberal borrowing requirements, but many lenders have other programs and special deals that may also have relaxed income and/or down payment requirements.

Secret #27
How to Buy a Home With Just 3 Percent Down

One of my favorite special loan programs is the Fannie Mae Community Home Buyer's Program. (Fannie Mae does not lend money directly to home buyers; it sets mortgage standards for lenders and buys loans on the secondary market from lenders that meet those standards.)

With the Community Home Buyer's Program, you can borrow up to $203,150 and put down only 5 percent. Plus, only 3 percent of the 5 percent needs to come from you; 2 percent can be a gift from parents, relatives, even your employer. And the loan requirements are much more lenient, allowing your monthly payment to consume as much as 33 percent of your gross monthly income and as much as 38 to 40 percent of your total monthly debt. What's more, you won't have to come up with two months mortgage payments in reserve at settlement, as most conventional loans require.

There is an income requirement: You can only participate if your income does not exceed 115 percent of the median income in your area. But the median income can be quite high in areas like Washington, D.C. and New York. And you don't have to be a first-time buyer to qualify for a Community Home Buyer's loan.

For more information, contact Fannie Mae at 800/732-6643.

Secret #28
A Single Source for Finding the
Best Mortgage Deal

Whatever mortgage you choose, you'll want to compare the rates and terms of several lenders in your area. If you don't have the time or inclination to call, contact HSH Associates at 1-800-UPDATES.

For $20, HSH will send you a listing of lenders with the best rates in your area (updated weekly) and a 42-page booklet, "How to Shop for a Mortgage."

Secret #29
Why One-Third of ARMs Cost Borrowers More Than They Should

Horror stories of incorrect ARM loan calculations abound. Some experts estimate that 50 to 70 percent of ARMs are calculated incorrectly! If you feel you've been overcharged, you can have a mortgage review company check into it for you. For example, Gaithersburg-based Loantech (800/888-6781) will review your mortgage papers for the entire term you've held the loan for a $95 fee. Then they'll issue a report, indicating whether or not mistakes have been made. You can then send the report to your lender with a letter asking them for a prompt refund. Loantech estimates 30 to 50 percent of the loans they review contain errors, and 99 percent of lenders rectify the situation promptly.

Secret #30
What a Home Inspection Won't Tell You

I am all in favor of having a home inspection—in fact, I'd recommend it even if you're buying a brand new home. But don't expect a home inspection to reveal every potential problem you may have with the home. The home inspector can't pull up carpeting or tear down walls to ensure everything is up to code through and through.

Inspectors will test and examine the condition of things that are clearly visible, such as conditions of the porch, gutters, chimney, downspouts, and roof. The inspector will also test the electrical, plumbing, heating, and cooling systems. And he will try to estimate how long items, such as furnaces, will last. But don't expect the inspector to be a soothsayer. He can't predict the future any more than you can.

Still, having an inspection is a good idea. After all, how else would you be able to discover flaws? At least you'll have some idea of the condition of what you're buying, and you'll be able to ask the seller or builder to correct problems before you go to settlement.

➤ **Inside Tip:** Don't use an inspector recommended by a realtor. These inspectors are notoriously broker-friendly. After all, continued referrals are contingent on satisfied clients, and if the broker is doing the referring, he's the client—not you. Find your own inspector through referrals from friends or relatives. That way, you can be sure the inspector is working for *you* and only you.

Secret #31
How to Slash Your Mortgage Interest Payments and Boost Your Net Worth at the Same Time

One of the smartest investments you can make is to prepay your mortgage. Prepayment is essentially adding additional payments to your principal, which increases your equity in the home and reduces the amount of interest you'll owe over the life of the loan. And the savings can be dramatic. For instance, if you prepay just $50 a month on a $100,000, 8.5 percent loan, you'll slash $3,722 off your loan in just five years. After 10 years, you'll save $9,407!

Plus, you're getting a guaranteed return on your money and you won't be taxed on your "gains" as you would be with stocks, bonds, mutual funds, or even a savings account.

Of course, you won't have access to your money the way you would with a savings account, mutual fund, or a stock, but that can be a good thing too. Having ready access to savings means being able to spend it easily too. Since you won't be able to "withdraw" your investment in your home until you sell, you won't be able to deplete it easily either.

Prepayment isn't for everybody, though. See Secret #32 to decide if it's the best use of *your* money.

Secret #32
What's Wrong With Prepaying Your Mortgage

When you prepay a mortgage, you're essentially making an invest-ment that earns the interest rate of your loan. So if you've got a 30-year mortgage with an interest rate of 10 percent, for every $100 you prepay you're essentially earning $10 (10%)—not a bad return. But there's a catch: You're also giving up a tax deduction. Because you'll be paying less interest on your loan, you'll also have less to deduct on your tax return.

In general, you want to put your money where it can work hardest for you. Ask yourself the following questions:

1. *How long have I lived in the home?* If you've lived in the home 20 or 25 years, most of your payment is already going toward principal. You aren't getting a huge tax deduction at this point anyway, so prepaying may make sense if you like the idea of being debt-free. On the other hand, your mortgage payment is low by today's standards. Plus, there's no need to rush to pay off the home if you could better invest the money elsewhere.

2. *How long do I plan to stay in the home?* If you plan to move soon and want to build up your equity in the home, prepayment is an excellent tool. It ensures that your savings goes toward exactly what you intend it for, and you won't be tempted to use the money for something else, as you might if you put it in a mutual fund, for example.

3. *How much do I have to invest?* If you have $500 or less to invest, it'll go much further if you use it to prepay your mortgage than it would if you bought stock, for example. Your $500 won't go far in buying stock once you consider commissions. With prepayment, all of your money goes to work for you.

4. *What is the interest rate on my loan?* In general, the higher the interest rate on your loan, the more benefit you'll get out of prepaying your mortgage. If your interest rate is relatively low (like under 10 percent) and you can get a higher return elsewhere, prepayment may not be for you.

5. *What kind of loan do I have?* If you have an ARM, two-step, or some other form of adjustable rate mortgage, prepayment is an excellent idea. Since each new adjustment is calculated on your remaining loan balance, the lower the balance, the lower your payment after the adjustment.

6. *What else could I be doing with the money?* You need to consider your other options. Do you have a high interest-rate credit card, for example? If so, paying off that debt first will yield you better returns than prepaying your mortgage. But if your alternative would be to put the money in a stock mutual fund, think twice.

First of all, your return isn't guaranteed. That 15 percent annualized return the fund is touting is an average, calculated over a long period of time, like 15 years. It doesn't mean that you'll actually make 15 percent. Also, you'll owe taxes on the fund's gains unless you shelter it in a retirement account.

Once you've considered these questions, you'll be able to see if prepaying your mortgage makes sense. And remember, it's not an all or nothing choice. You can prepay one month and then never again. Or you can use some of your investment money for prepayment and put the rest in a money market account or stock fund. The point is to try to put your money where it will work hardest for you.

Secret #33
Why You Shouldn't Take Your Bank's Offer for a Discounted Mortgage Payoff

As mortgage rates rise, banks will do whatever they can to get rid of low-interest-rate mortgages. That includes offering customers with low-rate loans a discount of 5 to 25 percent to payoff their mortgages early in one lump sum.

It's a great deal for the bank: It gets rid of a low-rate loan and gets to lend the money out to a new customer at a higher rate. Unfortunately, it's not such a good deal for you. If rates are high, you can probably earn more on your investments than you're paying out in interest. Plus, you're still getting a tax deduction for the mortgage interest. And if you pay off less than the full value of the debt, the IRS will tax you on the difference. So if the balance of your mortgage is $7,000 and the bank offers to let you pay it off for $5,000, you'll owe taxes on $2,000.

Reject the bank's offer. It's a bad deal for you any way you look at it.

Secret #34
How to Make Sure Your Mortgage Payment Is Always on Time

For most of us, paying the mortgage is top priority, and it should be. But it's also probably the largest bill you pay each month, so it doesn't make sense to pay it too early. For one thing, you may not have the money. For another, you'll lose use of that money and any interest you're earning on it once you send the check. That's why smart homeowners ask their mortgage lenders to debit their checking accounts on the day the mortgage payment is due.

Just about every mortgage servicer will comply with this request even if they don't have a specific direct debit program in place because it's cheaper for them. But more importantly, it's smart money management for you. It'll give you full use of your money until the date the mortgage is due. So if you get paid on the last day of every month and the mortgage is due on the first, you won't have to write a check before the money from your paycheck is actually in the account.

In addition, if you have an interest-bearing checking account, you'll gain interest on your money until it is debited. And you'll ensure that the mortgage payment is always on time. This is especially important if you have a very low-interest-rate loan or a special two-step loan where the mortgage servicer will be looking for any excuse to call the loan.

Secret #35
The Two-Percentage-Point Refinancing Myth

Homeowners commonly hear that it only makes sense to refinance if current interest rates are at least two percent lower than their interest rate. Nonsense! What matters is how much it'll cost to refinance compared to how much money you'll save and how long you plan to stay in the home.

Look at it this way: Say your current mortgage payment is $840 for a $100,000 loan at 9.5 percent. Your outstanding balance is $90,000 now, and you could refinance at 8.5 percent. Your new payment would be $692, which means you'd be saving $148 a month.

Now figure out what your closing costs will be. Say your closing costs will run around $1,500. It will take a little over 10 months to recoup that cost, given a savings of $148 a month. So even though the interest rate is only 1 percent lower, if you're planning to stay in your home longer than 11 months, it's worth it to refinance.

In fact, the longer you plan to stay in the home, the more it makes sense to refinance. Do the numbers yourself!

Secret #36
How to Refinance for Next to Nothing

When you refinance the traditional way, you'll have to pay many of the same closing costs you paid when you got your original loan: an application fee, credit report, appraisal fee, taxes, survey, title insurance, etc. But if you get a *streamline refinance*, you may be able to eliminate all but one or two of those fees.

FHA, Fannie Mae, and Freddie Mac all offer streamline refinancing programs that enable borrowers to shift to current market rates at a very low cost. To qualify, your loan must be FHA-insured or held by Fannie Mae or Freddie Mac. Check with your mortgage lender to see if your loan qualifies and what the costs are. It could save you hundreds of dollars.

Secret #37
How to Refinance With Less Than
10 Percent Equity

It used to be that you had to have at least 10 percent equity in your home in order to refinance. No more. Fannie Mae and Freddie Mac will now allow borrowers to refinance with just 5 percent equity in their homes. To qualify, you must live in the house, you must be getting a fixed rate loan, and you can't get any cash out of the refinancing. Check with your lender for details.

3
Let Your Feet Do the Talking: How to Demand the Best From Your Bank

Banks have a great thing going. I mean, if you're going to go into business, you can't go wrong selling money. Am I right? Even better, people don't seem to have very high standards for their banks. They don't demand price breaks or good service or even recognition of loyalty. It's a good deal any way you look at it—from the bank's perspective.

From your perspective, however, it's ridiculous. There's nothing wrong with being loyal to a business that has served you well, but if you aren't getting what you want, walk! You should be as demanding of your bank as you are of your local dry cleaners or pizza joint—at least! The following secrets will help you determine what to look for and how to get it.

Secret #38
How to Ensure Your Bank Is Safe

Worry about your bank's interest rates, worry about the service, worry about the monthly maintenance fee on your checking account, but you should never have to worry about your bank's safety. Above all else, a bank should give you that.

To check on a bank's safety, first find out if it's federally insured. State insurance isn't good enough. State insurance funds can go bankrupt and often provide less than the $100,000 insurance limit of the Federal Deposit Insurance Corporation (FDIC) and the National Credit Union Share Insurance Fund (NCUSIF).

But even if a bank is federally insured, it still may be troubled. For a $10 fee ($5 for each additional bank), Veribanc will give you an overall rating of your bank's health. Call Veribanc at 800/442-2657 for that extra peace of mind.

Secret #39
Why the Best Place to Bank May Be No Bank

What do you use a bank for? A credit card? Your car loan? A safe place to keep your cash and gain access to it on demand? Banks do provide useful services, but all too often they charge dearly for them. There are better, cheaper, and safer alternatives for your money. Credit unions top the list.

Credit unions tend to pay higher interest rates on savings and checking (share draft) accounts. They generally have very low service fees and minimum balance requirements. And they typically offer better interest rates on car loans, credit cards, and other loans. Plus, your money is guaranteed by the National Credit Union Share Insurance Fund up to $100,000 per credit union, just like the FDIC. (And unlike the FDIC, the NCUSIF is very well-capitalized.)

The only drawback: You have to be eligible to join a credit union. Credit union members share a common bond, usually through their employers or the military or a trade association of some sort. To find out if there's a credit union you may be eligible to join, write to the Credit Union National Association at Box 431, Madison, WI 53701.

Secret #40
The Only Five Questions to Ask When
Shopping for a Checking Account

Once you've found a few financial institutions you're interested in, there are really only five questions you need to ask to find a good deal on a checking account:

1. What is the minimum balance requirement? Start by asking what is the minimum balance you have to maintain in order to avoid a monthly service charge. Then ask how the minimum balance is calculated. Some banks will use the lowest balance of the month. So if your account drops below the minimum for even one day, you'll be assessed a fee.

➤ **A Better Way:** Choose a bank that uses an average daily balance method to calculate the monthly minimum.

2. What is the monthly fee if my balance drops below the minimum? If you choose a checking account that requires a minimum balance, the best way to ensure you always have it is to subtract that amount from your checkbook and just act like the money isn't there. But sometimes that isn't feasible. If you know your balance will fluctuate, be sure to find out what the fee will be if it drops below the minimum.

3. What other fees are associated with this account? Ask about per check fees, overdraft charges, automated teller machine (ATM) fees, and fees for point of sale (POS) debit transactions. POS debit is like using an electronic check. You use your ATM card to pay for things, and the amount is electronically debited from your account automatically. Most banks don't yet charge for this service, but I expect they will in the future. Some retailers also charge a nominal fee for POS transactions. You can find out about a retailer's POS fees at the time you make the purchase. It's best to find out about your bank's fees up front before you use the service.

4. How can I get a checking account that pays interest? Most banks offer interest-bearing checking accounts (also called NOW accounts), but they often require huge minimum balances of $5000 to $10,000. I find that outrageous! Ask if there are any other ways to get free checking with interest. For example, some banks will allow you to combine checking, savings, and money market balances to meet the required minimum. Others will even waive the minimum in certain circumstances. See Secret #41 for more ways to get totally free checking with interest.

5. How is the interest computed? If you have an interest-bearing checking account, it's important to find out how the bank calculates that interest. The best way is from day of deposit to day of withdrawal, compounded daily. That way, all of your money is working for you all the time.

Also, find out if the interest rate is tiered. Many banks offer a higher rate of interest if your balance goes above a certain floor, say $1000 or $5000.

Secret #41
How to Get Totally Free Checking

The ideal checking account would have no monthly service charges, no minimum balance requirements, no per check charges, and no ATM or POS fees. It would earn interest and offer you a higher rate for higher balances. Sound impossible? Au contraire. The trick is to ask for it!

Few people know it, but everything in banking is negotiable. Banks are just like any other business. If it's in a bank's best interest to give you totally free checking, you'll get it. So how do you make it in the bank's interest?

For starters, offer to have your paycheck directly deposited in the account (see Secret #4). Banks love direct deposit because it saves them money. Paper checks are inordinately time-consuming and expensive to process. With direct deposit, banks simply receive an electronic message to deposit a certain amount in your account, and boom—it's done! No fuss, no muss, no expensive back-office processing. Ask the bank to waive the minimum balance (or monthly service charge) if you agree to have direct deposit of your paycheck.

If that doesn't work, try the loyal customer routine. Explain that you have a CD or a savings account and you'd be willing to roll that money over into a new account with the bank if you could get free checking. Or mention that you'll be in the market for a car loan or mortgage in a few months, and you'd be willing to get it from the bank if you could get free checking. Or say that you already have a car loan or student loan or savings account with the bank and you'd like to get a break on your checking account.

Sometimes all you have to do is ask. Think of it as having your house painted. You'd certainly get the painters to bid for the job, wouldn't you? Well, banks are in business just like painters. Let them know they have to ask for your business, and they will.

Secret #42
How to Shave 60 Percent Off the
Cost of Your Checks

Most people think they have to buy their checks from a bank. Nonsense! This is just another myth banks like to perpetuate so they can make extra money. Think about it: What is a check? A piece of paper with printing on it. That's all. There's nothing magical about it. So why would you go to a bank to buy your checks? After all, the bank isn't in the printing business. The bank will just send the order out to a printer anyway, so why not cut out the middleman?

A number of check-printing companies sell directly to the public, including Custom Direct Check Printers (800/272-5432), Designer Checks (800/239-9222), Current Inc. (800/533-3973), and Checks in the Mail (800/733-4443). Most charge around $4.95 or $5.95 for a 200-check order (regardless of the pattern or style you want) and a $1 to $3 shipping and handling fee. Compare that to the $15 to $20 charged by most banks.

Secret #43
How to Avoid ATM Fees

I love ATMs. I think they're one of the greatest inventions of the twentieth century. But I'm not willing to pay $1 a pop for the privilege of using them. And you shouldn't be either. If you go to an ATM just twice a week, that's $100 a year in fees! If I handed you a $100 bill, would you throw it out the window? Of course not. Yet that's exactly what you're doing when you pay for ATM transactions. As the former editor of a publication that covered ATM technology, I am the last person to advocate you give up the convenience of ATMs. I just want you to use them smarter.

First, find out from your bank if it allows any free ATM transactions. Most banks will let you use their own ATMs without paying anything. They typically only charge when you use another bank's ATMs. If that's the case, use only your bank's ATMs. Other banks will allow you a certain number of free ATM transactions per month. If so, try to stick within that range.

If your bank doesn't offer any way to get free ATM transactions, I'd switch banks. I'm serious—there are just too many banks out there offering free ATM usage for you to have to pay for it. Then take the $100 you'll save in fees and invest it in yourself. You deserve it!

Secret #44
Why You May Be Paying ATM Fees
Even If Your Bank Doesn't Charge Them

There's a sneaky little ATM charge very few people know about, and it may be costing you big bucks. It's called an ATM surcharge. Unlike typical ATM fees, which are assessed by *your* bank, a surcharge is levied by *the bank that owns the ATM you're using*. So even if your bank charges no fees for using other banks' ATMs, you could still be paying an ATM transaction fee. And if your bank does charge a fee for using other banks' ATMs, you could be paying for one ATM transaction *twice*. Here's how it works:

Say you bank with Smallsville Bank, which charges you $1 for ATM transactions. You're in the airport, desperate for cash, and you spot a Megabucks Bank ATM. You use it to get $60. Three weeks later, you get your bank statement, and it has a $2 fee for ATM usage. Did Smallsville Bank suddenly double the fee for its ATM transactions? No. Megabucks Bank levied the additional $1 fee.

Surcharging is not yet widespread, but it is growing. Most banks that surcharge typically do so only in prime locations, like airports, casinos, and hotels. To avoid surcharges, read the screens on the ATM and notices around the machine carefully. Banks are required to disclose surcharge fees there. Look for phrases like, "This transaction may cost you $1." If you see such a phrase, it's a surcharge *in addition to* what your bank normally charges for ATM transactions. If you can, use a different machine. It's bad enough to have to pay once for ATM transactions, but twice is unbearable!

Secret #45
The Cheapest Way to Get Cash Abroad

Forget the traveler's checks. Pack your ATM card for the cheapest, most convenient way to get cash abroad. Like traveler's checks, your ATM card gives you a secure way to access cash overseas (as long as you don't keep your Personal Identification Number [PIN] with your card), but it's much cheaper because you'll get the wholesale exchange rate (the rate banks charge each other, not the rate they charge customers). Plus, you'll save on commissions and other fees banks charge retail customers to exchange money. Of course, you'll still have to pay whatever ATM transaction fee your bank normally charges for using other bank's ATMs, so avoid getting cash in small increments.

To make sure your ATM card can be used overseas, look to see if it has a Plus or Cirrus logo on it or call your bank and ask if it's a member of Plus or Cirrus. These are the international ATM networks. Then make sure you have a four-digit numerical PIN. If you don't, ask your bank to issue you one. Foreign ATMs don't use five-digit or letter PINs. Finally, ask your bank how well represented its network is in your destination country. Both Plus and Cirrus have plenty of affiliated banks in most of the top travel spots, but some destinations favor one network over the other.

Secret #46
What's Wrong With Debit Cards

I'm a big proponent of debit cards. I use my debit card to buy gas, groceries, and anything else that I would have paid cash for (as long as the merchant accepts it). But debit does have one drawback: You lose float—the time between when you make a purchase and when you pay for it. Despite the fact that debit cards are touted as electronic checks, they really aren't. For unlike a check, where you'd gain at least two days between the time you write it and the time it clears, a debit transaction is posted almost immediately. Like cash, the money is removed from your checking account the minute you make the purchase.

So if you're using a debit card in place of a check, say, at the grocery store, be sure you have the money in your account to cover the transaction. Otherwise, you could be hit with a nasty overdraft fee.

Secret #47
How to Use Debit Cards and Still Gain Float

There is a little-known kind of debit card that allows you to pay for purchases electronically and still gain the float of a check. It's called an *offline debit card* and can be found under the Visa Debit or MasterCard Debit logos.

Just like a Visa or MasterCard credit card, Visa Debit and MasterCard Debit cards are accepted at thousands of locations worldwide—everywhere that Visa or MasterCard credit cards are accepted, in fact. The Visa and MasterCard debit cards even look like Visa and MasterCard credit cards. But there's one important difference: When you "charge" a purchase, the money is automatically debited from your checking account.

You do not get a bill at the end of the month. You do not write a check to pay for the month's purchases. And you do not have the option of carrying over a balance to the next month. It is a debit card, and as such, it is tied to your checking account and is only available to you from your own bank (unlike a credit card, which you can get from any bank). But unlike most debit cards, these offline debit cards have float built into them—sometimes as much as two weeks—because they are processed through the normal credit card channels. That also means that you can use your Visa Debit or MasterCard Debit card anywhere that Visa or MasterCard is accepted. The merchant won't know whether it's a credit or a debit card, and it doesn't matter.

▶ **Inside Tip:** To gain all the benefits of a debit card with the float of a check, call your bank and ask if it offers a Visa Debit or MasterCard Debit card.

Secrets #48–50
Three Common Myths About Lending—
They Could Be Costing You Big

Perhaps it's the blue pinstripe-suited vice presidents, the marble lobbies, or the imposing loan application forms. Whatever the reason, banks just have a way of intimidating folks. There's no reason for it, of course. Banks are just a business like any other. Yet this aura of we're-doing-you-a-favor-for-allowing-you-in-here still surrounds many banks. And truth be told, I think they like to perpetuate it. And why not? It's a great business tool for them. Only problem is it could be costing you big time. The following secrets will help you separate banking fact from fiction, and could save you a ton of money in the process.

Secret #48
Banks Need to Lend More Than
You Need to Borrow

I call the lending process "The Big Lie." Banks act like they're doing you a favor by granting you a loan, when in fact, nothing could be further from the truth. Banks need to lend money in order to stay in business. Lending is the way banks make money. Without loans, banks would go bankrupt! So next time you're applying for a loan and feeling intimidated, think about this: The loan officer is really a salesman. It just so happens his product is money. But just as if he were selling shoes, he needs for you to buy that money. If you don't, he makes no commission. Kind of sheds new light on the loan process, doesn't it?

Secret #49
All Loans Are Not Created Equal

Loans of the same type can differ dramatically from one another, not just in interest rate, but in terms, penalties, fees, and a number of other things. The most common misconception is that two loans with the same interest rate and same length of payments will cost the same. Not true. It depends on the type of loan and how the interest is calculated.

On a simple interest loan, interest is paid only on the loan balance outstanding. So if you pay off the loan early, you've only paid interest on the amount you borrowed, not the balance you paid off.

In contrast, most installment loans are front-end loaded, meaning you pay add-on interest on the original loan amount *throughout the life of the loan*. In calculating the loan this way, the dollar amount you pay in interest is significantly higher than you'd pay with simple interest. Plus, you get no benefit from paying the loan off early, because you'll still owe the same amount in interest.

So when you compare loans, ask how the interest is calculated as well as the APR and the length of the loan.

Secret #50
Loan Rates and Fees Are Negotiable

Most banks offer set rates and fees for each type of loan they make. But what they don't tell you is that the more attractive you are as a customer, the more negotiable those rates and fees are.

Before you approach a bank for a loan, get a copy of your credit report (see Secret #81 for how). Then shop around; get quotes from at least a dozen banks. Once you've narrowed it down, call the two or three with the best deals and ask if they can beat each other's best deals. If you have no blemishes on your credit report, use that as a selling point. If you are a loyal customer, mention that. If you are willing to have your bank account debited for the loan payments, offer that. You'd be surprised what great things come to those who ask!

Secret #51
How to Get a Loan With a Poor Credit Record

Getting a copy of your credit report before you apply for a loan is essential if you think you have a blemish or two on your record. You need to know where you stand before you try to get the loan. If, as you suspected, there are negative ratings on your credit report and you can't get them removed, tell the credit bureau you want to write a note of explanation to be attached to your report. By law, the credit bureau has to honor that request (see Secret #82). Then when you apply for the loan, let the loan officer know of your blemish right up front and explain the circumstances surrounding it. The bank will be much more willing to make a "risky" loan to someone who discloses a problem up front than to one who tries to hide problems.

Secret #52
The Worst Source for a Loan

I'm certainly no fan of using banks to borrow money if you can get a better deal elsewhere. But elsewhere *never* means a credit card. I know it's tempting to have a $2,000 to $10,000 credit line at your fingertips. No paperwork to fill out, no waiting period, no possible rejection. But believe me, you'll pay dearly for this convenience. Credit cards typically charge interest rates of 2 to 10 percent higher than the average car, mortgage, or home equity loan. That's $390 to $2,195 more in interest on a $5,000 loan over three years. You could go to the Caribbean on what you'd save! Now isn't that worth filling out a little paperwork?

Secrets #53–55
The Three Best Sources for a Loan

When you borrow, the name of the game is to get the loan at the lowest possible total cost to you. And remember, your costs include not only the interest rate, but the length and terms of the loan as well as closing costs and tax considerations. With an eye toward these criteria, check out the following low-cost ways to borrow:

Secret #53
Borrow From Your Retirement Plan

Your 401(k) is an excellent source for a loan because your borrowing costs are practically nil. You'll get a low interest rate. And everything you pay will go right back into your own pocket because essentially, you're borrowing from your own savings. One word of caution, though: If you leave your job, you'll be required to repay the loan in full or it will be treated as a withdrawal. Not only will you owe taxes on it, but you'll also have to pay a 10 percent penalty (unless you're over age 59fi). So avoid borrowing from a 401(k) unless you know you're planning to stay at your job at least as long as it will take you to pay it back.

Secret #54
Borrow Against Your Life Insurance Policy

The cash value of your life insurance policy is another super low-cost source of a loan. Not only do you get a competitive interest rate, but you can also take as long as you like to pay it back. The only risk you face in doing this is that you may lose some of your death benefit, depending on the type of life insurance and the amount of cash value build-up.

Secret #55
Get a Home Equity Loan

Home equity loans aren't just for putting on an addition or remodeling. You can use the money from a home equity loan for virtually anything. The big benefit of this type of loan is that the interest is tax deductible (see Secret #242 for details). And lately, banks have gotten so competitive in their quest for your home equity loan business, many have severely reduced—or even eliminated—the closing costs.

But before you rush out to get a home equity loan, consider this: You're borrowing against your home. Your home is essentially the collateral for the loan, and if you can't pay, guess what happens? That's right, you could lose your home. The best reason to use a home equity loan instead of another type of loan is if the total cost (factoring in closing costs and taxes) is significantly less than you'd be able to get elsewhere—and you know you'll be able to pay the loan back well before you plan to sell your home.

Secret #56
What a Home Equity Loan Has
That a Second Mortgage Doesn't

People often use the terms "home equity loan" and "second mortgage" interchangeably. But even though in both instances you are borrowing money and using your home as collateral, the two types of loans differ in some important ways.

With a home equity loan, you receive a line of credit but you borrow only what you need when you need it, similar to a credit card. You also only pay interest on the amount you've borrowed. By contrast, with a second mortgage, you borrow a lump sum, and you owe interest on the full amount right from the start.

When you need a large amount of cash all at once, it probably makes no difference whether you get a home equity loan or a second mortgage. But if you'll need the money at several different times, say twice a year for the next four years for your son's college tuition, then a home equity loan is the only way to go. That way, you'll have a credit line you can tap when you need it, but you'll only owe interest on the amount you've actually used.

Secret #57
Why You Should Never Borrow More Than
80 Percent of the Value of Your Home

Most lenders won't allow you to borrow more than 80 percent of the current market value of your home for a home equity loan. Unfortunately, as competition increases, some lenders will let you go further out on a limb. My advice: Don't. When you take out a home equity loan, you're essentially giving the bank back all the equity you've built up over the years. And when you borrow 80 percent or more, you could actually end up *owing* the bank money when you sell.

Say your home is currently worth $100,000 and the principal balance left on your mortgage is $15,000. You want to take out a home equity loan of $80,000, and the bank lets you. Now look at what happens when you want to sell two years later. Say you've paid back $5,000 of the home equity loan and another $5,000 of your original mortgage. But home prices in your area have plummeted. The best offer you've gotten on your home is $80,000. You want to take it. The only problem is you still owe $75,000 on your home equity loan and $10,000 on your original mortgage. If you accept the offer, you're now in the hole for $5,000. That's bad enough, but the real tragedy of this situation is that before the home equity loan, you had $85,000 equity in your home. Even with the drop in home values, you would have made a $65,000 profit from the sale.

Don't give the bank what's rightfully yours. If you decide a home equity loan is advantageous to you, fine. Just be sure to limit the amount you borrow.

Secret #58
Stay Away From Home Equity Loan Cards

In an attempt to attract homeowners to home equity loans, a number of banks now allow borrowers to tap their home equity lines of credit via a special home equity loan credit card. Like a regular Visa or MasterCard, you can charge anything you want. The only problem is you're not tapping the bank for credit as you do with a regular credit card, you're tapping your home.

I hate these cards because it makes it all too easy to put the equity in your home at risk for a couple of pairs of shoes or a night on the town. Credit cards are fine for nickel-and-dime purchases like these. Home equity loans are not.

What's worse, by putting the loan in the form of a credit card, many lenders are getting away with charging exorbitant interest rates. As of this writing, the average home equity loan rate is around 8 percent (before taxes). But some lenders are charging as much as 17 percent for their home equity loan credit cards. What's worse, they're advertising the rates as even lower (like 12.2 percent for people in the 28 percent bracket) because the interest is tax deductible!

This is absurd. If you want a home equity loan, fine. But when the lender asks how you'd like to tap it, say you want to set up an account and have the money deposited into it or have a check mailed to you. That way, you'll be sure to use the loan for the large purchases for which it was intended.

Secret #59
You Could Be Paying to Insure the Bank
Without Even Knowing It

Most customers don't realize it, but banks and other lenders often automatically charge you for credit life and disability insurance when you get a loan. It's really a selfish practice, since this insurance only benefits the bank (it guarantees the loan will be repaid if you were to die or become disabled). But what really makes it sneaky is that most banks don't even mention they've included it in the loan. What's worse, it's often exorbitantly priced—you could almost assuredly get the same insurance elsewhere for less. And in some cases, it's even written into the loan, which means you're actually paying interest on the credit life insurance!

Protect yourself by saying up front that you don't want any kind of credit life insurance. In most cases, banks can't require you to buy it as a condition of the loan.

Secret #60
Which Three Services Never to Buy From a Bank

Banks are fine for checking accounts and loans, but I would never buy insurance, stocks, or mutual funds through a bank. Banking is one of the most heavily regulated industries in the country, which means their costs for compliance are exorbitant. And guess who pays those costs? You do! So even if a bank representative seems to understand your insurance needs or your retirement goals (which is highly unlikely), and even if the bank has a good product to meet those goals (even more unlikely), you'll almost certainly pay more for it. Think of it this way: If you can buy a mutual fund directly from T. Rowe Price, and you can buy the same fund, managed by T. Rowe Price, from a bank, why would the bank want to sell it to you unless they were making money from it somehow?

But even worse than the fees is the way banks are using their stalwart, conservative image to sell products that are anything but stalwart and conservative. Take mutual funds. Banks recently won the right to sell mutual funds. Now customers who are used to buying CDs and savings bonds from banks are getting talked into rolling over their money into "high-paying" aggressive stock funds. Problem is, those aggressive stock funds aren't "high-paying" or anything-paying, for that matter. Stock funds may pay dividends, but most of their gains come from capital appreciation, which could just as easily be capital *loss*.

Don't buy insurance or investments from a bank. It's no safer than buying directly from an insurance company or a mutual fund. And it'll only cost you more.

4

Get the Credit You're Due

One of the great things about being American is the sheer joy of spending. It's an integral part of our culture in a way that style is a part of being French and good food is a part of being Italian. But the pleasure of spending is often followed by the shadow of debt.

Financial pros know that the judicious use of debt can be an integral part of a smart money management plan. But too much debt can become a crushing burden. Read on to see how to prevent your credit card spending from getting out of hand and how to use your credit cards to your best advantage.

Secret #61
How to Get Your Credit Card Issuer to
Lend You Money *Free*—No Fooling!

Credit cards are more than just a convenient way to pay for something. They provide you with instant access to hundreds—in many cases, thousands—of dollars every month. Upon filling out a single application, you get a short-term loan from a bank that renews itself every month as long as you don't exceed your limit. And if you know how to use it right, your credit card can be a tool for letting your bank pay your bills while your money sits in a savings account earning interest.

The key is float. Float is the time between when you make a purchase and when you pay for it. If you're paying with cash, there is no float. If you use a check, it can be as little as two days to many months, depending on when and where the payee cashes it. With a credit card, you generally have 15 to 25 days between bills. And depending on when the merchant actually submits the bill to the credit card issuer, it can be much longer.

The point is you can use your credit card to buy time. Let the bank pay the merchant right off the bat. In the meantime, wait for the bill to come and wait until it's due to pay it. In the interim, your money can be sitting in a checking or money market account earning interest. Just be sure to pay the entire balance in full. Otherwise, you'll owe the credit card issuer interest, and believe me, it'll be much more than you'll ever be earning in your savings account.

Secret #62
How Credit Cards Can Eat Away at
Your Purchasing Power
Without Your Knowing It

One of the smartest financial moves you can make is to pay off your credit card bill in full each month. Forgive me if I sound like I'm preaching—I just can't stand the idea of you paying 70 percent more for something than you have to.

How do I come up with that figure? Simple. The average credit cardholder carries a revolving balance of $3,300 according to the Bankcard Holders of America. Let's say you're not quite as credit-happy. Assume you're carrying *half* that balance on a credit card that charges 16 percent interest. That's 1.3 percent per month. Doesn't sound so bad. But if you had no new charges and only paid the minimum each month (say $30), it would take you *seven years and nine months* to pay that $1,650 off, and you would have paid over $1,140 in interest! That's because credit card issuers compound interest. That is, they charge you interest on top of interest.

So when you pay $30 the first month on a $1,650 bill, your bill the next month will say you owe $1,641.06, not $1,620, because you're charged interest. And if you pay another $30, your bill the following month will say you owe $1,632, not $1,601. You get the idea. The interest clock is always ticking, and your minimum payments can hardly keep up.

Secret #63
Once the Interest Clock Starts, It Doesn't Stop Until All Balances Are Paid in Full

The worst part about revolving your balance is that on most cards, you lose the grace period on all future payments until the balance is paid in full. That means once you carry over a balance—even as little as $5—most credit card issuers will charge you interest *immediately* for all new purchases.

So say you charge $400 in January and pay off $300 of the bill in February. You'll be carrying over a $100 balance to March. Then say you charge something for $250. Interest starts accruing on that $250 the day you make that purchase.

While it would only amount to a few dollars the first month, a pattern of carrying balances month to month—however small—and making new purchases each month can add up to hundreds of dollars over the course of a year.

Do yourself a favor: Pay off all your existing credit card balances as soon as possible. Start with the credit card that has the highest interest rate. Once that's paid off, move to the one with the next highest rate and so on. Make no new charges until all of your credit cards are completely paid off. Then, don't charge anything in the future unless you can pay for it in full when the bill arrives.

Secret #64
Why the Right Credit Card Is More Important Than Having a Lot of Credit Cards

One of the most common myths about credit cards is that the more you have, the better your credit record is likely to be. Utter nonsense! Having a lot of credit cards is not an advantage. In fact, it can be quite a disadvantage. For example, let's say you're planning to buy a house and you've got seven credit cards. They're all paid off, but each has a credit line of $2,500. To a bank, that's a possible debt of *$17,500*. After all, you could conceivably charge that much at any time.

And that leads to the second reason I don't like the idea of having a lot of credit cards. It's too much of a temptation. Whittle your credit cards down to two or three. You'll automatically reduce your chances of running up large balances you can't handle, and you'll spend that much less in interest.

Secret #65
The Best Credit Cards If You
Pay Off Your Balance

Even if you use your credit card primarily for convenience and pay the balance in full every month, there are still hidden costs you'll want to avoid and special perks you may want to take advantage of when you select a credit card.

At a minimum, you'll want a credit card with no annual fee and the longest grace period possible. The grace period is the amount of time you have each month before your credit issuer charges interest (see Secret #73). Since this is essentially your float, you'll want it to be as long as possible. In addition, if you can get extra perks like frequent flyer miles or special rebates, do it! As long as they aren't costing you anything and you still plan to pay your balance in full each month, they're just dandy with me.

Here are three of my favorite cards if you pay your balance in full:

- *The GM MasterCard (800/947-1000).* You pay no annual fee, get a 25-day grace period, and earn 5 percent of every charge toward the future purchase of any GM car except Saturn. Your rebate is capped at $500 a year for a maximum $3,500 over seven years. But the card also lets you earn 5 percent on all purchases at GM partners (Marriott, Mobil Oil, and MCI) above the annual $500 limit.

- *The GE Rewards MasterCard (800/437-3927).* Another no annual fee card with a decent grace period (24 days) that offers a perk: A 2 percent rebate in the form of coupons for retailers such as

Kmart, Foot Locker, Northwest Airlines, and Toys "R" Us. Unfortunately, you have to charge $500 just to get a $10 coupon, but it's not bad if you pay your bill in full every month and would like an occasional perk.

■ *The AFBA Industrial Bank Visa or MasterCard (800/776-2265).* This one has no perks, but it also has no annual fee, a 24-day grace period, and according to Gerri Detweiler, executive director of the BankCard Holders of America, this bank is known for its courteous customer service.

Secret #66
The Best Credit Cards If You
Don't Pay Your Balance in Full

If you keep a revolving balance, you want to go with the card with the lowest interest rate. Some picks:

■ Central Carolina Bank of Georgia (800/577-1680)
■ Amalgamated Bank of Chicago (800/723-0303)
■ Wachovia Bank of Georgia (800/842-3262)

For a current list of low-interest-rate credit cards and cards with no annual fees, send $4 to BankCard Holders of America Customer Service, 524 Branch Drive, Salem, VA 24153, or call 703/389-5445.

Secret #67
You Don't Have to Switch Credit Cards to
Get Lower Rates

While it makes sense to always try to get a credit card with the lowest rates and fees, if your card charges higher rates, don't assume that you need to switch to get a better deal. All you need to do is *ask*.

Although they don't like to publicize it, banks routinely waive annual fees and lower interest rates on credit cards for customers who are willing to negotiate. The trick is to find a better deal elsewhere, then ask your issuer to match it. Nine times out of ten, you'll get what you want—and if you don't, take your business elsewhere.

Secret #68
How to Get Credit When You
Have No Credit History

One of the great ironies of the credit world is you have to have credit to prove you're a good credit risk. But if you've never had credit before, how do you get it for the first time? Basically, you have two choices: (1) You can start with merchant cards or (2) you can get a secured card.

Although I prefer bank-issued credit cards (Visa and Master-Card) to credit cards issued by a single merchant (Mobil, Exxon, Sears), if you have a hard time getting a bank-issued card, it's fine to start with a department store or oil company card first. Just be sure to pay the balance in full each month—merchant cards are notorious for charging high interest rates. Then, once you've established a credit history with one or more of these merchant cards, try to get a Visa or MasterCard.

It's important to eventually get a Visa or MasterCard because these cards are better for establishing credit. Since merchant cards are generally easier to obtain, most credit grantors give them less weight than a bank card when assessing your creditworthiness. Plus, you'll have greater flexibility with a bank-issued card, since Visa and MasterCard are accepted all over the world.

Your other alternative is to go with a secured credit card. You can get a secured Visa or MasterCard card from a bank, and it works just like a regular Visa or MasterCard. In fact, to merchants, it appears just like a regular credit card. But instead of the bank issuing you a line of credit, you must make a deposit. Your credit line is equal to the amount of the deposit. As long as you pay your bills, your deposit stays intact and you build a good credit history. Eventually, after a period of timely payments, you will build a good credit record and be able to apply for an unsecured (regular) credit card.

Secured credit cards are also useful for people with poor credit records.

➤ **Potential Trap:** Secured cards have become big business for con artists. "Credit problems? Turned down for credit?," they advertise, "We'll repair your credit immediately. Just send $99." Beware of ads like these. Stick with banks you know.

For the help in finding the best deals on secured credit cards, contact the Bankcard Holders of America at 703/389-5445.

Secret #69
Beware of Super Low-Rate Credit Cards

Have you ever come across a credit card that has an interest rate that seems too low to be true? As my father told me when I announced in junior high school that I had discovered a way to travel to Paris for free, "If it sounds too good to be true, it probably is."

In the case of the Paris trip, it turned out that I would have to work as a chambermaid for six months to get the free trip. As for low-interest-rate credit cards, it generally means that the low rate you see when you sign up isn't likely to stay low for very long. In some cases, those low rates are introductory rates that will go up after a certain period of time. In other cases, they are variable rates that are pegged to a specific index, like 3-month Treasury bills. The problem with variable rate cards is that when interest rates go up, the interest you pay does too. Then suddenly your low-interest-rate card isn't so low after all.

Be sure to ask if the interest rate is either a special introductory rate or a variable rate. If it's a special introductory rate, find out when it will go up and by how much. If it's a variable rate, I'd steer clear of it. After all, why get locked into a deal that could go sour at any time when there are better, more stable cards around?

Secret #70
Beware of Phantom Low Interest Rates

Another trick credit card issuers use to suck you in is offering a low interest rate that is only good if you never revolve your balance! They advertise interest rates of 2 to 6 percentage points lower than average, but the rate immediately jumps 2 to 6 points if you don't pay your balance in full! This is nothing short of ridiculous.

Once again, you can protect yourself by asking if the interest rate can change. If it can, it's probably not such a great deal after all.

Secret #71
How a Credit Card Can Slash
1 to 2 Percent off Your Grocery Bill

Having a credit card that gives you frequent flier miles or store coupons is nifty, but what about a credit card that gives rebates on one of life's necessities, like groceries? Enter the Kroger MasterCard.

The supermarket chain has teamed up with Cincinnati's Fifth Third Bank to give cardholders a 1 percent rebate on the first $2,500 they spend at Kroger each year and 2 percent on purchases over $2,500, up to a maximum rebate of $500 per year.

I like this idea as long as you plan to pay the balance in full each month. The card has no annual fee, so it costs you nothing, and it might become a good way to track how much you spend on groceries each month. But again, if there's any chance that you won't pay your balance in full, avoid this card like the plague. It's bad enough to pay interest on new shoes, it's ridiculous to do so on groceries!

Secret #72
What's Wrong With American Express

American Express is not a credit card per se. It is a charge card, meaning you can charge purchases from month-to-month with no limit, but you must pay the balance in full each month. So you can't stretch out your payments over many months, you're not building a credit history, and it's costing you $55 just to have the darn thing! As a rule, I would avoid American Express for these reasons.

➤ **Inside Tip:** The only exception is if you're interested in using your credit card to earn frequent flyer miles. American Express has a Membership Miles club that lets you earn frequent flyer miles on any of four airlines: Continental, Delta, Northwest, or Southwest. You have to pay $25 on top of the $55 annual fee, but the $25 is waived for the first year. I recommend this only if you're saving miles for a particular trip *and* you don't know which airline you want to use. Call American Express for details at 800/297-6453.

Secret #73
The One Credit Card to Avoid at All Costs

When you use a credit card, your bank makes money in two ways: (1) from the merchants each time you charge a purchase and (2) from interest if you don't pay the balance in full each month. While the money coming in from merchants is certainly nothing to sneeze at, it isn't nearly as profitable as the interest income. That's why credit card issuers like it when you don't pay your balance in full each month. They want to get the most profit possible out of every purchase. And some banks will try just about anything to get that interest income from you.

The worst offenders are the ones that charge you interest from the minute you make the purchase. With these cards, even if you pay your entire balance the day you get your bill, you'll owe interest.

How do you spot a bank that does this? When you apply for a credit card, look to see what the "grace period" is. "Grace period" is the term banks use to describe how much time you have before interest is levied on your purchases (essentially, the amount of time between due dates on your bill).

Most credit cards have a 25-day grace period, but there are some that have no grace period at all. I would avoid such credit cards—even if you don't plan to pay your balance in full every month. After all, why should you pay one dime more in interest than you need to?

Secret #74
Why Credit Card Issuers Love People
Who Don't Pay Their Bills

You would think the bank hates it when you pay your credit card bill late, right? Wrong. Some banks love it when you pay late because then they can charge you late fees. Arguing that it takes them more time in processing, the bank will charge as much as $10 or $20 to process a late fee! I think this is ridiculous. At most, it costs a bank $2 or $3 to process a late payment. That means they're making a 400 to 900 percent profit on your late fee!

Don't fall for this. No matter how small it is, get your payment in on time. You don't need to give your bank a bonus payment just for being late.

Secret #75
Why Some Banks Love People
Who Go Over Their Limits

When you go over your credit card limit, most banks will simply send you a notice and ask you to pay the amount over your credit limit in full. But others will levy fees. This is absurd because the bank is not only making money from you in interest, but it is also making money from the actual purchases themselves.

Don't take over-the-limit fees lying down. If you have a good record of payment and this is the first time you've gone over the limit, call the bank and ask for the fee to be waived. Chances are, just asking for it will get the fee wiped out. But be sure not to go over the limit again. Few banks will extend the same courtesy twice.

Secret #76
The One Credit Card Service
You Should Never Use

A few years ago, I was travelling with a friend and she stopped to get cash at an ATM. I assumed she was using her ATM card, but instead she used her MasterCard. A few weeks later, the bill arrived. Her $200 withdrawal cost her *$8*. Can you imagine paying $8 for an ATM transaction? It's absurd.

Of course, the banks love to tout cash advances. That's because they not only charge you a high (2 to 2.5 percent) fee for the privilege, but most also start the interest clock on cash advances immediately. And oftentimes, that interest rate is much higher than the interest rate charged on regular credit card purchases. Of course, there are some card issuers that don't charge interest for cash advances, but their cash advance fees are generally so high you end up paying just as much.

➤ **A Better Way:** Use your ATM card to get cash. That way you won't pay high interest rates, and you won't spend more than you have in your checking account.

Secret #77
What Credit Card Insurance Is Really Good For

Credit card life and disability insurance is another favorite gimmick banks are touting to credit card customers. "If you were ever to become disabled or die, we'd pay off your outstanding balance up to $5,000," the advertisements read. And how much do you have to pay for that wonderful privilege? Oh, somewhere in the neighborhood of $10 a month.

Who are they kidding? The cost of the insurance far outweighs any benefit you may receive (and that benefit is very questionable). Plus, it is an inefficient way to get life insurance. If you need life insurance, get life insurance protection for *all* of your debts—not just your credit card. If you don't, skip it entirely. Like cash advances, the only one benefitting from this service is the bank.

Secret #78
Why "Month Off" Credit Card Programs
Are No Vacation

Another favorite trick credit card issuers use to suck you into the interest rate cycle is to offer to give you a month off. To make matters worse, they'll butter you up by telling you this is an exclusive offer, only for people with good payment records. Don't buy it! Whether a minimum payment is required or not, the interest clock is still ticking. What this type of offer really amounts to is an extra month of interest for the bank—at your expense.

Secret #79
How Frequent Flyer Credit Cards Can End Up
Costing You More Than They're Worth

One of the most attractive credit card perks the banks have ever come up with is letting you earn frequent flyer miles for your credit card purchases. To me, this is one of the best deals around today. The problem is it could end up costing you more than it's worth if you aren't careful.

You see, most frequent flyer credit cards have high annual fees, high interest rates, and don't offer the flexibility of being able to choose between the different airlines. For example, with the Citibank AAdvantage Card, you pay a $50 annual fee and earn a mile on American Airlines for every dollar you charge. Similarly, with a Mileage Plus First Card, you pay a $60 annual fee and earn a mile on United Airlines for every dollar you charge.

So if you don't fly at all, and you only charge say, $5,000 a year, it takes you five years to earn a free ticket (most airlines require 25,000 miles for a free ticket), and you've paid between $250 and $300 in annual fees, not to mention any interest you've incurred.

The best way to use these cards is with introductory deals and in combination with air travel. From time to time, most of these cards will offer bonus miles for signing up. Take advantage of these. And if you travel a fair bit, you can use your credit card to inch your way toward a free ticket. For example, say you're 2,000 miles away from a free ticket and you don't plan to travel any more this year. You'll spend $50 or $60 to get a frequent flyer credit card, but you'll probably rack up enough purchases in one year to put you over the top for a free ticket. Then you can cancel the credit card.

And if you do plan to hold your frequent flyer credit card for a few years, just make sure the free trip you end up taking costs you more than the money you spent in annual fees and interest.

Secret #80
Why You Should Always Pay for Car Repairs and Airline Tickets by Credit Card

Credit card companies don't care what you buy with the card; they just want you to keep on charging. But *you* should care because there are certain times when paying by credit card can give you much more than a couple weeks of float.

For instance, when you buy something from a mail order company or car repair shop and you pay by credit card, you can refuse to pay if you aren't satisfied with what you've received.

Under the Fair Credit Billing Act, as long as you've tried in good faith to work it out with the seller, you can refuse to pay both the amount of the purchase and the associated finance charges too. Pay by check, and you can kiss your money goodbye.

Secret #81
How to Get a Copy of
Your Credit Report for Free

Your personal credit history, complete with your payment behavior, is available to businesses and banks through credit reporting agencies and credit bureaus. Credit bureaus do not assess your creditworthiness. They typically just provide creditors a computerized report of your credit history, which banks and merchants use to assess your creditworthiness.

Under the Fair Credit Reporting Act, you can get a copy of your credit report free if you've been denied credit. Get the name and address of the credit reporting agency that was used by the merchant or bank as well as the reason for the denial, and send the credit reporting agency a notice within 30 days after your rejection. If you wait too long, the credit reporting agency does not have to honor your request.

Since so many people have had a hard time with mistakes on their credit reports, Congress is currently considering legislation that would require credit reporting agencies to give consumers a free credit report on request. Right now, TRW (800/392-1122) is the only credit reporting agency that provides free reports on request. Send your request with your full name, social security number, current address, previous address, spouse's name, and date of birth to P.O. Box 2350, Chatsworth, CA 91313.

Secret #82
How to Correct Mistakes on
Your Credit Report

What happens if you get your credit report and you notice a horrible mistake? Something that could keep you from getting a mortgage on the house of your dreams? Under the Fair Credit Reporting

Act, you have a right to dispute any information on your credit report within 30 days, and the credit bureau must investigate and correct the information within 60 days.

Many credit bureaus are trying to handle problems even faster. In fact, the 1400-member Associated Credit Bureaus trade group, whose members include the big three—TRW, Equifax, and Trans Union—recently adopted a policy of investigating disputes within 30 days of notification and reporting the results to consumers within five days of completion of the investigation. This is probably an effort to avoid the legislation Congress has been considering for some time that would require credit bureaus to investigate disputed information within 30 days or delete it. Regardless of the reason, however, it is a step in the right direction.

But what if the credit bureau investigates and says your complaint is all wet? Do you have any power to change your credit report? The answer is yes—sort of. The Fair Credit Reporting Act provides for your right to attach a note of explanation to an area of dispute on your credit report. The reporting agency must include the note in all of its files on you. The problem is that most of the time creditors use computers to scan the reports, so your note may never even be read. Still, it's better than nothing. And when you apply for a loan, you can provide your own explanation to the lender at that time (see Secret #51).

5
Get Everything You Deserve From Your Job and More

I once read that people are more willing to talk about their sex lives than their salaries. Think about Madonna. She's the very symbol of sex in popular culture, but I hear she refuses to disclose how much she makes per year. It's no wonder most folks have a hard time figuring out how to get what they deserve from their jobs.

Well, that's what this chapter is all about. I have talked with some of the best career advisors and negotiators in the country to discover how they ensure they get everything they deserve from their jobs—and more.

Secret #83
The Best Time to Talk Salary

When most companies conduct a job search, they use a narrowing down process to select the ideal candidate. They cull from a huge number of applicants a few reasonable prospects. If you're one of them, you're selected for an interview, perhaps even two or three interviews. Then comes the offer. Now look at where the company is at this point. If they're making you an offer, they've already weeded out most, if not all, of the other candidates. They may have even already written the other candidates rejection letters! This is the ideal time to talk salary *because they've already decided they want you.*

You may want them too, but you're still in a position to walk away. Indeed, you're in a better position to walk away than they are. You can just continue your job search; they have to start a candidate search all over again while having an empty position in their organization.

So try to keep salary questions at bay until this point. If the issue comes up sooner, be as vague as possible. Say something like, "I'd certainly be interested in discussing that with you when I have a better idea of where I'll fit into the organization."

Most interviewers won't press you to name a figure until they know they want you. Think of it this way: If you know you want to buy something, you need to know how much it costs. Until that point, price can only distract you. You don't want to distract the interviewer. First establish the value of your product (yourself), then talk price.

Secret #84
What's Wrong With a Negotiation That Focuses Solely on Salary

When it comes time to talk compensation, don't fall into the trap of focusing only on salary. There are numerous potential issues in any negotiation, and any time you narrow the negotiation down to one issue, there has to be a winner and a loser. This is particularly bad when it comes to salary because if you lose, you resent your new employer before you've even taken the job. And if you win, your new employer resents you.

A better strategy is to have a clear idea of what you want and the compromises you're willing to make. That way, you may have to concede some points on one issue, but you'll be much more likely to get what you want on others.

The fact of the matter is getting the highest possible salary may not give you what you really want. Think about what you'll do with the money. Will you use it to pay for daily living expenses, such as food, rent, or transportation costs? If so, you may be able to get your new employer to pay for your parking or give you an expense account for lunches. Perhaps you'll need it to pay for day care and other child rearing costs. If so, see if the company has a flexible spending account, which allows you to set aside pretax money to pay for child care (see Secret #88). Perhaps you would use the money to expand your own horizons, to travel, or go back to school. If so, you'll want to negotiate an extra week of vacation or tuition reimbursement.

There are forms of compensation other than salary, and by knowing exactly what you want, you'll be in a much better position to get it.

Secret #85
Why It's Important to Let Your Feelings Show in Salary Negotiations

Okay, so you've waited for the ideal time to discuss salary and you've asked for the moon, now it's the company's turn to respond to your proposed figure. The company comes back with a counteroffer. Ouch. It's less than you expected. You try to remain calm, forcing back the feelings of disappointment bubbling inside. Stop! This is one of the biggest mistakes you can make. The company is waiting for your reaction. If you don't show some sign of outrage or even uneasiness, they'll assume everything is just dandy.

A first reaction is like a first impression; it will immediately convey acceptance or rejection. If you don't react with disappointment, you're signaling acceptance. If you let some disappointment show, you're signaling rejection. And believe me, it's a whole lot smarter to let that disappointment show when the salary offer is first proposed than later on after you've accepted the job.

Secret #86
The One Thing Never to Do When You're Offered a Job

So what do you do when the company comes back with a salary offer that's *more* than you ever expected? Breathe a sigh of relief and accept it before the company can take it back? No. Even if the offer is more than you expected, I don't want you to accept it immediately.

No matter how excited you are, no matter how good it sounds, no matter how badly you want the job, I want you to refuse to react at all. Be silent for a moment. Take a deep breath. Then say something like, "Hmmm. That sounds interesting. Is that your very best offer?"

At this point, the employer is likely to be a bit shocked. Expect it, and just remain silent. Give him a chance to digest your words. After all, you've presented a challenge. Let the employer meet it. If he says, "That's my best offer," it probably is. And you can either accept it or decide to think about it. (I'd think about it—a night's sleep can do wonders to clear the mind.)

On the other hand, it's likely he'll say something like, "I'll have to get back to you." At this point, you've struck gold! By asking for more (or in this case, just by not accepting the first offer), you're showing that you're *worth* more. And nine times out of ten, the employer will come back with a higher offer.

Secret #87
The Most Underutilized Employee Benefit

Salary isn't the only form of compensation. There are a plethora of employee benefits you can negotiate for yourself, including health insurance, disability insurance, retirement plans, stock options, company car, tuition reimbursement, country club memberships, and on and on. But of all the benefits available to you as an employee, one of the most valuable ones is often ignored: health reimbursement plans.

I don't know anyone who hasn't been hit in some way by rising health care costs. The irony is many people have the ability to cut their out-of-pocket expenses by 30 to 60 percent, yet they don't! All you need to do is participate in your employer's pretax *flexible spending account* (health reimbursement plan). About half of all large employers offer such plans, which allow you to withhold a certain amount of money from your paycheck each month to cover unreimbursed medical expenses. You select an amount at the beginning of the year, say $25 per paycheck, and it is deducted right off the top—before taxes and before Social Security (FICA).

The money is put into a special account for you to access throughout the year as you need it. You don't even have to wait to build up a certain amount in your account before you can use it.

For example, say you get paid twice a month and you elect to have $25 deducted per paycheck for a flexible spending plan. Then say you go to the doctor January 10 for a check-up, and it costs $75, but it isn't covered by your health plan. You can get reimbursed from your flexible spending account right away, even though you've only "contributed" $25 to the account so far.

The major drawback of these plans is that you can't change the amount withheld during the year unless there is a change in your family status (you get married, divorced, have a child, etc.). And they have "use it or lose it" rules: If you don't use all of the money you've set aside by the end of the year, you lose it. (You do generally have several months after the year ends to submit claims for expenses that were incurred in the plan year, however.) There is also a risk that you will leave your employer during the plan year. If that happens, any amount you haven't claimed is forfeited. But by the same token, any amount you've been reimbursed for that has exceeded your "contributions" to date is yours to keep at the company's loss.

The trick is to try to accurately assess your expenses for the year, then estimate an amount slightly lower to be withheld. You want to be conservative, but you also want to sock away every penny that you will spend. Since you don't have to exceed a floor (as you do if you were to deduct medical expenses on your federal tax return), every penny you withhold represents significant savings: For most of us, it translates to a discount of 30 to 50 percent in the cost of the services when you figure savings from both federal and state taxes as well as Social Security deductions.

The maximum amount you are allowed to set aside in a flexible spending account is currently $5,000. As of this writing, flexible spending accounts are still legal, but Congress has repeatedly threatened to get rid of them. So if your employer offers you the option, take advantage of it while you still can!

Secret #88
How to Use the Same Technique to Slash Your Child Care Costs

Many employers also offer flexible spending accounts for child care expenses. The maximum allowable amount you can contribute to a child care flexible spending account is also $5,000 (in addition to the $5,000 for your medical expenses). In most other respects, the two plans work exactly the same way, except that you may not be allowed to be reimbursed for contributions you haven't yet made to a dependent care flexible spending account.

In order to qualify for a dependent care flexible spending account, both you and your spouse must work, unless the non-working spouse is disabled or a full-time student.

Secret #89
Why You Should Beware of
Independent Contractor Arrangements

In this era of downsizing and corporate layoffs, it's likely that benefits may not even be available to you. In fact, many companies have started hiring people as "independent contractors" in an effort to save the cost of health insurance, payroll taxes, unemployment taxes, and a whole host of other benefits. For the worker, such an arrangement translates into a higher paycheck (since nothing is withheld). But it also gives you the responsibility for filing estimated taxes and paying for your own health insurance.

Even though you may be willing to accept the higher costs of such an arrangement, I'd be very careful about accepting this deal. The IRS is cracking down on employees who are treated as independent contractors, assessing penalties not only to the employers who promote such arrangements, but also to the "employees" as well. Here are the IRS' twenty rules for what constitutes an employee.

1. Must comply with the employer's instructions for doing the work.
2. Receives training from the employer or at the direction of the employer.
3. Provides services that are integral to the employer's business.
4. Provides services that must be rendered personally.
5. Hires, supervises, and pays workers for the employer.
6. Has an ongoing working relationship with the employer.
7. Must follow set hours.
8. Works full-time for the employer.

9. Works on the employer's premises.

10. Must do work in a sequence set by the employer.

11. Must submit regular reports to the employer.

12. Receives payments of regular amounts at set intervals.

13. Receives payments for business and travel expenses.

14. Relies on the employer to provide tools and/or materials.

15. Doesn't have a major investment in resources for providing services.

16. Can't make a profit or suffer a loss from providing services.

17. Works for one employer at a time.

18. Doesn't offer services to the general public.

19. Can be fired by the employer.

20. Can quit work at anytime without incurring a liability.

The IRS will give different weight to each criterion, depending on the case, but don't expect leniency. If there is any question in your mind that your arrangement is not an independent contractor one, reject it. You don't want the IRS coming after you when you're not even the one benefiting from the deal!

Secrets #90–92
Three Simple Steps to Getting a Good Raise

When you first accept a job and the proposed salary is less than you had hoped, your alternative is clear: You don't have to accept the job. But what about when you've already taken the job? How do you negotiate for a raise when you can't (or don't want to) threaten to leave?

Secret #90
Find Out What Your Value Is on the Open Market

Your first step is to find out what you're worth. What are other people in your position making? Read the classified ads in trade publications to see what salary ranges are being advertised now for people in your position. Get a copy of *Working Woman's* annual salary survey. It includes average salaries by job title and is broken down into male and female categories. *Money* also occasionally does salary surveys. Call the editor of a trade publication and ask what she knows (you may be surprised what journalists can find out). Contact a headhunter to find out what kind of salary ranges are common for people with your experience and education.

If possible, get a sense of what other people at your level in your company are making too. How successful you are at this depends a lot on what the company culture is. If it's highly secretive, you may not have a prayer.

But it may just be easier than you think. My brother once worked for a government lab in California. Although the people there never thought of themselves as government employees, technically, they were. And as such, their salaries were available to the public. When it came time for his review, my brother just trotted down to human resources, paid $1 and got a list of what everyone in his department was making! Although that list was available to anyone who asked, nobody had ever asked for it before!

Most of us aren't in a position to be able to do what my brother did. But it does make you realize how easy it is to know where you stand *before* you go in to ask for a raise.

Secret #91
Demonstrate Your Value

Once you have a clear idea of what you're worth and what you want, the next step is to demonstrate your value to the company. Try to find specific, measurable ways you've impacted the company's bottom line in the past year. There isn't a business out there that isn't looking for two things: (1) ways to save money and (2) ways to make money. Your goal is to demonstrate that you've done one or both in a significant way.

When you have three or four key accomplishments, put them in a memo and give it to your boss before your review. That will give her a chance to consider how valuable you are before she decides on a specific figure.

Secret #92
Let Your Boss Be the Hero

What happens when you get to the review and your raise isn't what you wanted? At that point, you need to let your boss know you are disappointed—but be very careful in how you show that disappointment. Blurting out, "I can't believe you think you can get away with this!" isn't your best bet. I say this not because you shouldn't show your frustration, but because *it puts your boss in a position of defending herself.* Once you do that, you've erased any hope of getting what you want.

Instead, express your disappointment, but make it easy for your boss to give you what you want. Say something like, "Frankly, I'm not very happy with this raise. I'd like to give you some things to think about before we go on with this review." Then restate the contributions you've made to the company, ending with something like, "I'd like to do even more to prove my value in the future. Can we discuss that after you've reconsidered my raise?"

That way, you've set the tone for reopening the discussion about salary without forcing your boss to defend her initial offer.

Then when she comes back with a higher raise, thank her and congratulate her! Tell her she did a good job. You want her to take credit for your raise so that next time, she will feel that getting you more money is an accomplishment for her as much as it is for you.

Secret #93
How to Deal With a Difficult Boss and Get Everything You Deserve

Ideally, proving your value to your boss will always yield great rewards, but there are some bosses who are just plain difficult to deal with. Nothing pleases them, and the very idea of giving you something you want somehow goes against the very fiber of their beings. Nationally-known negotiating expert Roger Dawson calls these people "street fighters."

According to Dawson, the street fighter is someone who can win only if the other person loses. This kind of person is not interested in win/win negotiating, and even if the street fighter gets most of the concessions, he doesn't feel like a winner until the other person has lost.

I once worked for a street fighter. Boy, getting anything from this guy was brutal—even if what I wanted would be good for *him.* I would go in and try to explain how whatever I wanted would benefit him, and he would always veto it even if he agreed that it would benefit him. I never did figure out how to deal with him, but

I learned an important lesson: Never assume you know what the other person wants. In this case, he wanted to win. Pure and simple. Nothing else mattered. For him, my getting what I wanted would have meant him losing face.

How do you handle a street fighter? According to Roger Dawson, the only way is to show them they've won by proving how much you'll lose. You complain how much the proposed agreement will hurt you. You accept whatever you get grudgingly. You look sad. You essentially prove to the street fighter that you're lying on the ground, bleeding, and he can claim victory.

Just by positioning yourself as the loser, the street fighter automatically becomes the winner, which is all he wants anyway. So don't be afraid to fight a street fighter—just make sure he thinks you've lost.

Secret #94
Why You Should Always
Leave Them Wanting More

When you're ready to leave a job, don't make the same mistake I made when I left my first job. I had been working as a secretary for a large trade association. From the time I took the job, I had no intention of keeping it very long—I thought of it as a stepping stone (and a way to feed and clothe myself) before I moved onto a real job where I could write. As luck would have it, I was able to land a writing job within about 15 months. Indeed, within 10 minutes after I found out I had the job, I had my resignation letter on my boss' desk. Then I spent the next two weeks fluttering around the office, chatting with my friends about how exciting my new job would be, and ignoring most of the work that had to be done in my current position.

"Who cares?" I said to myself. "I won't have to worry about this in three weeks anyway. Why should I bother fixing it?" I had the classic short-timer's syndrome.

About a week after I started my new job, my new boss called me into her office.

"Remember that background check we did on you?" she asked.
"Yes."

"Well," she said, "I think we have a small problem."

I started to get that sinking feeling in my gut.

"It seems your old boss wasn't happy with you. She said you had an attitude problem."

I could feel my face growing hotter. My throat started to close. My mind started racing. What had I said or done to my old boss to make her say such an awful thing? At my annual review, she was full of compliments. What had gone wrong and what would happen to me now? Was I going to lose my new job over this?

Well, I didn't lose my job. But I learned one of the most valuable lessons of my career: Last impressions last forever. I had done a fine job in my first position. It wasn't my overall skills that made my old boss so angry; it was how I left. Just by leaving in such a sloppy way, I had jeopardized my new job, which was the only chance I had to break into what I really wanted to do: write.

The point is when you're ready to leave a job, work in your last few weeks as professionally and thoroughly as you did in your first. I learned the value of that lesson when I left my second job. I not only completed all of my projects before I left, but I prepared notes and material for my replacement in order to make the transition easier. So instead of getting the kiss-off, when I did leave, I got a wonderful send-off party with many beautiful gifts. What's more, by leaving on a good note and keeping in touch with my former colleagues, I'm still able to solicit their advice on projects and problems I'm facing today.

So the next time you leave a job, fight the urge to succumb to short-timer's syndrome. If you put everything you've got into those last few weeks, you'll be well-rewarded down the line.

Secret #95
What to Do About Health Insurance
When You Leave Your Job

Under the Consolidated Omnibus Budget Reconciliation Act (COBRA) of 1986, if you were covered under your employer's health insurance plan, you must be allowed to extend your coverage for up to 18 months after you leave. You pay 102 percent of the group-rate premiums, which is generally lower than you'd be able to find on your own—but not always. Before opting for the coverage, ascertain your needs and check out what insurers in your area would charge.

Are you primarily interested in major medical coverage in case you had an accident or were suddenly diagnosed with a disease? If so, your employer's plan may be more expensive. It may provide all sorts of goodies like a prescription plan, dental care, or maternity benefits that you don't need.

As with any type of insurance, the purpose of health insurance is to pay for illnesses that would be financially devastating to you if you had to bear the cost yourself. If your company's plan offers a $100 deductible, ask yourself, for example, if it would be financially devastating to you if you had to shell out $250 or $500 or even $1,000 for your health expenses during the year. If the answer is no, shop around for other plans that offer higher deductibles. You may be able to find one that's cheaper.

A word of warning: No matter what plan you choose, it *never* pays to go without health insurance. Most people are particularly vulnerable when they leave one job to go to another. The coverage they received from the former job stops, and the coverage under the plan at the new job hasn't started. It pays to get some kind of interim temporary plan even if it costs you several hundred dollars. Think of it this way: Do you really want to risk getting appendicitis—or worse—in the two weeks when you aren't covered? Even if you wait to have the surgery until your new health insurance starts, it won't matter. It'll be a preexisting condition and won't be covered. Don't put yourself in that situation—maintain health insurance coverage at all times.

Secret #96
What It Takes to Make It as an Entrepreneur

Ah, to be your own boss, the captain of your ship, commander of your destiny. To be accountable to no one and available to everyone. To work when you want and loaf when you don't. Lots of people dream of striking out on their own—many even have terrific ideas for new businesses. Yet more people fail in new businesses than succeed. So how do you know if you've got what it takes to be one of the lucky few success stories? Ask yourself the following questions:

- Do I get more done when I work alone than when I work with a team?
- Do I have a clear vision of what I want to do and do I have the skills necessary to succeed in doing it?
- Do I have a plan for achieving my goals?
- Am I the kind of person who gets things done when I say I will?
- Am I able to withstand rejection and keep going in pursuit of my goal?

If you answered "yes" to all of these questions, you have the personality of an entrepreneur. But before you quit your job, you'll need to consider a few other things, like:

- Do you have an idea for a product or service that people are willing to pay for?
- Who is your target market?
- How will you reach your market?
- How will you finance the operation?

As you can see, you'll need more than an entrepreneurial personality to make it on your own. One of the best ways I know to test your idea is to write a business plan. Not only will it force you to test the marketability of your idea, but it will also help you decide if you're willing to do what it takes to make the idea work. Remember, it doesn't cost anything to have a great idea, but a viable business can't run on good ideas alone.

For help on how to write a business plan, check out David E. Gumpert's *How to Create a Really Successful Business Plan* (*Inc.* Publishing: 1990).

Secret #97
The Smartest Way to Start Your Own Business

There tends to be a common thread among the stories about failed entrepreneurs: They quit their jobs, use all the money they've saved or borrowed to buy snazzy office equipment and business cards, then wait for the clients to come knocking down their doors.

Okay, maybe that's a bit exaggerated, but it is true that in the heat of their excitement, many entrepreneurs do decide to quit their jobs.

In order to start some businesses, that may be a necessity. But there are hundreds of other businesses that don't require you to quit at all. And if you don't have to give up your paycheck (I don't know about you, but I kind of like the idea of money showing up in my checking account on a regular basis), why do it?

I say the smartest way to strike out on your own is to do it when you're not on your own. Launch your business in the evenings or on weekends and see how it goes. Find out if you can make a go of it before you really have to. That way, you'll see if you really are cut out to be an entrepreneur, and if you aren't, you haven't lost as much.

For more information on what it takes to start your own business, contact the Small Business Administration at 202/606-4000 and ask for a starter kit.

6

The Pain-Free Road to Buying and Maintaining a Car

The first time I fell in love was on a car lot. There it was right in front of me: a black, newly-painted, five-speed Toyota Corolla GTS. It had a sun roof, pop-up headlights, and a terrific stereo system. I just had to have it.

The salesman was a nice sort of fellow. Calm, easygoing. He said the car drove real well. I had to take his word for it, since I couldn't drive stick shift at the time.

"How much do you want for it?" I asked, dewy-eyed.

"$9,000."

"Well, I only have $7,000. I guess I'll have to borrow the rest."

"I think we can work something out," he said, leading me into his office.

And we did. I borrowed $2,000 that day. And 12 months later, I had paid it all back—at $200 a month.

I was happy to do it. I loved the car, and I could afford the $200 a month payment. It was only years later that I realized I'd been paying over 20 percent in interest.

I'd like to believe I was never that naive. But I was. I don't want you to ever have to suffer the same fate. So read on.

Secret #98
The Smartest Move You Can Make
Before You Go Car Shopping

Before you even set foot in a showroom, it's a good idea to visit your local bank or credit union. You'll not only find out how much car you can afford, but—and this is important—you'll be able to take the question of financing out of the car buying process. This is important because car dealerships often try to lead you into discussions about financing as a way to confuse you about the price of the car (see Secrets #119 and #120). You can avoid this problem by getting financing elsewhere.

Even if you do want to get the loan from the dealership (which may be worthwhile if you have bad credit or don't have a credit history), it's still a good idea to visit a bank first so you'll have a basis for comparison. Chances are, the bank will quote you rates of 1 to 2 percent lower than you'll find at the dealership.

Secret #99
The Three Most Important Questions to
Ask When Shopping for a Car Loan

It's a good idea to call three or four financial institutions to get quotes for your loan. When you call, there are really only three questions you need to ask:

1. What is the annual percentage rate (APR)?
2. How is the interest calculated?
3. Are there any other charges and if so, what are they?

Of the three questions, the first is most important. That's because the APR is the only real way you can compare loans from different sources. Banks and finance companies quote interest rates all the time, but the only rate that matters is the APR because it tells you the true annual interest rate you'll be paying as a percentage of the loan. By law, banks and finance companies must disclose the APR when they make a loan. But they don't have to disclose it on the phone if you don't ask. So be sure you're getting the APR when you get your quote.

The next question you'll want to ask is what the conditions of the loan are. The right answer: simple interest, single payment loan paid monthly over the term of the loan. That means you'll only pay interest on what you borrow, and you can pay off the loan early if you want (see Secret #49 for details).

Finally, find out if there are any other lending charges. Fees for credit checks, application processing, and other lending fees are common, but you don't necessarily have to pay them. Remember, banks are a business just like any other business. If you find the fees unreasonable, say so. You may get them knocked down.

The trick is to shop for a loan just like you'd shop for anything else. There's no reason to feel inferior to the bank. Remember, without you, they don't have a business!

Secret #100
The Single Most Important Number to Know
Before Walking Into a Dealership

In addition to having financing lined up in advance, you'll also want to know the dealer cost before you go shopping. The dealer cost is the actual price the dealer paid for the car. The dealer's sticker price is, well, how can I put this nicely ... a complete fabrication. Seriously, you'll see pigs fly before you'll find a sticker price that actually reflects the dealer's cost.

So if you can't find the dealer cost on the sticker, where can you find it? Aye, there's the rub. Car dealers don't want you to know what they actually paid for the car; after all, then you'll know how much profit they've padded in. So you'll have to do a little digging.

You'll want to buy a copy of *Edmund's Car Prices Buyer's Guide*, available at your local bookstore for about $5. This little gem lists the retail and wholesale cost of every car and every option on the market today. Simply look up the wholesale cost of the cars you're interested in, add in the wholesale price of the options, plus about $100 for advertising (annoying as it may be, dealers do charge you for their advertising), about $50 for gas (yup, they charge you for that too), and voila, your target price of the car.

Oh, did I forget to account for dealer profit? Silly me. I guess it's reasonable to allow 3 percent for dealer profit. What's that?

You're afraid 3 percent is too low? The dealer will go out of business with a 3 percent margin? I wouldn't worry too much. As you'll see in Secret #114, even 3 percent over invoice still allows the dealer to make a healthy profit.

➤ **Inside Tip:** Before you set your target price, find a car on a dealer's lot and copy down the *list* price and options from the Manufacturer's Suggested Retail Price sticker and compare them with the list prices in your Edmund's Guide. If they don't match, you have an old book. This can easily happen, since prices do change frequently. Just adjust your wholesale price upward accordingly.

And for heavens sake, be sure it's the MSRP sticker you're looking at, not the dealer sticker. Both stickers are padded with extra profit for the dealer, but the MSRP sticker is required by law to include the list price of the base model car and the list price of the options. These are the only numbers you need for now. When we get to Secret #110, we'll talk about how to shave off extra profit padders from the dealer sticker.

Secret #101
How to Determine Dealer Cost With a Single Phone Call

If the process of determining the wholesale price of a car sounds too time-consuming for you, I have just the solution for you. Each of the following pricing services will send you a computer printout including the dealer cost, retail cost, and the cost of options of any car you're interested in:

- Car/Puter International (800/221-4001) charges $23 to have the printout mailed to you, but you can get the same information by calling 900/226-CARS for $2 per minute. You can reach Car/Puter 24-hours a day, but if you call between 8:30 a.m. and 10 p.m., Eastern time, you'll be able to talk to someone who can also let you know if there are any special factory rebates going on right now.
- The Consumer Reports Auto Price Service costs $11 for the first car, $20 for two cars, $27 for three cars, and $5 more for each additional car. Call 800/933-5555.

- Nationwide Auto Brokers (800/521-7257 charges $11.95 per quote and also offers a car buying service (see Secret #132).

- Auto Advisor (800/326-1976) takes the process a step further with its TargetPrice service. Call 800/326-1976 with the car and options you want. Auto Advisor will research your local market and give you the dealer cost plus what your target price should be, taking into account local supply, demand, value, and price. The cost of the service is $49.95.

Secret #102
No Question Is Meaningless to a Car Salesperson

No question from a salesperson is meaningless. Each one is designed to either gain your trust (ever try to say no to a friend?) or find out what type of buyer you are. Period. So while you're thinking you're making small talk, the salesman is already formulating strategy based on what he's observed about your attitudes and your needs.

Meanwhile, you've gotten nowhere because you've been busy responding to the salesperson and haven't found out a thing about the salesperson, the car, or the dealership, all of which could help you in negotiating your deal.

So for starters, don't assume that the salesperson's questions are innocuous. They aren't. He's trying to size you up, figure out what your hot buttons might be, what he can say that will make you buy the car. Expect this, and decide what you want to reveal beforehand.

For example, you may want the salesperson to think you're a serious buyer, so you say, "I live right around the corner, but I've been all over looking for a car. And now I'm ready to get down to it." That way, you've given the salesperson an incentive to try to sell you the car, but you haven't revealed anything you don't want him to know.

At the same time, you want to find out as much about the salesperson as possible. The best way to do this is by turning one of his questions around. So if he asks you about your job, you might say, "Oh, my job isn't very interesting, but I bet you have a few stories you could tell. How long have you been in this business anyway?"

This way, you're giving the appearance of being friendly, but you've revealed nothing about yourself, and you've gotten him to reveal something about himself. Keep asking questions to try to find out how the dealership does business, how long a particular car has been sitting on the lot, and what *his* hot buttons are.

Of course, I'd take all of the salesperson's answers with a grain of salt. Most have no problem lying straight out. But the important thing is that you've maintained some control. And as you will see in the following secret, the salesperson's best weapon is control. By taking that away, you're also taking away his influence over you, and you'll be able to maintain a clearer focus on your own goals.

Secret #103
You're in Charge!

Most people think car salespeople are sleazy predators who'd sell their souls to the devil for a good deal. And most car salespeople have done nothing to prove otherwise. Yet amazingly, they are *still* able to cut terrifically profitable deals for themselves. Why? Because they know how to take control.

Car salespeople succeed because most car buyers find them intimidating. Think of it this way, suppose you were involved in a business deal and you knew the other side had a reputation for being cutthroat. You go in armed with every piece of ammunition you can muster, yet you still feel anxious. Why? Because you know you're about to be put through the emotional equivalent of boot camp. No one wants to go through that. Not for a business deal. Not for a car.

Even the toughest, sharpest, shrewdest negotiators like to play nice. So when they know the other side won't, they feel anxious, intimidated, out of control. And because they feel this way, they are.

Now let's get around to the other side of the dashboard. What is the car salesperson feeling when he sees you? *Easy mark, my-commission's-in-the-bag, let-me-call-my-travel-agent-to-book-that-cruise-to-Alaska?*

No, he's thinking, I've got to sell a car today. If I don't, I won't be able to pay the mortgage. I could even lose my job. I sure hope these buyers will give me the sale.

Now who's got the power? You see, like any negotiation, buying a car is at least 50 percent psychological. If you put yourself in the right frame of mind, determine what you want, and remember that you have ultimate control over the sale, you'll find the process a whole lot more enjoyable—and rewarding.

Secret #104
Cultivate an Attitude of Indecision

Being decisive may be an asset in most aspects of your life, but it is nothing but detrimental to you in negotiating a car deal. That's because once the salesperson realizes you're set on a particular make or model or style, he can use that information against you.

"Oh," he'll say, "I only wish you wanted such-and such. If you did, I'd have no problem getting that for you. But this car/option/whatever is in such hot demand, I just can't do a deal. Frankly, I've had no trouble getting the full asking price on it."

You can avoid getting sucked into this trap by leading the salesperson into believing you know exactly what you want, then vacillating throughout the negotiation. For example, ask to see a Toyota Corolla. Say you know it's reliable, fuel efficient, and has relatively good resale value. Then when you hit a point where the salesperson seems unwilling to budge, wonder aloud if you should buy a used car instead. Or leave the salesperson's office and start wandering around the lot, seeing if they have anything better.

The idea is to keep the salesperson guessing. If he knows that at any moment you could change your mind and the whole deal could fall through, he'll be much more likely to give you what you want.

Secret #105
Shop With a Friend

No matter how independent you are, I highly recommend bringing another person with you when you go car shopping. This serves several purposes. First, it makes it harder for the sales team to out-number you. The salesperson may be able to bring in one other salesperson under the guise of needing some help, but pile three or four salespeople into one office and you have the impression of staring at circus animals.

Second—and most importantly—bringing along another person gives you much more negotiating leverage. All your friend needs to do is drop in a few negative comments at opportune moments, so you can distract the salesperson and steer the conversation where you want it to go.

I'd even plan the comments in advance. That way, you'll know what to expect, and while the salesperson is busy trying to answer your friend's bogus objections, you can reassess your strategy.

Secret #106
How to Choose a Car Salesman

I like my car salespeople young and dumb. I'm serious. I want someone who is inexperienced, who hasn't learned all of the tricks of the trade yet and who will get flustered when he can't pigeon-hole me into a category.

Even better, since their livelihood is based on how well they can produce, young salespeople will be more eager to make a sale— any sale— to prove to the manager they can cut it.

Of course, starting with a young salesperson does not guarantee you'll stay with a young salesperson. Virtually all dealerships use some form of the turnover tactic (bringing in a more experienced salesperson or manager to work you over and close the deal). But starting off with a young salesperson will give you confidence. You'll be more likely to get what you want in the beginning, and you can be more stubborn about keeping it.

Secret #107
The Best Time to Buy a Car

Some people are convinced you can practically steal a car from a dealership if you buy at the right time. Don't believe it. A good negotiator will be able to buy a car at a good price *any time.*

However, there are certain times when the dealer is under pressure to sell: at the end of the month, mid-week (when business is slow), the end of the model year, and Christmas time. Rainy days are good too (people seem to stay away from dealerships when it's raining). If it's convenient for you to shop at one of these times, by all means, do it. It's always smart to use any advantage you might have. In the end, however, you'll get the best deal on a car by *negotiating for it*—not waiting for a rainy day.

Secret #108
Start With a Ridiculously Low Offer

When you finally get to the point of talking price, start with a ridiculously low offer. That way, you're giving the salesperson plenty of room to negotiate with. This is important. You want him to spend hours just trying to talk you up to your target price. So even if it sounds ridiculous to you, even if you know the dealership can't make a profit, start with a super low offer.

Otherwise, you'll just be giving the salesperson license to squeeze you for more money. Think of it this way: If you go in with your best offer, the salesperson has no choice but to either accept it on the spot or to try to talk you up from there. Which one do you think he'll pick?

Secret #109
Bring a Good Novel With You

It's important to expect the negotiation to take some time. Car salespeople know that most buyers find the whole negotiating process distasteful and want to get to the bottom line as soon as possible. That's why they spend hours trying to wear you down. It isn't that they don't know what the manager will accept. It isn't that they have to consider your offer carefully. They shuttle offers back and forth between you and the sales manager so they can wear you down, pure and simple.

I'm sure you've been through the routine. You make an offer, and the salesperson says he has to check with his manager. He may actually talk to the manager or he may just get a cup of coffee. But he wants you to think he's meeting with the manager. He takes a good, long time—long enough for you to think he's in there fighting for you.

Then he finally returns, shaking his head, complaining how difficult it is to deal with the boss today and telling you how hard he fought to get you a couple hundred dollars off. Then he gives you his best you-know-what-it's-like-to-deal-with-management looks, and being a kind-hearted sort, you sympathize with the poor working stiff. Maybe you've already been through several rounds of these shenanigans, and you don't feel like going through another. Whatever the reason, you decide to accept the offer just to get it over with.

Stop! You've just been a victim of what I call the "Good Guy/Bad Guy, I'll-keep-you-here-until-it-kills-you" routine. Let's break this tactic down into parts. First is the Good Guy/Bad Guy part. I'm sure you've heard of this one. The salesperson winks conspiratorially at you in the presence of his sales manager, agreeing to see if "he" (the sales manager) will go along with what "we" (you and the salesman) are proposing. This is absurd! Who's working for whom here? Who's getting the commission? Who's shelling out big bucks? The salesperson is no more on your side than Bob Dole is on Bill Clinton's. It's just a tactic to try to get you to let your guard down.

Good Guy/Bad Guy is so common it's hard not to have fallen prey to this tactic at least once in your life. But fortunately, it's also easy to counter. When the salesperson says, "I hope 'he'll' go along with what 'we' have in mind," just simply say, "Why wouldn't he? You both work for the same dealership." Just calling them on this is usually enough to stop it.

Now for the "I'll-keep-you-here-until-it-kills-you" part of the routine. This is the part where you'll need a copy of a Tom Clancy novel. As soon as the salesperson begins to get up to talk to the sales manager with the offer, pull out your book. Open it eagerly, as if you can't wait to get back into reading it. Project to the salesperson that you've got all the time in the world. You might even tell him to take his time. Then just as he starts to leave, adjust yourself in your chair, as if you're getting comfortable for a good, long read.

This technique can work miracles. After all, the salesperson is really just as anxious—if not more anxious—than you are to close the deal. Once he realizes that he can't wear you down, you'll have the upper hand.

Secret #110
How to Spot Hidden Dealer Profit

When the salesperson gets tough on price, pick out items on the dealer sticker that you don't understand or haven't asked for. Start with abbreviated things, like ADP, MVA, or DVF.

In reality, you'll find that many of these important-sounding codes are nothing more than ways to pad in extra profit for the dealership. You know what ADP stands for? Added Dealer Profit. MVA? That's Market Value Adjustment—translation: something-that-sounds-official-but-has-no-purpose-whatsoever.

Then there's my personal favorite, DVF. Remar Sutton talks about this one in his book, *Don't Get Taken Every Time: The Insider's Guide to Buying or Leasing Your Next Car or Truck* (Penguin Books), a must-read for anyone in the market for a car: DVF stands for Dealer Vacation Fund.

Bottom line: Question every item on the dealer's sticker. If the salesperson balks or tries to make you feel petty or guilty, stand firm. If you know something is pure profit, say so. The salesperson will have no choice but to eventually back down.

Secrets #111–113
Three Tricks Car Dealers Use to Squeeze
More Money Out of You

Perhaps you've gotten the impression that I don't trust car dealers. It's not that I find the business inherently distasteful, it's just that they routinely employ tactics designed to squeeze as much as they can out of you. Here are a few more to watch out for:

Secret #111
Beware of the Option Trick

This comes into play when the car you're interested in has a radio, CD player, or some other option you don't want. You tell the salesperson you want the car without the option. You ask him to take it out. He shakes his head, gives you his best you'll-be-sorry look and says, "All of our cars come with a radio (or CD player or whatever). I'll have to special order a car without it, and that could take months!"

First of all, remind the salesperson that it is an *OPTION*. Option means it's a choice, and you are choosing not to buy it. Tell the salesperson that if he finds it so annoying to order the car without the option, you'll gladly take a car with the option installed— as long as you don't have to pay for it. My guess is that somehow he'll be able to remove the option or order you a new car within a reasonable time frame.

Secret #112
Don't Pay Extra for Items That Are Standard

Another favorite tactic some car dealers use is to try to get you to pay extra for standard items. For example, they'll order cars for the showroom without carpeting and then claim you have to pay extra for carpeting. Protect yourself by reading the brochures carefully. The brochures will list every item that's included in the price and every option that costs extra.

Secret #113
Don't Pay for the Same Thing Twice

It's bad enough that the prices on the dealer sticker are inflated, but what's worse is that some of the items on the sticker have already been included in the dealer invoice cost. Take the dealer prep charge. All domestic manufacturers include prepping in the price of the car, and some imports do too. Don't pay an extra $100 to $500 for something you're already paying for.

Advertising fees are another example. As with most products, the cost of advertising is already included in the dealer invoice price (since most car advertising is done by the manufacturer, not the individual dealer). But that hasn't stopped some dealers from trying to charge extra advertising fees of 1 to 1.5 percent of the price of the car! Don't fall for it. If the dealer won't remove the advertising fee, walk out. Remember, there are plenty of other dealerships that will gladly take your money.

Secret #114
You Can Buy a Car at Dealer Invoice Cost

My ultimate goal would be to buy a car at dealer invoice cost. I'd be flexible enough to give the dealer 3 percent— even as much as 5 percent— over invoice, but I'd still shoot for dealer invoice cost.

Why would a dealer be willing to sell you a car for his cost? Simple. Because he can still make a nice profit, thanks to a little thing called "holdback."

Holdback is a kickback given to the dealer from the manufacturer as an incentive to sell. Typically 2 to 4 percent of the manufacturer's suggested list price, the holdback is distributed to the dealer several times a year in a lump sum. So even if the dealer sells the car for the invoice price, he's still making a 2 to 4 percent profit on the car.

In addition, manufacturers often give dealers special cash incentives to sell certain cars. These incentives or rebates are typically used to stimulate sales of less-popular cars, and like the holdback, they are 100 percent profit for the dealer.

Now, it's highly unlikely you'll be able to get the dealer to part with his holdback or cash incentive. And I'm not suggesting that you do. What I am suggesting is that you let the knowledge of that holdback and any other special cash incentives give you the confidence to negotiate a lower price on the car.

➤ **Inside Tip:** Not all cars have a holdback—just about all American cars do, but many foreign cars do not. Many of the pricing services listed in Secret #101 can help you figure out whether or not the car you're interested in has a holdback, a factory rebate incentive, or other special incentives for dealers.

Secret #115
Why You *Won't* Get a Better Deal on a Car That's Been Sitting on the Lot for Months

A popular car buying myth is that it's better to try to buy a car that's been sitting on the lot for months. That way, the reasoning goes, the dealership will be dying to sell it. Sounds logical—in fact, the dealership *is* probably dying to sell it. Problem is, the dealership won't be willing to give you a good price for it because the dealer has more invested in the car.

You see, most dealers today don't buy cars outright. They finance them, paying the manufacturer a "floor plan fee" or interest every month. So the longer they've had the car on the lot, the longer they've been paying interest. If the car stays on the lot for two months, they may have only paid $400. But if it stays on the lot for six months, they've already shelled out $1,200. And that floor plan fee is charged against the dealer's 3 percent holdback (see Secret #114). So the dealer is not only incurring the interest charge, but also losing an extra profit booster too.

Secret #116
Why You Can Get a Better Deal If You Order a Car

For the same reason you won't get a better deal on a car that's been sitting on the lot, you *will* get a better deal if you order a car. Since the dealer doesn't have to shell out a dime in floor plan interest, his cost is less, which means your cost should be less too.

I say "should" because you still have to negotiate for it. A dealer isn't going to automatically give you anything. But if you bring up the fact that ordering saves the dealer interest, you're more apt to get the deal you want. And ordering means you'll get the exact car with all the options you want too!

Secret #117
How to Get the Best Price for Your Trade-In

Before you even get to the point of discussing a trade-in with the dealership where you're buying a new car, take your old car around to other dealerships and used car lots to see what it's worth. Tell them you're thinking of selling, and ask what they would give you for it.

Hint: Don't expect to get a price based on the "blue book" value. Blue book figures are based on average selling prices across the country. They're used for insurance purposes—not for selling a car. You may have a car that's in great demand today and would command a much higher price than is listed in the blue book. Or (and this is most often the case), you might have a car that looks like it's been through a tornado. No matter what the blue book says, it's going to be difficult to move.

So take it to the market instead. You'll have a much better idea of what to expect when you are ready to trade it in, and if the new car dealership won't give you the best price, you'll be able to sell it elsewhere.

Secret #118
How to Get Rid of Your Old Car With No Sweat— And Gain a Tax Deduction to Boot!

Don't want to deal with the hassle of trying to sell your trade-in? No problem. Here's a way you can get the full market value of your trade-in with no negotiating, no selling, no hassle: Donate the car to charity. You get a tax write-off for the full fair market value of the car, and the charity gets to use your car as it wishes. A number of charitable organizations will take your car. One of the ones I like is called Best Buddies, which is a sort of big brother/big sister program for mentally retarded and handicapped children. This program, which is currently only available in Florida, Maryland, Virginia, Washington, California, and Delaware, will even come to your home to pick up the car. Whatever they can get from fixing it up and selling it or selling the parts goes to Best Buddies. Call 800/213-8800 for details.

Secret #119
Why a Dollar a Day in Carspeak is Really $536 to You and Me

A favorite trick of car salespeople is to talk about money in utterly ridiculous terms. For example, you'll ask about the price of antilock brakes, and the salesperson says, "Oh, about a dollar a day." So you say to yourself, "A dollar a day, hmm. That's less than I'd spend for a hamburger. It's worth it."

Problem is, it isn't a dollar a day. It's $365. And if you're financing the car, it's $536 on a five-year car loan at 8 percent interest. That's $536 in cold, hard cash. Hardly the cost of a hamburger. Don't let the car salesperson talk in funny-money terms. Always get price quotes in real dollars.

Secret #120
What's Wrong With a Low Monthly Payment

Talking in terms of monthly payments is another favorite trick of car salespeople. "How much do you want to pay per month?"

they'll ask you. The idea here is to get you to avoid looking at the big picture—the total cost—so they can make a killing off you.

Oh sure, the salesperson can get you a car for $150 or $200 a month. Problem is, you'll be paying $200 a month for *six* years! If you don't discuss the price in total dollar terms, the salesperson can set the price at virtually any figure he wants, because he can just keep stretching out your payments.

The only reasonable response to the question of how much you want to pay per month is: Nothing. Explain that you're buying a car, not a monthly payment. Refuse to allow the salesperson to talk in monthly payment terms. In fact, the only time the issue of monthly payment should arise is *before* you set foot in the showroom when you're shopping for a loan. At that point, you'll want to calculate how much you can afford to put down and how much you can afford to pay per month, so you can arrive at an acceptable price. Once you've done that, the total price of the car should be the focus of your discussions, not a monthly payment.

Secret #121
The Dealership's Secret Weapon—And How to Prevent It From Being Used on You

Tactics like talking in funny-money terms (it'll only cost you a dollar a day) or getting you to talk in terms of a monthly payment are all part of the salesperson's key weapon in the battle for your money: confusion. Confusion is the salesperson's best friend. The more he confuses you by coming at key issues from weird angles, the more likely you'll get taken in the deal.

Be on the lookout for this. It will happen just as you ask a pointed question about the trade-in appraisal or just as you're getting close to agreeing on a price. Just when you thought you were talking about one thing, the salesperson switches to something else. It can be maddening!

The way to combat this tactic is to clear your mind. Get a cup of coffee. Go to the bathroom. Think things over. Sort through what the real deal is. Price, financing, and trade-in are all separate issues. Each one should be dealt with separately.

The salesperson won't want to do this. He'll try to answer your question about the price of antilock brakes by saying he could allow you $1,500 on the trade-in, which makes them virtually free.

Don't believe it! Keep bringing him back to the issue at hand. Press for direct answers. If you're persistent enough, you'll win out in the end.

Secret #122
Car Salespeople With Starving Families
Should Get Out of the Business

When the salesperson really wants to close the deal, he'll start using some especially dirty tricks on you. A favorite one is the sympathy ploy.

"Listen, I've had kind of a bad time of it lately," the salesperson will say to you with puppy dog eyes. "I haven't been able to sell a car all month, and I'm afraid if I don't sell this one, I'll get fired. Help a guy out, huh?"

Help a guy out alright—all the way to the bank! If a salesperson tells you he can't pay the mortgage or feed his family, it's probably a lie. Even if it isn't, frankly, that's his problem, not yours. I'd answer the sympathy ploy with a sweet, but firm, "Gee, that's really tough. Now am I going to get this price/interest rate/whatever or not?"

Secret #123
The Most Powerful Negotiating Tool Any Car
Buyer Can Have

There is a point in just about every negotiation when you cross the line. You decide you want the car, you want it today, and you're going to do whatever it takes to get the best deal possible. Stop! You have just reached the point at which you are most vulnerable because you aren't willing to walk away.

As nationally-known negotiating expert Roger Dawson once explained to me, the single biggest negotiating mistake most people make is not being willing to walk away. They become so emotionally invested in whatever they're negotiating that they develop the mindset that they're going to get it no matter what.

Don't fall into this trap. Say to yourself, "This is not the only dealership in America. I can always go somewhere else if things don't work out here." Repeat it until you believe it. And just as you're about to give in on something, remind yourself of this. Be especially wary if you've been working with a particular dealership for several hours or even several weeks. Don't let them wear you down. You'll always fare better if you stay firm on your price and terms and be willing to walk away if you don't get what you want.

Secret #124
What's Wrong With 2.9 Percent Financing (and Other Unbelievably Low Rates)

When a dealership offers you a loan at a rate that sounds too good to be true, chances are it is. It's not that the manufacturer's finance companies are *lying*, it's just that hardly anybody can qualify for these unbelievably great rates. They typically have tough restrictions, like requiring a high down payment or a perfect credit record. And even if you do qualify, they're generally so short term (like one or two years) it isn't worth it.

Here's what I mean: Say you were planning to borrow around $12,000. At 7 percent, a four-year loan would cost you around $300 a month. But if you had to pay off that same loan in two years, even with a 2.9 percent rate, it would cost you around $540 a month. $540 a month! Doesn't make that 2.9 percent look so attractive anymore, does it?

Dealers use these unbelievable rates to suck you into the dealership, nothing more. And if they figure you can meet the restrictions required for one of these unbelievably low rates, they'll usually just pad the price of the car elsewhere to make up for the loss in interest. It's a sour deal any way you look at it. Don't fall for it.

Secret #125
The Truth About "Free Payments"

You know that old saying, "Nothing in life is free?" Well when it comes to car dealers, it should be: "Nothing in buying a car is free. And if you think it is, it's probably costing you a bundle."

Take so-called "free payments." The car salesperson offers to make your first payment for you if you promise to close the deal today. Isn't he nice? *Not!*

Oh sure, you'll get a nice check for the $200 or $300 payment, but the salesperson will turn right around and tack that $200 or $300 onto your car loan. Now you're not only paying the $200 or $300, but you're paying interest on it too!

Like the other tactics mentioned in this chapter, "free payments" are just another way to suck you into closing the deal.

Secret #126
Keep Your Money to Yourself

You're close to getting the deal you want, and now the salesperson is pressing for a deposit.

"If I could show my manager that you're serious, I know I'll be able to get him to agree to your figure," he says smoothly. "You wouldn't have to put down much, just $500 or $1,000."

$500 or $1,000? I don't think so. There is simply no good reason to give a dealership one dime of your money until you've agreed on a price—*in writing*. That means a buyer's order, approved and signed by the manager. And even then, there's no need to put down anything close to a $500 deposit. Remember, these are the same folks who'll let you drive the car home tonight with a wink and a smile (well, practically).

Pressuring you for a deposit is simply another tactic to get you to close the deal. A deposit won't do a thing except require you to go back to the dealership and haggle more. And if you decide you don't want the car or don't want to buy it at that particular dealership, a deposit merely means you'll have to make one more trip to the dealership to ask for your money back.

If you feel you must put down a deposit, make it small. I'm talking like $50 or even $10. Of course, the salesperson will draw back in horror at the mere mention of such a low figure, but rest assured, he'll recover. More importantly, you'll feel less locked in if you decide to change your mind.

Secret #127
How to Pin Down the Deal

Okay, you've finally gotten the salesperson to agree on a reasonable price. Ah, time to relax, right? Not so fast. Even after you think you've agreed on a price, the salesperson will probably still try to squeeze you for more.

You're especially vulnerable if you reach agreement over the phone. Then you risk coming into the dealership and having the salesperson withdraw the offer. "I'm sure I wouldn't have agreed to that price," he says in that guilty politician's tone. "We couldn't possibly agree to that." Now you're back to square one.

To avoid this frustration after you've agreed to a price, have the dealership give you (or fax) the purchase order for the car. Make sure it has the agreed upon price, the vehicle identification number, and the signature of the salesperson or sales manager. If the salesperson tries to weasel out of giving you the purchase order, say you need it for the bank to get your loan. That puts the salesperson in the position of either giving you the agreed upon price or letting the whole deal fall through. It's a good bet he'll choose to give you your price.

Secret #128
Car Salespeople Are Notoriously Bad at Math

One of the sleaziest tricks in the car business is what I call the "calculation fleece." Here's how it works: You negotiate your heart out and finally reach agreement on a price, trade-in allowance, financing terms, everything. All that's left is the paperwork. That's when the salesperson nabs you. He "mistakenly" extends the number of payments by a year. He adds in disability insurance and credit insurance "automatically." He "clumsily" transposes the second and third figures on your trade-in allowance (to the dealer's advantage, of course). In essence, he's raking you over the coals and hoping you won't notice. And as slimy and unbelievable as it sounds, it's used on car buyers every day.

The only way to protect yourself against this tactic is to check every figure on the buyer's order, including the

- Year and date of the car you're buying and your trade-in
- Make and model of both cars
- Serial numbers of both cars
- Asking price

- Trade-in allowance
- Amount to be financed
- Annual percentage rate
- Number of payments
- Amount of payments
- Taxes
- Any other fees

If even one number is off, if there is even one dollar unaccounted for, bring it to the salesperson's attention. Remember, he's testing you. He wants to see how careful you are. If you act like you'll sign anything, he'll take that as a signal to find other places to line his pockets. You may feel a little silly for being so particular, but isn't it better to feel a little silly *before* you sign the contract than finding out you've been cheated *after* you sign it?

Secret #129
The Sale Isn't Over Until
You've Left the Dealership

Congratulations! You've negotiated a great deal on a new car. You've signed the buyer's order, and you're feeling pretty good. There's just one more person the salesperson wants you to meet at the dealership, and you'll be on your way.

Stop! Before you get too relaxed, remember the sale isn't over until you've left the dealership. Car dealerships make money in lots of different ways. Profit on the price of the car is just one way. The trade-in is another way. Financing is yet another way.

And even if you're planning to finance the car elsewhere and you're selling your old car to a neighbor, the dealer will still try to get you to meet with the business manager or customer relations representative whose job it is to squeeze you for even more money.

A friend of mine just bought a black four-door Corolla. The salesperson had just finished telling her how reliable the car is. Then he escorted her over to the manager to "fill out some paperwork." When she got to the manager's office, he spent 45 minutes detailing all of the things that could go wrong with the car and trying to get her to buy extra maintenance and service warranties. Finally, she stood up and said, "I thought this car was supposed to be reliable. If I'm going to need all these extra maintenance warranties, maybe I shouldn't buy it!" The manager got the hint.

Remember, no matter what the tactic is, everyone you meet at the dealership has one goal: to get more of your money. Don't buy anything unless you've had time to think it over and you know you need it.

Secret #130
Three Car Options Never to Buy

Every dealer sells them and many buyers buy them, but the following options are essentially pure profit-padders with little, if any, real value.

Take the ever-popular rustproofing/undercoating/glazing option. If this is so necessary, then why don't the manufacturers just put it on in the shop? Oops! They do! Hence, the reason why most experts believe these services are basically useless. Even if you buy from a manufacturer that doesn't do a great job of rustproofing, I'd urge you to still take a pass on buying it from the dealership. I've seen dealers try to charge as much as $1,200 for this service. What a waste! You can get it from a good shop for around $200.

Then there's the infamous extended warranty or service contract. I really hate this one. First of all, most new cars come with very good warranties these days, and some used cars do too. What's more, you could end up shelling out $600 to $1,200 for something you may never use that may not even cover what you need. I say stash the money in a good money market or short-term bond fund instead. That way, you'll have some cash for future repairs, and it'll be earning interest to boot.

Finally, avoid buying alarm systems or security devices from the dealer. If you want an alarm, but it elsewhere. You'll save 50 to 70 percent off the dealer's price.

Secrets #131–132
Two Ways to Buy a Car With No Negotiating

Buying a car without haggling is a mouth-watering proposition for most consumers. What wants to go through the hassle of researching prices, shopping around, spending hours with too-well-manicured salesmen when you could get the whole thing over within an hour? If the idea of having a root canal is more appealing to you than dickering with car dealers, try one of these strategies:

Secret #131
Buy a Saturn

You've got to hand it to Saturn. They saw a crying need for honest and straightforward dealing in the car business, and they filled it. And quite profitably too, I might add. According to *Kiplinger's Personal Finance,* Saturn's no-dicker prices are *11 percent* over dealer cost—no small mark-up. But the sale is quick and easy. And from what I hear, customers are quite pleased with the car. If you're willing to pay an 11 percent mark-up for the promise of no negotiating, buy a Saturn.

Secret #132
Use a Car-Buying Service

In my opinion, the best no-haggle deals come from car-buying services. They do the bargaining, and you get a car for just $100 or $200 over invoice. Here's a quick rundown of the major services:

- AutoAdvisor (800/326-1976) has two services. The Simple Buyer's Service (for $279) is designed for buyers who know exactly what they want. You just call up, tell the operator the make, model, color, and options of the car you want and when and where you want to take delivery. Then they go to work, researching and negotiating a deal for you.

    The Enhanced Service ($359) gives you up to an hour with a car professional who can give you advice about the features and options of all the cars you're considering.

When I called for information, I got a coupon for $35 off any buying service in the packet they sent me.

■ Car Bargains (800/475-7283) will take the make, model, and style you want and then get bids from at least five local dealerships for a $135 fee. For each bid, you'll get the invoice price of the car plus options, including the amount over invoice the dealer agreed to sell you the car. You'll still have to go to the dealership to pick the car up, though.

■ Consumers Automotive (703/631-5161) charges $195 to $295 depending on the price of the car you buy and promises to deliver the vehicle to your door. You never even have to visit a dealership!

■ Nationwide Auto Brokers (800/521-7257) offers to get you a car for $50 to $125 over invoice plus its fee of $50 to $150. The good thing about this service is it automatically deducts factory-to-dealer incentives from your price—so you get the dealer's rebate! So if the manufacturer is giving dealers a $500 rebate, you'll get the car for $375 to $450 *under* invoice.

Secret #133
What You Should Know If You Decide to Use a Car-Buying Service

As good a deal as car-buying services may get you, they are still far from perfect. First, most won't handle your trade-in for you. And the ones that do are not likely to give you the best price. Also, you may have difficulty getting the best-selling models, and delivery may cost you extra (unless you live in Detroit).

Finally, if you have to pick up the car from a dealership, you may have to withstand high-pressure sales tactics before you can drive it home. One couple I know used a car-buying service to get a Ford Explorer for just $100 over invoice. But when they went to pick up the car, they had to listen to a 45-minute spiel from the customer relations manager on the benefits of rustproofing and spend another hour with the finance manager, who kept assuring them he could beat their credit union's rate— as long as they *leased* the car.

To be sure, car-buying services aren't an ideal solution for everyone. But they can generally provide you with a fair price with much less hassle than you'd find going it alone.

Secret #134
What's Wrong With No-Haggle Dealerships

Despite the success of Saturn and car-buying services, most dealers still haven't changed the way they do business much. Even the "no-haggle dealerships," which promise set prices, don't seem to get it. Sure, they'll offer you a no-haggle price, but it's often much higher than you could get if you bargained at a traditional dealership. And if you try, you can even bargain with the no-haggle dealership.

Which leaves you in the same place you'd be in if you went to a regular dealership. That's why I don't place too much faith in no-haggle dealerships. Until they start offering truly low prices and refuse to negotiate, they're the same as any other dealership as far as I'm concerned.

Secret #135
How to Slash 20 to 25 Percent Off the
Cost of a Car Without Breaking a Sweat

Most new cars drop 20 to 40 percent in value the minute you drive out of the showroom. Doesn't it make sense then, that you could buy a newly-used car for 20 to 40 percent less than the price of a new car? Indeed, you can.

Now the point I want to emphasize here is *newly used*. We're talking about an alternative to a new car, so you want to make sure the car you buy is in good shape. Good shape doesn't always mean the lowest mileage. You could easily find a low mileage car that's a lemon or one with relatively high mileage (50,000) that rides like a dream. Good shape is good mechanical condition. And the only way to find out is to have a mechanic look it over.

Before you even shop for a used car, I'd find a mechanic who'd be able to give it a thorough evaluation, including engine, fans and belts, cooling system, battery, brakes, exhaust, suspension, differential fluid, and a test drive. Mention these specific items when you talk to the mechanic, and get the mechanic's price up front.

If the car does need repairs, don't automatically rule it out. Find out what the repairs will cost, and just subtract that from the price you offer on the car.

Secret #136
What to Ask When You're
Shopping for a Used Car

When you go shopping for a used car, the following questions will help you narrow down your choices:

- Why is the car being sold? If you're buying from a dealership, I'd take the answer with a grain of salt—I'm sure they have no qualms about lying to you. But if you're buying directly from the owner, pay close attention. If the words "need something more reliable" or "can't keep up with the repairs" slip out, you know you're in trouble.
- Is there a service and repair record? The ideal, of course, would be meticulous records of proper maintenance.
- Has the car been in any accidents?
- Has the car been repainted recently? If so, it could be covering up serious rust damage.

In addition, you'll want to inspect the car for the condition of the tires, upholstery, headlights, and any cracks in the tail pipe (which your mechanic should also pick up).

Secret #137
How to Check Out a Car's Reputation

The National Highway Traffic Safety Administration has an Auto Safety Hotline that allows you to order a variety of reports on car safety, including recall reports, vehicle crash test reports, and tire quality grading reports. Call 800/424-9393 for details.

Secrets #138–141
Four Ways to Get the Best Repairs
for the Lowest Price

My idea of heaven is having a car that never breaks down, never needs a repair that costs over $100, and lasts 200,000 miles. Hey, I can dream, can't I?

Seriously, though, to me there is no more frustrating feeling than having to take a car for repairs. I never know if the problem has been diagnosed correctly. I have no idea whether or not the price is fair. And I have to go on faith that the mechanic actually did the work.

Fortunately, I have learned a few tricks from folks in the know about finding a good mechanic and getting a decent price, like:

Secret #138
Find Out How the Mechanic Is Compensated

Before you take your car into a shop, ask on the phone how the mechanics are compensated. Ideally, you want to avoid mechanics that are paid on commission, especially in high-pressure franchise operations. These shops often operate under a system, pressuring mechanics to sell a certain number of oil changes, alignments, or whatever per week. You want your mechanic to fix what's wrong with your car, not sell you something you don't need!

Secret #139
Give the Mechanic the Guilt-Trip

If at all possible, try to talk to the mechanic in person—ideally, *before* the diagnosis is made. That way, he has a face to put with the car, a face he can think of when he thinks about charging you for unnecessary work.

When you meet the mechanic, call him (or her) by name. Tell him you trust him. Explain that your car's future is in his hands. And when he makes his diagnosis, try to be there in person. Have him show you what's wrong. Ask questions. Ask him to explain what you could have done to prevent the problem or take better care of the car in the future. All of this is designed to get the mechanic to take a personal interest in you and your car, to want to help you and—you hope—to want to avoid cheating you.

This is why I like independent shops. They may not have the volume of the franchises or all the diagnostic equipment of a dealership, but the mechanic has to talk to you face-to-face. He can't hide behind a service advisor. He has to look you in the eye when he makes a recommendation, and he knows his livelihood depends on your future business.

Secret #140
Get a Second Opinion

If you drive your car into a repair shop, you ought to be able to drive it out for a second opinion. A lot of mechanics have an annoying habit of getting you to authorize one repair, then calling you later when the engine is completely taken apart and recommending other repairs. At this point, you're very vulnerable, and they know it.

Don't let any mechanic take advantage of you this way. Say you want a second opinion. If he says he can't put the car back together without doing the work, tell him that's his problem. You drove the car into the shop, you ought to be able to drive it out.

Secret #141
Look Into Secret Warranties

Have you ever gotten a repair and then heard three or four other people talk about needing the same work on the same kind of car? If so, chances are there may be something wrong with the way the car was manufactured, and you may be eligible for a free repair.

Before you get any kind of major work done, check with the manufacturer to see if it's covered under warranty. Even if your warranty has expired, check anyway. A lot of manufacturers will cover the repair if a significant number of their cars have the malfunction. But don't expect them to publicize this, you'll have to ask about it.

7

From Small Potatoes to Big Bucks: How to Take $100 and Turn It Into a Six-Figure Nest Egg

I read an interesting story about young entrepreneurs recently. At the ripe old age of 20 or 21, these young adults had shunned cushy corporate jobs in favor of starting their own businesses. Each of the three people profiled was extremely successful, having generated between $50,000 and several million dollars in income within three years.

But what amazed me was how willing these young people were to take risks. One fellow had started his own tour bus company to service Colorado's new gambling industry. Each bus cost over $200,000! I couldn't imagine making that kind of financial commitment. But when asked about the risks, the young man replied, "There's very little financial risk for me at all. I lease the buses. And I use other people's money to pay for it."

Another entrepreneur, a young woman, booked rock bands for a living. When asked about the risks she took to go into business for herself, she said, "Yeah, it was pretty scary. But I didn't move out of my parents' house until I was bringing in over $50,000 a year."

I guess what appears "risky" on the surface isn't always so risky after all. It's the same with investing. Many people assume investing is risky. They think the least risky way to invest is to hide money under a mattress. But of course, that's more risky.

Hiding your money under a mattress subjects you to risk of theft and loss of purchasing power (your money doesn't grow, but inflation does, so what you have doesn't buy as much tomorrow as it does today).

On the other hand, investing in the stock market is no different from lending $1,000 to your Uncle Max to open up a pickle stand. Essentially, you're lending money to businesses to help them grow and expand, just as a bank does. And like a bank, by understanding and quantifying the risks, you can ensure gains are maximized and losses are minimized.

Secret #142
Where to Stash Your Cash for the Best Return

Whether you're new to investing or an old hand, it's important to have a safe, accessible place to put your cash where you can get a decent return. My choice? Money market mutual funds. Like bank savings accounts and certificates of deposit (CDs), money market funds are safe (they aren't federally-insured, but they do maintain a constant $1 per share value). But unlike savings accounts and CDs, they are as liquid as checks (in fact, all you have to do to access your money market fund is write a check), and they tend to have higher yields.

When choosing a money market fund, look for one that: (1) comes from a good no-load mutual fund family so you can switch in and out of it depending on your investment needs, (2) pays a decent yield, (3) has low check-writing minimums ($100 to $500 is standard; anything higher is too much), (4) has a low minimum initial investment, and (5) does not invest in derivatives (ask when you call for an application). Some of my favorites are:

- Benham Government Agency Fund (800/472-3389; $1,000 minimum initial investment, $100 minimum check)
- Benham Capital Preservation Fund (800/472-3389; $1,000 minimum initial investment, $100 minimum check)

- Twentieth Century Cash Reserve (800/345-2021; $1,000 minimum initial investment, $500 minimum check)
- Vanguard Money Market Prime (800/523-7731; $3,000 minimum initial investment, $250 minimum check)

You'll notice that all of these are money market *mutual funds* not money market *deposit accounts* from banks. I prefer money market *funds* because they have higher yields.

Secret #143
Why Playing It Too Safe Can Be Risky Business

Putting your money in a savings account or money market fund is the safest way to invest, right? Wrong. Certainly, a portion of your money should be held in safe, liquid investments, such as money market funds. And you should certainly not venture beyond money markets until you have three-to-six months' living expenses in reserve. But for your retirement money and other *investments*, keeping it all in money markets, CDs, and bank savings accounts is just plain risky.

You see, these so-called "safe" investments have a major downside: They rarely earn enough to beat inflation. Like termites in a basement, inflation slowly eats away at your nest egg, year after year, almost without you even knowing it. It's insidious, and if you include the effect of taxes too, you could actually be losing money!

The best way to build a nest egg is by putting a healthy portion of your assets in *growth* investments, like stocks and stock mutual funds. Over time, stocks have outperformed money markets, bonds, and other fixed income vehicles, hands down, turning in an average 10.3 percent annually since 1926.

So how much of your nest egg should you keep in stocks? Clearly, it depends on your investment time frame. The longer you have before you need to use the money, the more you can put in stocks. If you're saving for retirement, a good rule of thumb is to take your age and subtract it from 100. Invest that amount in stocks. So if you're 20, you can invest 80 percent of your retirement money in stocks. If you're 50, 50 percent of your retirement money should be in stocks or stock mutual funds.

Secret #144
How to Grow Rich $25 at a Time

You don't have to be rich to invest. With as little as $25 or $50 a month, you can build a sizeable nest egg. Just look at how your money will grow if you invest a set amount per month and earn an average 9 percent per year:

Monthly Investment	5 yrs.	9% Average Annual Return Over 10 yrs.	15 yrs.	20 yrs.	25 yrs.
$25	1,899	4,874	9,531	16,822	28,238
$50	3,799	9,748	19,062	33,645	56,476
$100	7,599	19,496	38,124	67,290	112,953
$150	11,398	29,245	57,186	100,934	169,429
$200	15,198	38,993	76,249	134,579	225,906
$250	18,997	48,741	95,311	168,224	282,382
$500	37,995	97,483	190,622	336,448	564,765

As you can see, even as little as $50 a month can grow to more than $56,000 over time. And if you set up an automatic investment plan, your money will grow, even if you forget about it! See Secret #187 for my favorite mutual fund families with automatic investment plans.

Secret #145
Four Characteristics of Successful Investors

In my work, I get an opportunity to talk with hundreds of individual investors each year. One of the most striking things I've noticed is that the most successful investors aren't necessarily any smarter or better at analyzing financial data than anyone else. They don't have degrees in business or financial planning; in fact, many don't have degrees at all! The secrets to their success are really quite simple:

1. *Successful investors have a plan, and they stick to it.* It's easy to get tempted by a neat story, to want to buy the latest hot stock touted by *Money* magazine or CNBC. But that isn't the way successful investors make money. Successful investors assess their own needs first. They look at their goals, time frame, and knowledge of investing to come up with a plan to suit their needs. If they

are 50 years old, for example, and have 15 years until retirement, they set up a 15-year plan.

Then they read as much as they can and invest in things they know about and are comfortable with. If, for example, they hear about the terrific return potential of zero coupon bonds, but don't really understand how they work, they don't buy them.

They don't allow themselves to get sidetracked by hot tips. They buy only investments they've researched or that someone they trust has recommended, and they shut out the noise of the financial press. In this way, they can be sure of sticking to the plan they've developed.

2. Successful investors invest regularly. Successful investors do not expect to hit home runs with their investments every time. They know that one home run plus lots of strikeouts (little losses) adds up to a lot of time on the bench. To succeed year after year, successful investors know they must keep their money growing. They use two methods to do this: First, they invest in stocks or stock mutual funds. They know that stocks are the only investment with the long-term power to grow their money year in and year out. Second, they invest regularly. I love this method because it's guaranteed to work for everyone. Even a spendthrift like Babe Ruth could have grown a fortune just by socking away a little on the side every month. And what a powerful edge! You're always adding more to your principal, so your nest egg can't help but grow. It's virtually *guaranteed.*

3. Successful investors are patient. Often, it will take time for a good investment to show its true value. Successful investors understand this, and consequently, they do not get caught up in the daily ups and downs of the market. They know that to succeed in the long run, they have to be patient. They do not jump in and out of investments, trying to time the market perfectly. They buy investments that have good value and hold on to them until the market realizes that value. They do not expect to see instant growth, so they are not disappointed by temporary setbacks.

4. Successful investors do not marry investments. To be successful at investing, you must be unemotional. No matter how much they like a stock or a mutual fund, no matter how promising that investment was when they first bought it, successful investors know that selling at the right time is as important as buying.

It's hard to sell something that has done nothing but lose money. But successful investors do not try to recoup their losses. They know that if an investment is not panning out, holding on will not help. They cut their losses and move on.

Likewise, if an investment has made a lot of money, they know how to protect their gains. It's emotionally hard for someone to part with something that has done nothing but go up, yet that's precisely the best reason to sell. Nothing goes up forever.

Secret #146
The Best Time to Start Saving for Retirement

It's never too soon to start saving for retirement because the sooner you start, the more you'll be able to take advantage of the single most powerful investment weapon there is: time. Time is a wonderful thing in investing. It allows you to take a little money and let it grow into tens—even hundreds—of thousands of dollars through the magical power of compounding. With compounding, you can multiply your return many times over because you're earning gains on top of gains on top of gains.

And the more time you have, the less you need to invest to achieve your goals. Consider this: You can turn a one-time $5,000 investment for your 10-year-old into a $600,000+ retirement nest egg just by letting the magical power of compounding work for you over time. With just a simple $5,000 initial investment at age 10, your child would have a *$692,957* nest egg when she retires at age 65 (assuming a 9 percent average annualized return). And that's if she never added one red cent after the initial $5,000 investment!

➤ **Inside Secret:** To really supercharge this investment, you could set up an Individual Retirement Account (IRA) for your child. This will allow her money to grow tax-deferred until she begins withdrawing (see Secret #150 for details). Anyone can set up an IRA; the only requirement is that your yearly contribution be no more than your annual earnings or $2,000, whichever is less. If your child can earn some extra money babysitting, delivering papers, even mowing the lawn, that counts. And she doesn't even have to use her own money to fund the IRA. You can use your money to set up her IRA as long as you don't invest more than she earned for the year. Even if you set aside just $500 a year for five years and then stopped at age 15, she'd still have a nest egg worth $291,931 by the time she reached age 65 (assuming a 9 percent average annual return). Now that's what I call a real gift for the future!

Secret #147
The First Rule of Investing

It's easy to fall into the trap. You hear a hot stock tip at a cocktail party, read about a gangbusters mutual fund in *Money* magazine, or see a neat company being touted by a money manager on "Wall Street Week" or CNBC. So you buy it. Only problem is, you didn't realize it was just a tax shelter that would require you to tie up your money for 15 years or that the zero coupon bond you bought doesn't pay current interest, but is taxed as if it does or that the bank mutual fund wasn't FDIC-insured.

Investing can be complicated. Even professional money managers get tempted by eye-popping returns sometimes and buy things they don't understand (does the word "derivative" ring a bell?). But that doesn't mean *you* should. The only sure-fire way to invest for success is to buy *what you understand*. That goes for individual stocks, as well as bonds, mutual funds, and even CDs. You need to know how an investment works (when it matures or pays dividends, for example), what the risks are (e.g., could the bond be called or does the fund invest in a select industry like utilities that could be hurt by rising interest rates), what the tax implications are (e.g., zeros pay no current income, but are taxed as if they do), and, most importantly, *what fundamental reason does this investment have for growing now*?

The beauty of this approach is that you get to use the knowledge you have of the companies and products you know to grow your own wealth. Nowhere is the value of this approach better illustrated than in the story renowned investment expert Peter Lynch tells in his book, *Beating the Street* (Simon & Schuster, 1993), about a group of seventh graders at St. Agnes School in Massachusetts. After learning to read the financial papers and researching companies they were interested in, the teens picked a group of 14 stocks in January, 1990. The portfolio was full of names like Nike and Topps, L.A. Gear and Mobil, companies the seventh graders understood well. Not all the picks were winners, but by the end of 1991, the portfolio had earned a whopping 69.6 percent! Outperforming the S&P 500 over the same time period by more than two-and-a-half times!

If a group of seventh graders can do that, you can too. Before you plunk down your hard-earned money to buy some plexi-tech, superconducting, gigabyte-whiz stock you heard about at a cocktail party or read about in *The Wall Street Journal,* think of those seventh graders. Ask yourself if you understand why the company in which you're about to invest your savings will grow. If you don't have the answer to that question, don't invest. Only with a solid understanding of the investments you're buying can you truly expect to grow your money over the long term.

Secret #148
The Truth About Diversification

Diversification is a popular concept. If you buy a bunch of things, the theory goes, when one or two go down, you won't be hurt because you'll have three or four others that are going up. The problem is if you buy a bunch of investments where some are designed to go up while others are going down, you could very well cancel out your gains entirely. It's like winning at the slot machines in Vegas, then getting robbed on the elevator up to your room. You're right back where you were when you started—only more frustrated.

A better way to diversify your risks without potentially canceling out your returns is to look for investments that are all poised to go up, but have different fundamental risks and different reasons to perform well.

For example, say interest rates are rising and inflation is heating up in the United States, but European countries are just emerging from recession. You may put together a portfolio that includes: 30 percent cash to take advantage of rising U.S. interest rates, 10 percent gold to benefit from inflation, and 60 percent European stocks to take advantage of economic growth and potentially lower interest rates overseas. None of these investments is linked to the same fundamentals as the others, so they don't share the same risks. But each one may have a good reason to perform well at the same time. That's how diversification should work.

Secret #149
What's Wrong With Tracking
Your Investments Daily

Once you buy a few investments, you'll want to see how they're doing. I know people who look up their stocks and mutual funds every day in the newspaper. But there's a danger in doing this. It's like weighing yourself when you're on a diet. Sure, you may have made progress or had a setback in the short-term (and checking daily is *very* short-term), but that's not what counts. What matters is how well you're progressing toward meeting your goals, and short-term fluctuations won't tell you that. Even worse, short-term fluctuations in investing may cause you to get scared and sell an investment that really has good value.

Don't monitor your investments every day. Ideally, you want to check your progress every month. That way, you can be sure you're staying on top of changes in trends without getting sucked into making an emotional decision based on short-term volatility.

Secrets #150–152
Three Ways to Let Uncle Sam Boost Your
Investment Returns

As any serious investor knows, taxes can take quite a bite out of the average savings plan. Fortunately, the federal government, in its infinite wisdom, has recognized this and decided to give taxpayers a break in the form of three IRS-approved tax-deferred investment plans.

These tax-deferred investment vehicles allow you to sock away money for your retirement and not pay one dime in taxes on your gains until you begin withdrawing at age $50\frac{1}{2}$ or later. In a word, this is a godsend. It allows the wonder of compound interest to work to the max for you. You'll earn interest on top of interest and not pay a penny in taxes until you begin withdrawing. There is simply no better way to build a nest egg.

Secret #150
An IRA Is a Terrific Way to
Grow Your Money Tax-Deferred

With an Individual Retirement Account (IRA), you can invest up to $2,000 per year (that's the max allowed by law) in virtually anything you choose, from a bank CD to individual stocks or mutual funds. All you have to do is let the financial institution (bank, stockbroker, mutual fund) know that you want your investment to be sheltered in an IRA. You report your investment on your tax return, but you pay no taxes on your gains until you withdraw at age 59 1/2 or later. You can even switch in and out of investments in your IRA over time.

What's more, you can deduct your entire $2,000 annual investment as long as you earn less than $25,000 per year ($40,000 if you're married). And if you earn between $25,000 and $35,000 ($40,000 to $50,000 for married couples), you can take a partial deduction. So you get a tax deduction right off the bat, plus tax-deferred compounding to boot!

[Note: Even if you aren't eligible to deduct your IRA, you can still make up to a $2,000 contribution to your IRA each year.]

Secret #151
Let Your Employer Fund Your Future
With a 401(k)

A 401(k) plan is even better than an IRA because you can invest up to around $9,500 (it's adjusted upward slightly each year to account for inflation) annually and it comes right off the top of your paycheck. You never see the money, so you never have to make the decision not to save. But the biggest benefit of a 401(k) is that many employers match or partially match your contribution, so you get pretax investing, tax-deferred compounding, *and* an extra bonus from your company! This is without a doubt the best of all tax-deferred retirement plans. If a 401(k) is available to you, I urge you to take advantage of it. (Nonprofit employers offer a similar plan called a 403(b). This is essentially the same arrangement as a 401(K); the difference in the name is simply because it is part of a different section of the tax code.)

Secret #152
The One Investment That Guarantees
You Won't Outlive Your Money

How would you like to be able to sock away as much money as you want for retirement, have your earnings grow tax-free, and be guaranteed to have a steady stream of income for as long as you live? Sound like a dream? Well it's all possible with a variable annuity.

An annuity is sort of like an IRA and a life insurance policy rolled into one. Like an IRA, an annuity allows you to earn interest and capital gains on your money without paying one dime in taxes until you begin withdrawing. And you must wait to withdraw until you reach age 59 1/2 or you'll face a 10 percent penalty.

But unlike an IRA, you can make unlimited contributions—up to $1 million per year if you want. Your contributions are made with after-tax dollars, however, so you don't get the tax deduction benefit you get with an IRA or 401(k). But since an annuity is essentially an insurance product, once you begin withdrawing money ("annuitizing" in insurance lingo), you are guaranteed to receive income for the rest of your life. That means you'll never outlive your money!

➤ **Inside Tips:** To get the max out of these tax-deferred retirement vehicles, use them like the pros do:

1. If it's available to you, invest in a 401(k) first. You simply can't beat it because: (a) Your investment comes right off the top of your paycheck before taxes; (b) all of your earnings compound tax-deferred; (c) many plans offer matching employer contributions—that's like free money from your company; (d) your investment is automatically deducted from your paycheck; you never see it and you never have to make the decision not to invest; (e) many plans allow you to make penalty-free withdrawals for certain expenses like buying a home or funding a college education. You may have to repay the money with interest, but that interest is going to you.

2. Once you've invested the maximum amount in your 401(k), invest in an IRA even if your investment is not tax-deductible. Your earnings still accumulate tax-deferred, you have an exceptionally wide variety of investment options available to you, and IRAs typically charge much lower management fees than annuities.

3. After you've maxed out your 401(k) and IRA contributions, look into a variable annuity. The key here is *variable.* All annuities are underwritten by insurance companies, but if your money is in a variable annuity, the funds are kept separate from the rest of the insurance company's assets. So if the insurance company goes under, you won't lose your money. By contrast, the money in a fixed annuity is commingled with the rest of the insurance company's assets. And if the insurance company went bankrupt, you could lose your money. What's more, variable annuities offer you more investment options, so you have more control over your investment returns.

Secret #153
The One Big Drawback of Annuities

Because annuities are quasi-insurance products, they tend to have higher fees than typical investment products. In addition to high management fees, front-end loads (commissions), annual fees, and a whole host of other fees, many annuities also carry back-end surrender charges.

Surrender charges are fees you pay if you sell or switch out of the annuity within a certain time period. You typically have five to seven years, and the surrender charge usually declines per year. For example, if you buy an annuity with a 6 percent declining surrender charge over six years, you'll pay 6 percent if you sell or switch out of the annuity the first year, 5 percent the second year, 4 percent the third year, and so on.

The best way to avoid getting socked with this fee is to choose an annuity that has no surrender charges, such as Vanguard's Variable Annuity (800/522-5555; minimum investment: $5,000) or Scudder's Horizon Plan (800/225-2470; minimum investment: $2,500).

This is important because even if you don't plan to tap your annuity for many years, you still may want to roll it over into another annuity. And if you have a surrender charge, that rollover will be treated as a sale, and you'll have to pay the surrender fee.

Secret #154
Three Things to Look For in a Variable Annuity

Okay, so you've decided to buy a variable annuity. Before you plunk down your hard-earned money, get the literature from several different annuities and ask yourself the following questions about each one:

1. What investment options does it offer? This is the most important question—after all, this is what will determine how fast your money grows. My preference is for an annuity that has well-known subfunds you can follow in the financial press. An annuity sponsored by a mutual fund family, such as Vanguard, Fidelity, or Scudder, is a great choice because the subaccounts are all funds that mirror well-known Vanguard, Fidelity, and Scudder funds, and you can analyze and track them easily. Many insurance companies offer well-known subfunds in their annuities too. Lincoln National, for example, offers funds in its annuity that mirror Fidelity Equity Income II and Janus Fund.

But just because a fund is well known does not mean you should buy it. Even funds that have good, long-term track records can turn into portfolio duds. That's why it's best to look for an annuity with as many different investment options as possible. Ideally, you'd have a blue-chip growth fund, an aggressive small company growth fund, an international fund, a short-term bond fund, a long-term bond fund, a growth and income or asset allocation fund, a gold fund, and a money market fund. This should give you the broadest range of choices to switch in and out of as the economic climate changes.

2. What are its fees? As I mentioned in Secret #153, high fees are the biggest drawback of annuities—there are lots of them, and they're much higher than the fees you'd pay to invest in a regular mutual fund.

To start with, avoid all funds that have front-end loads, commissions, or sales charges. Next, look at the expense ratio (fees that go to the insurance company or fund company to manage the annuity). The average variable annuity expense ratio is 2.28 percent. Try to find one that's below the average, like the Vanguard Variable Annuity (1 percent expense ratio). Next, look at the surrender charges. As I said in Secret #153, I prefer annuities with no surrender charges, but if there is one, make sure you plan to keep your money there until after the surrender charge disappears. Finally, ask about annual fees, switching fees, and any other fees. Although a $30 annual fee may seem small when you think about your whole nest egg, think of it this way: If someone stole $30 out of your wallet, how would you feel? Remember, one of the best ways to build wealth is to find ways to keep more of what you start with!

3. *What are the payout options?* Here, you're looking for as much flexibility as possible. When it comes time to take your money out, you want to be able to have choices as to how fast or slow you do so. The more payout options the annuity has, the more control you'll have of your money in the future.

Secret #155
How to Grow Your Money Tax-Deferred
After You Retire

Retirees take note! You can still gain all the benefits of tax-deferred compounding even if you're 70 or older by investing in an annuity. IRAs require that you start withdrawing your money at age 70 1/2, but some annuities, such as Vanguard's Variable Annuity, allow you to keep making contributions to age 75 and beyond.

Secret #156
How to Avoid Getting Taxed Twice on Your IRA

It's vital that you keep track of all of your IRA investments—if you don't, you could end up paying taxes on the same money twice. Here's why: When you first open your IRA, you may fund it with tax-deductible dollars. Since you haven't paid taxes on this money, you'll owe taxes on it when you withdraw. But later, you may be adding to your IRA with contributions that aren't tax-deductible. Since you have already paid taxes on this money, you'll only owe taxes on the gains you've made—not the principal you invested initially.

The secret to avoiding the double tax trap is accurate record-keeping. By keeping track of both your pretax investments and after-tax investments, you can be sure Uncle Sam won't get the best of you!

Secret #157
How to Deduct Your IRA Even If You Make Over $35,000

It's true that if you're covered by a pension plan and you earn more than $35,000 ($50,000 for married couples), you can't deduct your annual contributions to your IRA. But if you aren't an active participant in a pension plan, you can deduct the full $2,000 annual limit even if you make $100,000 a year!

▶ **Inside Tip:** There's a lot of confusion regarding what constitutes being an active participant in a pension plan. If, for example, your employer offers a 401(k) plan, but you choose not to participate, does that mean you aren't an active participant? Generally, yes—as long as your employer makes no contributions on your behalf.

Say, for example, your employer offers a 401(k) plan that matches your contribution dollar-for-dollar, but you choose not to invest. As long as you aren't participating in any other pension plan, your IRA contribution would be deductible. But if your employer made contributions to the plan, whether you chose to participate or not, your IRA contributions would *not* be deductible. Call the IRS (800/TAX-FORM) to get a copy of Publication 1602, which explains the rules in detail.

Secret #158
When It Makes Sense to Choose an IRA Over a 401(k)

If a 401(k) offers the ability to make higher contributions and the potential for a matching investment from your company, why would you ever elect not to participate? In most cases, you shouldn't. But if you don't like the investment options in your 401(k), and you don't plan to contribute more than $2,000 a year, you may find it's better to set up an IRA on your own. You'll have the flexibility of choosing whatever investments you want and your investment may be tax-deductible to boot (see Secret #157 for details).

Secret #159
The One Investment Never to Put in an IRA

You can put virtually any investment in your IRA, from CDs to commodities. But there's one investment that you should never put in an IRA: municipal bonds. The main advantage to investing in munis is that the income you receive is tax-free. But this advantage does you no good when it's sheltered in an IRA (because you don't pay taxes on your earnings in an IRA). And since munis pay lower yields than their taxable counterparts, you'll just be earning less income.

Save your municipal bond and tax-free money market money for a regular account, and put your investments with the greatest capital gains potential, like stocks, in your IRA.

Secret #160
What Nonprofit Retirement Plans Have
That 401(k)s Don't

A 403(b) is essentially the equivalent of a 401(k) for employees of nonprofit organizations. Like a 401(k), a 403(b) allows you to make regular contributions of your choice to a variety of investment funds that grow tax-deferred until you retire. But unlike a 401(k), a 403(b) allows you to invest your money elsewhere if you don't like the way your plan portfolios are performing. You can make the switch without retiring or leaving your job.

All you need to do is to set up a 403(b)(7) custodial account with the mutual fund or brokerage firm of your choice. Then have your 403(b) plan administrator transfer the funds from the plan portfolio into your new account.

There is a catch, however. Since most 403(b)s are invested in annuities, you may face surrender charges if you transfer money out within your first five to seven years with the plan. Check with your plan administrator to see if you'd face any penalties before making the move. Even if there are penalties, you may be able to move part of your money (the money you put in first, for example) or you may be able to take 10 percent out each year without penalty under the annuity's free withdrawal clause. Many annuities have such a clause, which allows participants one free withdrawal of up to 10 percent of the account without incurring charges. Check with your plan administrator for details.

Secret #161
How You Can Get Fleeced Investing in Stocks If You Don't Know How

You know I believe stocks should be an integral part of every investor's portfolio. There is simply no better way to grow your money over the long-term. But that doesn't mean buying individual stocks is necessarily the way to go for every investor.

Individual stocks must be bought through a broker, and that means you'll have to pay a hefty commission. Full-service brokers can charge hundreds of dollars to execute a single trade. Think of it this way: If you pay $250 for a round-trip trade (buy and sell) on a $5,000 investment, you'd have to make 5 percent just to break even! A $50 stock would have to rise to $52.50 before you could even start making money!

That's why I recommend buying individual stocks only if you have a very large (like $25,000 or more) portfolio. Otherwise, you're spending too large of a percentage of your investment in commissions.

Secrets #162–166
Five Ways to Cut Commissions on Individual Stocks

Smart investors know that using a full-service stockbroker can be a mighty expensive way to play the market. Fortunately, there are a number of excellent ways to invest in stocks without paying big commissions. Here are a few of my favorites:

Secret #162
Ask for a Discount

As simple as it seems, so few investors negotiate commissions with their brokers. Instead, they accept the rates as set in stone and don't even bother to question them. It's a real shame, since most brokers will gladly discount commissions, especially if you have a large portfolio. So *ask!* After all, what have you got to lose except a couple hundred dollars in brokerage commissions!

Secret #163
Use a Discount Broker

Merrill Lynch and Dean Witter aren't the only stockbrokers around, you know. There's a whole slew of discount brokers out there that will execute trades at 25 to 70 percent less than you'd pay with a full-service broker. You won't get the same level of research and advice you'd get from a full-service broker, but a number of discounters do offer some services that come close, including free research materials, no-fee IRAs, and branch offices. And many offer services you can't even get from a full-service broker, like no-commission trading on mutual funds. Here are a few of my favorites:

- Charles Schwab (800/435-4000) is one of the biggest discounters around, with a nationwide network of 200 branch offices where customers can drop off a check, pick up some research reports, or just watch the ticker. Schwab also has 24-hour service, allowing you to place a trade with a live person at 3 a.m. if you like. And if you want to make your trades by phone, Schwab will slash 10 percent off your commissions.

- Jack White (800/233-3411) offers low commissions, computer and telephone trading, and handles a number of investments many other discounters won't touch, including commodities and precious metals.

- Barry Murphy & Co. (800/221-2111) is a bare bones discounter, offering razor-thin commissions and specializing in foreign trades. If you like buying foreign stocks, this is the one to go with.

- Fidelity Discount Brokers (800/544-6666) offers a wide range of services, 24-hour telephone and computerized trading, and the ability to trade a number of Fidelity mutual funds without paying a commission.

Secret #164
Reinvest Your Dividends

What do Exxon, IBM, and Coca-Cola have in common? Certainly not product lines! But they do all offer dividend reinvestment plans (or DRIPs, for short). DRIPs are a great way for investors to save money. They allow you to use the money you earn from dividends to buy additional shares of stock without paying a dime in commissions. And some companies even offer a discount on the stock price, too. So you save on the brokerage commission and get a below-market price to boot!

It's a great way to build a stock portfolio at a low cost. To find out if a company you're interested in buying offers a DRIP, call the company directly. (As you can imagine, brokers won't be too interested in passing on this information to you.) Ask for the Investor or Stockholder Relations Department. Since every DRIP program has its own rules and requirements regarding minimum and maximum investments, be sure to get the restrictions clear before you act.

Secret #165
Buy Shares Directly From the Company

A few companies not only allow you to reinvest your dividends without paying a commission, but they allow you to buy additional shares directly too! These programs are called Direct Stock Purchase Plans or Voluntary Investment Plans (VIPs), and they're fantastic. You can buy your very first share from the company directly—and often, at a very low minimum. Mobil, for example, requires only a $250 minimum initial investment to buy shares in its direct stock purchase plan.

➤ **Hidden Trap:** But be aware, if you buy directly from the company, you give up a serious advantage you have with a broker: time. A trade with a broker can be ordered, executed, and completed within minutes. Going directly to the company may take weeks. And you may have difficulty when you sell.

For more information about using VIPs and DRIPs, read Charles Carlson's *Buying Stocks Without a Broker* (McGraw-Hill, 1992).

Secret #166
Buy Through First Share

If the idea of investing through a DRIP appeals to you, but the stock you're interested in requires you to own at least one share, don't buy from a broker—buy from First Share. First Share is a low-cost program that allows investors to buy single shares of stock at a nominal cost in order to be able to participate in the company's DRIP. You pay $24 to join First Share. That enables you to request to buy single shares of stock from other First Share members. You pay First Share a $4 request fee and a $7.50 transaction fee, which goes to the seller. Call 719/783-9377 for details.

Secret #167
A Simple Strategy to Avoid
Buying at a Market Top

Everyone knows that the way to make money in the stock market is to buy at a bottom and sell at a top. The problem is figuring out when the stock has hit a bottom or top. And even if you could, most investors just can't stomach buying something that has just plummeted 60 percent. Indeed, it's much easier to buy something that has just soared 60 percent. But clearly, if it has just soared 60 percent, you aren't getting in at the bottom, are you?

There is no accurate way to predict a stock's bottom or top. That has led many investment experts to a strategy that, while not guaranteeing you get in at the bottom, will at least help you avoid buying at a top. It's called dollar-cost averaging. It's a simple principle. You invest a set amount per month or per quarter or whatever, buying whatever number of shares that dollar amount currently purchases. The effect is that when the share price is high, you buy fewer shares, but when the share price is low, you buy more shares. Over the long-term, your average share price will certainly be lower than if you bought at the top, and will tend to be lower overall. Here's an example:

		Stock ABC	
Date	*Amt. Inv.*	*Current Price*	*No. of Shares Bought*
April	$100	$29	3.4
May	$100	$25	4
June	$100	$22.50	4.4
July	$100	$22	4.5
August	$100	$27	3.7

Total Amount Invested: $500
Total Shares Owned: 20
Average Price Per Share: $25

As you can see, if you had invested the entire $500 in April, you would have bought at the absolute top, and your account as of August would be worth just $465 (at the August share price of $27/share). If you had known that July was the bottom, you could have invested the entire $500 then and your investment would now be worth $612. But as I said earlier, it's practically impossible to pinpoint exactly when the bottom will be. By dollar-cost averaging, you now own 20 shares, purchased at an average price of $25 per share, and your investment is now worth $540.

Dollar-cost averaging does not guarantee that you'll buy at the lowest share price, but it does help ensure that you don't buy at the highest price. In this example, you were still able to make a profit, even though you started buying the stock at its top. Indeed, many experts say dollar-cost averaging works best with volatile stocks, like gold.

➤ **Inside Tip:** You can also dollar-cost average into mutual funds. The easiest way is, of course, by setting up an automatic investment plan. But if you don't like the idea of having your bank account or paycheck drafted, you can still dollar-cost average by sending a check to the fund for a specified amount every month.

Secret #168
The Simplest Way to Spot a Winning Stock

One of the quickest and easiest ways to spot a winning stock is to look at the activity of the insiders. Every Wednesday, *The Wall Street Journal* reports insider trading activity. When there's a lot of insider buying of a particular stock, it usually means it's a great time to buy the stock. After all, who would know better what the company's future prospects are than its own staff? And if the insiders are confident enough to plunk down their own money, I'd say it's a good bet the company will do well. Plus, insider ownership serves to unify management's and stockholder's interests. No longer are the head honchos only concerned about their salaries and bonuses; they now have a vested interest in earnings growth and share price appreciation, just as shareholders do. And unlike individual shareholders, insider shareholders must believe the company will do well over the long-term because they're required by law to hold their shares for at least six months. So if they're buying now, you can bet they believe the company is headed for long-term growth.

➤ **Hidden Trap:** The reverse is not necessarily true when insiders sell. Indeed, insiders routinely sell twice as many shares as they buy, often for very personal reasons, like a need to raise cash to buy a house or a boat. Don't view insider selling with the same weight as insider buying, unless it's accompanied by other fundamental reasons for the stock price to fall.

Secret #169
When It Doesn't Pay to Listen to the Experts

When the headlines are screaming "Buy, Buy, Buy," and the investment advisors are singing "Happy Days Are Here Again," it's time to get out of the market. There is nothing worse for a bull market than rampant optimism by the professionals. It's a sure sign the tables are about to turn.

It's like the gourmet food craze of the 1980s. Restaurants began serving sun-dried tomatoes and raspberry/basil/red wine vinegrettes with everything. Little gourmet shops began popping up all over town. Even my local grocery store began carrying shitake mushrooms and arugala. Then boom! People got tired of dressing up to go out and decided they could find better things to do with $10 than spend it on a bottle of vinegar, and what do you think happened? Meatloaf came back into style! Little 1950s style diners crept up everywhere, and the cocooning trend started.

When did the mood shift? When everybody finally got on board. By the time my local grocery store started hawking arugala, I knew the gourmet food craze was over. It's the same with stocks. By the time *everyone* has jumped on the optimism bandwagon, it's a sure sign all the profit potential has been squeezed out of the market. And if the market hasn't turned down yet, it surely will. So sell while you can.

Secret #170
The Truth About Stock Splits

If I had a dollar for every time I heard, "Buy XYZ stock. It's doing great. It just split," or something like that, I'd be a rich woman. Stock splits do *not* signal good buying opportunities. In fact, if anything, they may signal a stock has peaked and is about to fall.

Here's why: Companies issue stock splits when their stock price rises to a level that makes it unattractive to many potential buyers. Say, for example, a company's stock rose from $40 a share to $70 a share within two years. With a price that high, many investors might be scared away, so the company issues a 2 for 1 split. The stock price is reduced to $35, and each shareholder now owns two shares for every one share he owned before. The value of the stockholders' shares has not changed at all. But now the stock may be more attractive to investors because they only need to shell out $3,500 to buy 100 shares as opposed to $7,000. The problem is that by the time the company decides to issue the split, the stock has already risen significantly. If you buy after a split, you're certainly not getting in on the ground floor of anything, and you may be getting in at the very top.

On the other hand, the split is designed to make the stock more attractive to more buyers. If it does, the increased interest could bid up the price.

The point is a stock split doesn't guarantee anything. In and of itself, it shouldn't be used as a buy indicator, and if you already own the shares and have realized significant gains, the split may even signal it's time to sell.

Secret #171
What Every Investor Should Know About Bonds

Bonds are one of the least understood investments around. Contrary to popular opinion, when a bond yield rises, it is not a good sign. In fact, it means you are losing money. That's because when bond yields rise, bond prices *fall*.

Here's how it works: Say you buy a $1,000 bond that yields 9 percent at issue. You'll receive an interest payment of $90 a year. That $90 amount never changes. But the price of the bond does change. It changes every day, in fact. Say the price of the bond were to fall to $900 the next year. Your yield would have risen to 10 percent ($90 divided by $900 = 10 percent), but if you sold the bond that year, you would actually lose money. Your total return for the year would be only $990 ($90 for one year's interest plus $900 from the sale of the bond), which is $10 less than you paid for the bond.

Don't mistake rising yields for rising prices. Remember, when bond yields rise, bond prices go down—and you are losing money.

Now you could hold the bond to maturity, in which case, your loss would only be a paper one. But remember, bonds are fixed income investments. If you hold a bond to maturity, you'll get your principal back, but the interest you've earned better be more than inflation and taxes were over the same period of time or you'll still end up with a loss in real dollar terms.

Secret #172
What's Wrong With Bond Funds

Most people assume bond funds are safer than stock funds, just as they assume bonds are safer than stocks. If by safe, you mean a guaranteed return of your principal, bonds are safer than stocks. But bond *funds* are not.

Unlike individual bonds, which can be held to maturity and redeemed at face value, bond funds never mature. Only the individual bonds within the fund mature, and it's unlikely that a portfolio manager would pursue a strategy of buying and holding all the bonds in the portfolio to maturity.

So when you buy a bond fund, think of it as buying an individual bond that you can't hold to maturity. You may gain a nice stream of income while you hold, but you'll also have to watch the fluctuations in bond prices because you'll eventually have to sell since there is no maturity date.

Secret #173
The Only Kind of Bond That
Lets You Lock In a Guaranteed
Compounded Annual Return

One of the problems with bonds is that you have to reinvest the interest income you receive at current rates. So if you own a $1,000 bond with a 9 percent coupon, you'll earn $90 interest a year. But what do you do with that $90? You have to either spend it or reinvest it. If you spend it, you lose the power of compounding (because you're only letting your principal grow, not your earnings). If you decide to reinvest, you must do so at current interest rates. If they go up, you're fine. But what if they go down? You'll earn less on that $90 and every $90 you have to reinvest at lower rates for as long as you own the bond.

But there is a special kind of bond that lets your earnings compound at the coupon rate—guaranteed. It's called a zero coupon bond. Zero coupon bonds are sold at a deep discount to face value. They pay no current interest. Instead, the full return is realized when the bond is sold at maturity. For example, you can buy a zero coupon bond today for $473 that's worth $1,000 at maturity in 2004. You'll gain $527 in earnings, which is a guaranteed 7.7 percent compounded annual return over 10 years.

Zeros are an excellent way to lock in a guaranteed compounded annual return. Your only risk is the risk of default of the corporation issuing the bond. To eliminate this, I recommend you buy only Treasury zero coupon bonds. Like regular Treasuries, Treasury zeros are backed by the full faith and credit pledge of the U.S. government.

Secret #174
The Smartest Way to Buy Zeros

Zero coupon bonds do have two major drawbacks. One, they can be expensive to buy and two, even though you receive no current income, you are taxed as if you did. But there are ways to get around both problems.

First, the high commissions. Stockbrokers have a nasty habit of quoting the prices of zeros in dollar terms rather than yields to maturity. "I can sell you a zero for $575," they'll say. That's great, but if it takes 15 years to mature, you're getting a whopping 3.75 percent yield. With that kind of return, you'll end up *losing* money faster than you'll make money, thanks to the wonderful power of inflation.

Don't let a broker do that. Ask for the "net yield to maturity" after commissions to find out what you'll really be earning. Chances are, your best bet will be to go through a discount broker to get the lowest commission.

As for the tax problem, you just need to make sure you only buy zeros in a qualified retirement plan, such as an IRA or 401(k). It's imperative that you do this. Otherwise, you will owe taxes on money you never see until the bond matures.

Secret #175
How to Invest in Zero Coupon Bonds
With as Little as $100

Like the idea of zeros, but don't have the cash to buy individual bonds? No problem. The Benham Group offers a unique series of zero coupon bond mutual funds. These bond funds are unlike any other bond fund because they actually mature. There are currently six different portfolios within Benham's Target Maturities Trust Fund, each of which matures at a specified date. Within each portfolio are zero coupon bonds of a specified maturity date; for example, the Target Maturities Trust 2010 portfolio only invests in zeros that mature in 2010. When 2010 arrives, the bonds mature, and the fund is dissolved. So you get the same safety of eventual maturity that you get with an individual bond. Better yet, the minimum to get into the fund is only $100 for an IRA account ($1,000 for regular accounts).

Scudder, Stevens & Clark also has a zero coupon bond fund that matures. The IRA minimum for its Zero Coupon 2000 Fund is $500 ($1,000 for regular accounts).

➤ **Inside Tip:** If you have the money and plan to hold zeros to maturity, mutual funds will not likely be your best bet because you'll be paying management fees every year you own the fund. But there is another smart way to invest in zero coupon bonds: Buy them for outstanding capital gains when interest rates are falling.

The price of zeros fluctuates wildly, much more than the price of individual bonds with the same maturity. So when interest rates are rising, the price of zeros will fall more than the price of regular bonds of the same maturity. But when interest rates are falling, the price of zeros will *rise* more than the price of regular bonds with the same maturity. Zero coupon mutual funds are a terrific way to play this trend because they can be liquidated at the drop of a hat. And you still get a measure of safety if interest rates work against you because you can still hold on until maturity.

Call Benham at 800/4-SAFETY or Scudder at 800/225-2470 for more information and a prospectus.

Secret #176
Your Gains From Muni Bonds Aren't All Tax-Free

People invest in municipal bonds because they have a major advantage: The income they earn is tax-free. But that doesn't mean all your gains from a muni bond will be tax-free. As with any kind of bond, you can profit from munis in two ways: interest income and capital gains (if the price of the bond goes up and you sell). The interest income is 100 percent free of federal taxes, but the capital gains are fully taxed.

This is particularly important for municipal bond fund investors because the fund may experience capital gains without you knowing it. Unlike an individual bond, which you have to sell in order to realize the gains (and you have control of whether or not you sell), muni bond funds buy and sell bonds within their portfolios throughout the year. If the fund realizes gains from those sales, the gains are fully taxable to you.

To figure out whether your muni bond fund had capital gains during the year, look to see if your fund paid any "capital gains distributions" on the tax statement you receive at the end of the year. If so, then you owe federal taxes on that money. Of course, your interest income is still tax-free.

Secrets #177–179
Three Mutual Fund Myths That Could Be
Costing You a Fortune—Literally

Mutual funds are a great way to get into the market if you don't have the thousands of dollars required to buy individual stocks and you don't want to pay huge commissions. Plus, they give you professional management and instant diversification. But just because mutual funds are diversified does not mean all mutual funds are the same.

Indeed, there are more than 5,000 mutual funds on the market today, all with vastly different investment goals, management styles, track records, fees, and risks. There are blue-chip stock funds, small cap stock funds, value funds, growth funds, high grade bond funds, junk bond funds, overseas funds, gold funds, sector funds, and every variety in between. The days of saying, "My money is in a mutual fund" have long since passed, for the differences between two funds with the same objectives" can be dramatic.

Reams have been written about picking mutual funds, but unfortunately, much of it is false. So the first thing we need to do is dispel the many myths surrounding mutual funds. The following secrets are designed to do just that, while showing you how to pick mutual funds the way the experts do.

Secret #177
This Year's Top Performers Are Likely to
Be Next Year's Losers

Open up any personal finance magazine and you're likely to find a list of top-ranked mutual funds. Hundreds of funds are listed in these mutual fund surveys, with all sorts of facts and figures. Now, which fund are you immediately drawn to? The 256th ranked growth fund buried near the bottom of the list or the number one fund?

It's only natural to want to buy the number one fund, but please, I'm begging you, don't. Because more likely than not, you'll be disappointed. Let's look at what happened to some number one funds in the past. In 1993, *Money* magazine put FAM Value at the top of its list of "12 Funds to Buy Now." How did it perform that year? Dismally. A $1,000 investment would have netted you $2.10, not even enough to cover cab fare to your local airport. Same with Vanguard U.S. Growth. The fund garnered *Morningstar's* highest rating—5 stars—as of December 31, 1992. But if you had bought it in January 1993 based on that recommendation, you would have *lost 1.4 percent* that year. What makes that performance even more disappointing is that 1993 was a banner year for most growth funds, with the average gain topping 12 percent.

Indeed, all to often, yesterday's top performers will be tomorrow's biggest losers. That's because the markets move in cycles. Vanguard U.S. Growth's blue-chip growth style served it well in 1989 and 1991 when the country was still in recession and big companies like General Electric were the only ones making money. But times change, and by late 1992, small start-up companies were gaining momentum, and funds that couldn't or didn't take advantage of the change (like Vanguard U.S. Growth) lagged.

Past performance *is* useful in telling you how a fund performed during past periods that are similar to the current one. It's also nice to see how a fund fared compared to the market averages and other funds like it (e.g., how a growth stock fund compared to other growth stock funds) over time. But from one year to the next, past performance tells you little.

A better way is to look at changes in interest rates, economic growth, and inflation. Here are a few general rules of thumb:

- When interest rates are rising and the economy is growing, money markets, short-term bond funds, and stock funds that invest in cyclical/industrial stocks tend to do best.
- When interest rates are falling and the economy is slowing, long-term bonds, zero coupon bonds, blue-chip stocks, and utility funds tend to do best.
- When inflation is rising, gold, precious metals funds, and real estate funds tend to do best.

The point is don't rely on last year's performance to select funds for tomorrow. If the fundamental economic situation hasn't changed much, you'll probably do fine. But if it has, watch out. You could end up buying a fund just after it has peaked and is set for a fall.

Secret #178
What a Portfolio Manager's Tenure
With a Fund Really Means

Checking portfolio managers' track records has become all the rage among mutual fund investors of late. The longer the manager has been with the fund, the better it will perform, according to the conventional wisdom. Problem is, it doesn't work. Portfolio Manager Roger Engemann has been with Pasadena Growth Fund since 1986, but that didn't stop the fund from *losing* a whopping 11 percent in 1993. Likewise, Fidelity Value got a new fund manager in 1992, and that didn't stop it from turning in a fabulous 21 percent that year and following it with another successful year of 23 percent gains in 1993.

The point is you can't predict a fund's performance based on how long the manager's been on the job. Sure, it's nice to see that the person responsible for investing your life's savings has been around the block a few times. It may be comforting to know that the manager has survived a few tough turns, like the bear market of 1973 to 1974 or the crash of 1987. But never, I repeat, never equate length of service with quality of investment style.

There are many things that contribute to a mutual fund's success. Good portfolio management is certainly right near the top of the list. But whether a particular manager has been with a fund for 10 years or 10 minutes doesn't tell you a thing by itself. If you want to take a closer look at the portfolio managers of the funds you're interested in, call the fund family and ask about their experience—on that fund and any others they've managed. Find out where they received their training and how they propose to do their jobs. If the manager is using a sound investment strategy and has a good track record—no matter where it comes from—that's all that counts. It's nice to see loyalty, but years of service with a particular fund are just that—and should be treated as such.

Secret #179
The Truth About Loads and Other Fees

Another popular concept touted in the financial press is the idea that no-load funds are better than load funds. Since you don't have to pay a load (up-front commission) to invest, more of your money goes to work for you from the start. That's true—it *is* cheaper to invest in a no-load fund from the start. But it isn't necessarily cheaper in the long run.

Even no-load funds have management fees (after all, they have to pay the help somehow, right?). And those management fees can really add up over time, even to the point where it's costing you more than a one-time load.

Say, for example, you invested $1,000 in two identical funds that returned 10 percent per year before expenses. One of the funds charges a 3 percent front-end load, but has an expense ratio (the management fee plus overhead) of just 0.75 percent. The other is a no-load fund, but has a 1.75 percent expense ratio. After five years, which account has more money? The load fund. You'll have $1,510 in it after expenses, but only $1,486 in the no-load fund.

Why does this happen? Because front-end loads are deducted only once up front, but management expenses are deducted every year. And most loads funds tend to have lower expense ratios than no loads. So don't judge a fund by its load. If it's a good fund that you plan to hold a long time (like more than five years), don't let a load stop you.

However, I would still avoid any fund with a load of more than 4.5 percent. That's just too much to pay right off the top. Remember, a front-end load is deducted right at the beginning. So if you invest $1,000 in a fund with an 8 percent load, only $920 of your money is going to work for you. That fund will have to earn at least 8.7 percent in the first year just for you to break even!

Secret #180
How to Buy a Load Fund That Costs Less Than a No-Load Right Off the Bat

Okay, so you know you have to hold a load fund for a few years in order for it to be cheaper or equal to what you'd pay with a similar no-load fund. But did you know that you can actually invest in a load fund that will be cheaper than a no-load from day one?

It's simple: All you have to do is put the fund in an IRA. Several fund families, including mutual fund giant Fidelity, waive their loads if you're buying the fund in your IRA. That way, all your money goes to work for you immediately, just like with a no-load fund, and you're paying less in expenses too (since most load funds have lower expense ratios than no-load funds).

Fidelity waives all of its loads for IRAs except in its Select funds, Magellan, and Millennium. Call Fidelity at 800/544-8888 for details.

Secret #181
When You Should Never Pay a Load

Some stock funds are worth the load, and if you hold them long enough, they can even be cheaper than no loads. But it is never worthwhile to pay a load for a bond fund. Bond funds tend to have lower expenses than stock funds, so the load you pay may not be outweighed by a lower expense ratio. Indeed, no-load mutual fund giant Vanguard has an abundant selection of bond funds with expense ratios as low as 0.2 percent.

Secret #182
How to Keep More of Your
Mutual Fund Profits to Yourself

Mutual funds are a great way to invest cheaply and conveniently. But when it comes to taxes, there is nothing simple about them. Indeed, calculating your profits can be downright complicated.

It all comes down to one key number: your cost basis. The IRS gives you three different ways you can calculate your cost basis: (1) average price per share, (2) first-in, first out, and (3) specifying shares. It's up to you which method you want to use, and you can use different methods for different funds. But once you decide on a method for a particular fund, you must stick with it as long as you own that fund.

It's worth it to calculate your cost basis using each of the three methods because each method will give you a different number. You'll want to select the method that gives you the *highest* cost basis. That means it cost you more to buy your shares, so your profit is less, and the tax you'll owe will be less too.

Let's take an example. Say you buy 10 shares of XYZ Fund at $10 a share. Then you buy another 10 shares at $15 a share. Then you buy another 10 shares at $8 a share. Now the price is $12 a share and you want to sell 10 shares. Do you have a gain or loss?

Your Investment in XYZ Fund

# of Shares Bought		Price Per Share	Value
10	×	$10	$100
10	×	$15	$150
10	×	$8	$80
Total Amount Invested:			$330

Current Value of Your Account

# of Shares Owned		Price Per Share	Value
30	×	$12	$360

If you used the average price per share method to calculate your cost basis, you would take the total amount you invested ($330) and divide by the number of shares you own (30). So your cost basis using this method would be $11. If you sold 10 shares at $12 a share, you'd have a capital gain of $1 per share or $10.

If you used the first-in, first-out method, you would sell the first shares you bought. That means your cost basis would be $10 per share because the first 10 shares you bought cost $10. In this case, you'd have a capital gain of $2 per share or $20.

Finally, if you used the specifying shares method, you could choose which shares you wanted to sell. If you chose the 10 shares you bought at $15 a share, you would actually show a capital *loss* of $3 per share (remember, the current price per share is still $12).

In this example, the specifying shares method would be the most advantageous to you. But remember, whichever method you choose, you have to stick with it as long as you own that fund. And be sure to pick a method *when you sell*—not when you figure your taxes—because that's when you have the most flexibility.

One final note: If you're using an automatic investment plan to invest a set dollar amount per month, you'll probably want to use the average price per share method. It's the easiest method to use when you're buying a lot of fractional shares.

Secret #183
A Hidden Tax Trap With Mutual Funds

Unfortunately, when you sell is not the only time you'll owe taxes on capital gains in a mutual fund. Unlike stocks, which only pro-

duce gains or losses when you sell, mutual funds can actually force
you to owe taxes on capital gains without your ever realizing a
profit.

Here's why: Mutual funds buy and sell stocks and bonds
within their portfolios throughout the year. Those sales result in
gains or losses for the overall fund. If the net gains outweigh the
net losses, the fund must distribute those gains to shareholders in
the year they're earned. That means if your fund earned money
and you haven't yet sold your shares, you'll still owe taxes on the
fund's gains.

It also means that if you bought the fund later in the year after
it had earned its gains, and the fund was now down, you would
owe taxes on profits the fund made that you never saw! You'd actually be holding a paper loss, yet still owe taxes on the fund's gains!

Most funds pay their distributions at the end of the year. If
you plan to make an initial investment in December, check with the
fund family first to see when the distribution will be. Then wait
until after the distribution to make your purchase.

You'll still owe taxes on gains the fund makes throughout the
time you hold it (the only way to avoid that is to invest in an IRA).
But at least you'll be sure you aren't paying taxes on profits that
never appeared in *your* account.

Secret #184
How to Slash Your Taxes on
Mutual Fund Capital Gains Distributions

Paying taxes on "paper profits" is a way of life with mutual funds.
But there is way you can minimize those taxes: Buy funds that
don't have big distributions.

Notice I didn't say buy funds that don't make big profits—
profits are different than distributions. Distributions are made
when the fund sells stock (or bonds or whatever) and realizes a
gain. But what if the securities the fund owns rise in value, but the
fund never sells?

Just like an individual, a fund can own a stock that has risen
in value and not sell. When it doesn't sell, it doesn't realize a gain
and therefore, doesn't have to distribute that gain to shareholders.

You, the shareholder, still get the benefit of the realized gain if you want to sell (since mutual funds have to value their assets on a daily basis, the share price would still rise). But you don't have to pay taxes on the fund's gains if you don't want to sell.

The trick is to find funds that don't buy and sell shares too often. In general, stock funds will buy and sell more often than bond funds. And aggressive stock funds will trade more often than less aggressive stock funds. The figure used to quantify how often a fund buys and sells in its portfolio is called "turnover ratio." The lower the turnover ratio, the fewer the sales, and the lower your distributions will be.

Most stock funds have turnover ratios of 100 percent or more. If you're concerned about taxes, I'd avoid funds with turnovers in excess of 100 percent.

Secret #185
How to Invest in High-Turnover Funds Without Incurring High Taxes

Funds with high turnovers (i.e., buy and sell their assets frequently) will cost you more in taxes because these funds have higher *realized* profits than funds that merely buy and hold assets. But fortunately, there is a way to invest in high-turnover funds without incurring high taxes: Put them in a tax-deferred retirement plan.

If you keep the funds that are most likely to realize big capital gains (like aggressive stock funds) inside your IRA, 401(k), or variable annuity, you'll still be able to own the fund you want, but you won't have to pay taxes on its gains until *you* realize them when you retire.

Secret #186
Why Switching Mutual Funds Can Be Costly

With mutual funds, switching from one fund to another can often be done with a simple phone call. And with the automated 24-hour trading and information services offered by many funds, it can get tempting to trade often.

But there's a danger in doing this too often: You'll get hit with a hefty tax bill. That's because switches are treated as sales. Even if you plan to keep every dime invested, you'll still owe taxes on the gains you realized from the sale of the first fund.

If you like the idea of switching in and out of funds often, do it in your IRA or Keogh account where it won't be taxed. Just make sure that the fund doesn't levy any fees for short-term trading.

Secrets #187–188
Two Ways to Invest in
High-Minimum Funds for Less

Ever hear about a mutual fund and wish you could buy it, but it has a minimum initial investment of $5,000 or more? It's infuriating. It's hard to believe mutual funds were created for the smaller investor to play the game, when some have minimums that don't even let the little guy on the field! Fortunately, there are two little-known ways to get into high-minimum funds for less:

Secret #187
Participate in an Automatic Investment Plan

A number of fund families will waive their minimum initial investment requirements if you set up an automatic investment plan to have a set amount, say $50 or $100, debited from your paycheck or bank account every month. Here are some of my favorites:

- Twentieth Century (800/345-2021) waives its minimums as long as you sign up for its automatic investment plan. And you can invest as little as $50 a month.
- T. Rowe Price (800/638-5660) waives minimums for participants in its Automatic Asset Builder Plan, which requires a minimum $100 per month investment.
- With INVESCO's (800/525-8085) EasiVest plan, you can invest just $50 a month and avoid the minimum initial investment requirement.

Many other fund companies offer this service too. And some that don't have established plans will agree to waive the minimum if you agree to invest automatically. All you have to do is ask!

Secret #188
Buy It in Your IRA

Just about every mutual fund has a lower minimum investment requirement for IRA accounts than for regular accounts. Since by law, you aren't allowed to contribute more than $2,000 to an IRA in a single year, any fund with a minimum higher than $2,000 has to lower it for IRA accounts. And in most cases, that minimum is much lower.

For example, Vanguard requires a $3,000 minimum for all of its regular accounts. But Vanguard's IRA minimum is just $500. Same for T. Rowe Price. Minimums for regular accounts are $2,500; minimums for IRA accounts are $500.

Secret #189
What's Wrong With Investing in Big Mutual Funds

It seems comforting to invest in a big, well-known fund like Fidelity Magellan. After all, it's got a great track record, right? The problem is the bigger a mutual fund is, the less flexibility it has in choosing its investments. Millions of dollars flood in every month—dollars the fund manager has to find a place to invest. With so much money to invest, it's almost assured that the manager must buy big companies because if it invests in smaller ones, the very act of the fund investing so much money could bid up the price.

It isn't necessarily bad to invest only in big, well-known stocks. But smaller companies do tend to perform better over the long haul. For greater flexibility, invest in funds with $1 billion or less in assets.

Secrets #190–193
Four Ways to Slash IRA Custodial Fees

Most fund companies charge you an annual fee to maintain your IRA. Called a custodial fee, it typically runs around $10 to $20 per fund. And you'll pay it every year for every fund in your IRA. That can really add up over 10 to 20 years! But there are a few little-known ways to get around the fee, including:

Secret #190
Consolidate Your Accounts Under One Roof

Most fund families and discount brokers have caps on the total amount they'll charge you in IRA custodial fees. For example, Janus charges a $12 fee per fund, but it's capped at $36. So say you have four different IRAs with four different fund companies. If you consolidated your account with one company, like Janus, you could still invest in four different funds, but you'd only pay $36.

INVESCO has an even better deal. You'll only pay a flat $10 annual fee per IRA account no matter how many of INVESCO's funds you have in that account.

Secret #191
Pay a One-Time Lifetime Custodial Fee

Janus also offers a special plan that allows you to pay a $100 lifetime custodial fee that covers all the funds in your Janus IRA, plus any you might add in the future. This is a good deal if you like having the flexibility of being able to invest in different funds (like an international fund, a blue-chip stock fund, a bond fund, etc.) without incurring a lot of extra custodial fees, and you plan to keep all your money with Janus for quite awhile. It also allows you to deduct the entire $100 custodial fee in one year, which could be useful if you're trying to bunch deductions to meet the 2 percent miscellaneous floor (see Secret #227).

Just be sure you write a separate check to pay the custodial fee. If you allow Janus to deduct it from your account, you won't be able to take the tax deduction for it.

Secret #192
Use a Discount Broker

A number of discount brokers, including Charles Schwab and Fidelity Discount Brokers offer low-fee IRA accounts. You can invest in as many funds as you want and pay just $22 a year with

Schwab (800/526-8600) or $20 annually with Fidelity (800/544-8666). Each of these brokers also offers no-commission trading on hundreds of selected no-load mutual funds. (See Secret #194 for details.)

And you can get an even better deal if you have a high dollar-value account. Fidelity Discount Brokers waives its IRA fees altogether for accounts over $5,000. Schwab waives its fees for accounts over $10,000. Call for details.

Secret #193
Invest With Scudder

With a wide variety of funds to choose from and no annual custodial fees no matter what your account balance is, Scudder, Stevens & Clark offers one of the best IRA deals around. Call Scudder at 800/225-2470 for details.

Secret #194
How to Buy Mutual Funds Through a
Discount Broker and Pay No Commissions

In the early 1990s, seizing upon the phenomenal growth of the mutual fund industry, discount brokers came up with a great innovation to attract clients: They began offering fee-free trading of no-load funds. It's a great concept. You get to buy and sell hundreds of different no-load mutual funds through a single source and pay no commissions or transaction fees for the privilege. You get consolidated statements (a big plus, as you know, if you've ever owned more than one or two mutual funds), round-the-clock service, and the ability to switch between mutual funds from different families.

Charles Schwab's program, OneSource, offers no-fee investing in more than 270 mutual funds from more than 24 different fund families, including Benham, Berger, Dreyfus, Evergreen, INVESCO, Janus, Kaufmann, Stein Roe, Strong, Twentieth Century, and United Services. Fidelity Discount Brokers offers a similar program with no commission trading and no loads on more than 350 funds.

Call Schwab at 800/526-8600 or Fidelity Discount Brokers at 800/544-8666 for details.

8
The Smartest Ways to Finance a College Education

I have good news and bad news. The bad news is college costs are already outrageous and rising faster every day. I've even seen figures that estimate it will cost upwards of $200,000 to send a child to college in 18 years!

The good news is you don't have to let that stop you from sending your children, grandchildren, or even yourself to college. There are many ways to pay for college: parent loans, student loans, grants, work study, scholarships, savings, bartering, the list goes on. The secret is to plan ahead. Don't let fear of six-figure tuition bills stop you or your children from getting the best education available. Remember: Better-educated people earn higher wages. It's a fact. College *always* pays for itself in the long run.

Secret #195
The Single Greatest Asset You Have in Funding Your Child's College Education
(Hint: It's Not Money)

I know the idea of paying $80,000, $90,000, or more to send your son or daughter to college seems daunting. And it's even more daunting if your youngster is just a mere tyke today, for you can be sure the costs will only go higher—like into the six figures—when she gets ready for the Ivy League. But the first thing you need to know about financing a college education is that it is possible.

In fact, parents of toddlers have an asset that's even more valuable than money when it comes to paying for college: time. Look at it this way: If you start saving when junior is a newborn, and you put away $125 a month, you'd amass *$75,000* by the time the little genius is ready to head off to Harvard (assuming a 10 percent average annual return).

If you waited until junior's eighth birthday, you'd have to sock away $366 a month to reach that same $75,000 goal. And if you waited until junior turned 13, you'd have to stash nearly $970 a month to end up with the same $75,000.

Now I don't know too many people who have an extra $970 lying around at the end of the month, so start saving now!

Are you put off by even the $125 a month commitment? I don't blame you. That's a nice chunk of change to have to pull out of your monthly budget for the next 18 years. But even if you don't have $125 a month to save, you can still save something. Start with $25 or even $10 a month. It doesn't matter how much. Just do it *now*.

Consider this: If you save $10 a month for the next 18 years, it'll be worth over $6,000 when you need it (assuming a 10 percent average annual return). Now, can you find an extra $10 in your budget?

Secret #196
The Best Investments to Fund a College Education

All right, you've got a savings plan set up to fund your kid's college education. Now what do you do with it? Here are my favorite choices:

- *For toddlers:* Stocks and stock mutual funds are the best way to save for college when you have 10+ years to grow the money. There is simply no investment that can beat stocks for long-term growth.
- *For teenagers:* Once your pride and joy turns about 13 to 14, you'll want to start shifting assets into lower-volatility investments,

like Series EE savings bonds, certificates of deposit (CDs), and zero coupon bonds that mature in each of the four years your child will be in college.

Series EE savings bonds offer a number of special advantages to college savers. First, Series EE bonds are guaranteed to yield a specified minimum rate (currently 4 percent) as long as you hold them for at least five years. But if interest rates rise, it's possible to earn more since rates are adjusted every November and May based on the current average yield for five-year Treasuries.

Second, you don't receive the interest on Series EE bonds until you redeem them, and if the bonds are in your name and you use the proceeds to pay for your child's college tuition, the interest you've earned is totally tax-free for couples with incomes up to $68,250 ($45,500 for singles) and partially tax-free for couples that earn up to $98,250 ($60,500 for singles). For more information and current interest rates, contact any bank or call 800/US-BONDS.

If you buy CDs or zero coupon bonds, be sure to limit the maturities to the years in which your child will be in college. In other words, if your child is 15 now, don't buy a CD or zero coupon bond with a maturity of over 6 years (when your child turns 21 and is ready to enter her last year of college). You don't want to have to sell zeros before maturity and risk losses or cash in a CD before it comes due and face a penalty.

■ *For 16-year-olds and up:* At this point, any money that is still in stocks or stock mutual funds should be switched into a money market fund. Any new money to be invested should go into a money market fund. This is not the time to be taking chances with your college fund. You'll need it very soon, and you want to make sure when it comes time to write the check, the money is there.

Secret #197
The Worst Way to Save for College

Without question, life insurance is the single *worst* way to save for college tuition. I know, your insurance agent has painted beautiful pictures of five-figure sums growing tax-deferred. Suddenly, visions of Harvard and Yale (paid for!) are dancing through your head. You see your little one, going off in the world, to become a neurosurgeon or an astronaut.

That may happen, but you can bet junior's spacesuit it won't be because you used life insurance to save for it. The problem with using life insurance to fund a college education is once you deduct the high commissions and the cost of the death benefit, there isn't much left to go toward your savings.

Indeed, it takes something like 15 years to see any significant growth in the cash value of most life insurance policies. And if you add to that the fact that the interest rate you'll actually earn could very well be much lower than the rate that was projected and may not even beat inflation, and the fact that you are trying to build a college fund, not buy life insurance, you can see what a raw deal life insurance to pay for college really is! If you want life insurance, look into term protection (see Secret #284). If you want to save for college, use the investment strategies I recommend in Secret #196.

Secret #198
The Second Worst Way to Save for College

Even worse than buying a life insurance policy on yourself to fund a college education is buying a policy on your child. Now you're talking about spending money to provide insurance in case a 13-year-old dies! It's bad enough that some insurance companies try to sucker you into buying policies for children, but it's even worse when they try to do it under the guise of funding a college education! You'll do better setting up a separate college savings fund where all your money can go to work for you.

Secret #199
The Smartest Way to Use Life Insurance to Pay for College

There is one circumstance where you should consider life insurance to fund a child's college education: in the event of your death.

If you have dependent children, I do recommend you buy life insurance to ensure your family can meet all of its financial obligations should you die. And when you are calculating how much insurance to buy, the cost of your children's education should definitely be included. Just make sure you gradually decrease that part of your death benefit as your children pass through college and eventually graduate.

Secret #200
What's Wrong With Putting Your Kid's College Fund in His or Her Name

The Uniform Gift to Minors Act (UGMA) allows you to set up a custodial account that you manage for your child until the child turns 18 (or 21 in some states). It's a popular way to save for college. It allows parents to receive the favorable tax treatment associated with keeping assets in a child's name, yet still have control of the money until the child grows up.

However, this plan has two major drawbacks: First of all, when the child turns 18 (or 21), the money is his to keep. If he wants to run off and join a commune, he can take the $50,000 you painstakingly stashed away and give it to the Church of Money Extraction if he wants.

Second, it could prevent you from qualifying for financial aid. The financial aid guidelines expect 35 percent of a child's savings to be used to pay for college, while only up to 5.65 percent of parents' savings need to go to pay for college. That's a difference of $14,675 on a $50,000 investment!

If you think you have no prayer of qualifying for financial aid, go ahead and put the account in your child's name. But if there is any chance whatsoever that you can get aid, I'd rather see you pay a little extra in taxes now than blow your shot of getting free money or an advantageous loan in the future.

And remember, even in an UGMA account, earnings above $1,200 a year are taxed at the parents' rate until the child turns 14. That's when your real tax savings would start. But your earnings would have to be pretty substantial in order for the tax savings to offset the potential cost to you in lost financial aid.

Secrets #201-202
Two Ways to Grow a College Fund and Avoid Paying Taxes on Your Gains

There are two innovative ways you can set up a college fund in your own name and not pay taxes on your gains until the tuition bill arrives:

Secret #201
Buy Stock in Your Own Name and Give the Shares Later to Your Child

The smartest way to fund a college education for tax savings is to buy individual shares of stock (not a mutual fund) in your own name, hold them until your child enters college and then give the shares to your child when it's time to pay the tuition bill.

You avoid paying tax while you're building your college port-folio because you haven't taken any capital gains (although you will have to pay tax on any dividends you receive). And by giving the shares to your child when it's time to sell, your child pays the tax at his rate, presumably 15 percent. Plus, by making the gift just before it's time to write the tuition check, the stock will be counted as part of your savings, not your child's, so only up to 5.65 percent of it will be considered eligible to pay for college (rather than the 35 percent that would be allocated it if were in the student's name).

Just be sure you give no more than $10,000 per year to your child (anything more will trigger a gift tax to you). And of course, don't use this strategy if your child is irresponsible or there's any chance he won't use the money to pay for college.

➤ **Inside Tip:** You can use this strategy with mutual funds too, but you'll still have to pay tax on the fund's annual capital gains distributions (see Secret #183).

Secret #202
Open a "College IRA"

Today, more and more people are waiting until their late 30s, even 40s to have children. That means if you or your spouse is 39 or older when your child is born, you'll be eligible to begin withdrawing from your IRA when your child is still in college. (If you're 39 now, you'll be 60 when your child enters her senior year of college.)

So what better investment for a college fund than an IRA that grows tax-deferred until withdrawal? That way, you can invest as you like without regard to tax considerations, and even if your child never goes to college, you've built up a tidy sum you can use for your own future!

Secret #203
Why Taking Money Out of Your Retirement Plan to Pay for College Can Cost You Big

It may make sense to use a retirement fund to save for college if you're going to turn 59fi while your child is in school. But if you'll be younger when your children are in school, withdrawing money from your retirement plan to pay for college is a very bad idea.

You'll get socked with a 10 percent penalty right off the bat. On top of that, you'll have to pay taxes on the money you withdraw and if that's not bad enough, that money will be counted as extra income available to pay for college, which makes you less eligible for financial aid.

A better way: Use the strategies mentioned in Secret #196 to build a college fund and the strategies mentioned in Secrets #213 to #216 to pay for college.

Secret #204
How to Give Money to a Child or Grandchild for College the Smart Way

Anyone can give away up to $10,000 a year without having to pay a gift tax. But any amount over $10,000 a year means you have to pay taxes on the gift. So what if you want to pay for your grandchild's college education, but still want to avoid exceeding the $10,000 per year gift limit? Simply give the money directly to the college. When you pay an educational institution directly on behalf of someone else, you can exceed the $10,000 limit without incurring gift taxes.

Secret #205
What's Wrong With College Prepayment Plans

Prepayment plans are the latest wrinkle in an effort to help families finance college. Basically, they come in two varieties: state plans that usually allow the student to choose any school within the state and individual plans sponsored by private schools.

The way it works is you give the state or the college a certain amount of money now, and in return, you're assured that the college bill will be paid when it comes time for junior to matriculate. Even if inflation rises ten zillion percent, junior's tuition bill will be covered.

It all sounds so safe. *Not!*

What if your kid doesn't want to go to the college of *your* choice? What if she doesn't get accepted? What if she doesn't want to go to college at all?

These plans do provide for your principal to be returned to you if any of these situations occurs, but at what price? The college or state will have enjoyed full use of your money for all those years, and what will you get in return? Your principal investment and perhaps a token amount of interest?

I say no thanks! Unless inflation sends the cost of college soaring more than 10 percent a year, you'll do better investing the money yourself. That way, *you* reap all the gains, and your child isn't locked into a college that may not interest her.

Secret #206
The Early Bird Catches the Financial Aid Worm

If you wait until your child's senior year in high school to start thinking about financial aid, you've waited too long. Even if your young wonder doesn't have a clue what college he wants to go to, you need to start thinking about financial aid when he's a high school junior.

That's because colleges make their financial aid recommendations based on your income and assets during the calendar year before your child starts college. So if your son will start his freshman year of college in September of 1997, 1996 is your base year for financial aid.

And it's a good idea to start planning for financial aid even before your base year. Just as you arrange your finances to your best advantage for tax purposes, so should you arrange your income and assets to your best advantage for financial aid purposes. And the sooner you start, the more flexibility you'll have. See Secrets #207 to #212 for specific ways to manage your money so you qualify for the most financial aid.

Secrets #207–212
Six Ways to Manage Your Money
to Get the Most Financial Aid

Colleges use a standard formula designed by the federal government to calculate how much aid they'll give you. In a nutshell, the formula tallies up your income, your assets, the student's income, and the student's assets and determines how much you can afford to pay toward tuition. The difference between what the school costs and what you can afford to pay is your financial need.

For parents, the formula figures you can contribute 47 percent of your income above a certain living allowance toward tuition. The living allowance or income protection allowance, is set by the federal government, and it's supposed to be what you need to live on. Of course, the allocation is ridiculously low. The latest figures I saw gave a family of four $16,670 a year! Now, do you know any family anywhere who could live on $16,670 a year? It's a joke. Anyway, it's assumed that 47 percent of anything you earn above the income allowance can go toward tuition.

Then the formula totals your assets (e.g., savings accounts, money market funds, mutual funds, stocks, bonds) and figures that you can contribute up to 5.65 percent of what you have there. The "up to" is important. A chunk of your assets won't even be counted as available to pay for college and then any amount above that chunk will be considered available based on your income. So 5.65 percent is the *maximum* contribution you'd ever have to make from your assets.

What's more, your home and your retirement funds are not counted as assets anymore (very important—more on that in a moment).

Once the parent's income and assets are tallied, the same analysis is done on the student's income and assets—only the student is required to contribute a much larger portion of his money.

The first $1,750 of a student's *after-tax* income is not counted in the federal formula. It's essentially "free earnings" to the student. But for every dollar earned after that, it's expected that the student will contribute 50 cents or 50 percent toward tuition. And for every asset the student owns (e.g., savings accounts, mutual funds, stocks, bonds, etc.), it is expected that he will contribute 35 percent toward tuition. (Colleges that do not use the federal formula to calculate financial aid will have a different allocation for student income and assets.)

The good news is there are a number of ways you can shift your income and assets around so that you qualify for more financial aid:

Secret #207
Pay Off Consumer Debt

Even though the rest of the world considers credit card balances, car loans, and personal loans debts, the financial aid world does not. To the people who devised the federal financial aid formula, this debt just doesn't exist. That means even though you still have to pay off these loans every month, they pretend it's not an expense for you.

However, any money you have sitting in the bank *is* counted as an asset and is considered available to pay for tuition. That means it's in your interest to use any extra cash you have to pay off consumer debts.

I know, it feels better to have $5,000 in savings and a $1,000 balance on your credit card than to have $4,000 in savings and no balance on your credit card. But taking that $1,000 from your savings reduces your assets available to pay for tuition. Plus whatever interest you're earning on your $5,000—even if it's in a top-performing stock mutual fund—is likely to be less than what you're paying in interest on that $1,000 credit card balance.

Secret #208
Large Purchases Can Work to Your Advantage

If you've been considering a major purchase like a computer or furniture, and you know you'll buy it soon, do it now. By concentrating large purchases in base income years, you reduce the assets you have available to pay college costs.

I'm certainly not advocating you go on a spending spree, but if you need something and you were planning on buying it anyway, just make sure you do it in one of your base income years.

Secret #209
Shift Bonuses to Your Advantage

Are you lucky enough to be eligible for a bonus from your employer? If so, you may want to consider asking your employer to accelerate or defer your bonus for another year in order to reduce your income in the base year for financial aid.

Say, for example, you're eligible to receive a bonus in January of next year. But that will be your base year for financial aid (the year before your child expects to enter college). Instead of waiting until January, ask your employer if you can get the bonus in December of this year. That way, the income won't be included in your base year income.

Likewise, if you expect to receive a bonus at the end of your base year, ask your employer if you can defer it until January of the following year. Your child will still be in college, and the bonus will be counted as extra income in the financial aid officer's calculations for your child's sophomore year, but it will probably still work to your advantage.

First of all, you can't predict what will happen in the future. You could lose your job or your spouse could take a cut in pay next year, and the extra income from the bonus wouldn't end up being "extra" after all. Secondly, many colleges project out what aid they'll give you in future years based on what they decide to give you in the first year. Of course, that estimate isn't guaranteed, but it may mean money is being allocated for you. And once you know the money is there, it makes it that much easier to get it.

So the income you earn in your initial base year is even more important than your income in the other three base years during which your child is in college. Whatever you can do to reduce it will be well worth it.

Secret #210
Avoid Large Capital Gains in Base Income Years

When you have a financial asset, like a stock, part of it is considered available to pay for college. But the most you'd have to take from that asset is 5.65 percent (35 percent for the student). If you sell it in a base income year, you've now converted that asset to income, and a much larger percentage is considered available to put toward tuition (up to 47 percent for parents, 50 percent for students). What's more, the financial aid officer will count the same money twice: once as an asset and again as income.

If you do have to sell assets to raise cash, try to sell losing investments as well as winners. That way, you can offset your gains with losses, and the net addition to your income will be less.

Secret #211
Adjust Your Withholding So You
Don't Get a Big Tax Refund

Since state income tax refunds are included as income on your federal tax return, it pays to underpay the IRS in the years before your base years. That way, you won't get a state income tax refund (or you'll get a small one) in your base years, so you'll have less income to report on your federal tax return in your base years.

Secret #212
Avoid Making Contributions to Retirement Plans
in Your Base Year

The assets in your IRA, 401(k), 403(b), or Keogh are excluded in the financial aid calculations, but the contributions you make to the plan during your base income years are treated as part of your income. So even though the IRS doesn't count those contributions as income for tax purposes, the federal financial aid formula does and expects you to fork over up to 47 percent of that money to pay for tuition.

What's more, if the contributions are tax deductible, they reduce your overall tax burden, which increases the income you have available to pay for tuition. So essentially, if you contribute to a tax-deferred retirement plan in your base income years, you lose twice. It's an odd twist in the system that actually penalizes you for saving.

However, if you plan ahead, you may still be able to sock away the same amount of money for retirement, while enhancing your ability to get financial aid.

If you can, put as much as you can into your retirement plan *before* your base years. For example, if you regularly contribute $1,000 a year to your retirement plan, try to double that contribution in the four years before your base year even if you have to borrow from a regular savings account to do it.

The advantage: You'll continue to build your nest egg for retirement and by the time your base years roll around, you'll have fewer available assets because you took the money out of savings. Plus, since you aren't making tax-deductible contributions to your retirement plan in your base years, you're increasing the taxes you owe, which gives you less income available to pay tuition. And it's good for your nest egg too since your retirement money will start growing and compounding sooner, which means you'll earn more on it than you would have if you had stretched out the contributions.

Of course, not everybody can afford to increase their retirement fund contributions in those pre-base years. If that's the case, just simply stop making contributions in your base years. Most folks find they need that money just to pay their share of the tuition.

If that's not the case for you, then by all means, go ahead and add to your retirement fund. Just do it with the understanding that it won't reduce your income for financial aid purposes.

➤ **One More Tip:** With all this talk of reducing assets in order to be eligible for more financial aid, many people are led to believe it's useless to build a college fund at all. Not true! If you have the money and are living a lavish lifestyle, don't expect financial aid officers to throw thousands of dollars in grants your way. They'll have no sympathy.

If, on the other hand, you've worked hard and saved slowly and steadily over the years for your child's future, financial aid officers will be much more willing to help. After all, they are human. I'm not saying they won't count assets or income in their formulas—they will—but they'll be much more receptive to working out a plan if you have a long history showing a willingness to contribute what you can.

Secret #213
The Smartest Way to Borrow for College

There are oodles of loan programs available to pay for higher education, but as attractive as the interest rates and terms are, none allows you to deduct your interest payments on your tax return. That's why the most advantageous way to borrow to pay for college may not be a student or parent's loan at all. Rather, a home equity loan may be your best bet.

Since the federal financial aid formula no longer counts home equity as an asset, it pays to build it up as much as possible before those magical college years arrive. In fact, I recommend prepaying your mortgage as an excellent way to save for college.

Then when it comes time for junior to enter college, take out a home equity loan to pay your share of the tuition. The interest rates on these types of loans are usually very attractive. Plus, you'll get to take a tax deduction on all the interest you pay (see Secret #242 for details).

➤ **Inside Tip:** Now some colleges do count home equity in their financial aid calculations. If that's true for the college you're dealing with, you can still use a home equity loan to your advantage. Just be sure you take the loan in your base income year. That way, you'll be reducing your assets available to pay for college and getting an attractive loan to boot!

Secret #214
Another Good Reason to Take Out a
Home Equity Loan

Using a home equity loan to pay for college is smart, but using it to pay off consumer debt first is even smarter. Having car loans, credit card debt, even other student loan debt only adds to your monthly expenses. You get no credit for it when the financial aid officers assess your available income to pay for college, so it makes sense to reduce it as fast as possible.

With a home equity loan, you can consolidate all of your consumer debt, pay it off at a relatively low interest rate, and deduct every dime you pay in interest on your tax return.

What's more, if the college you're dealing with considers home equity in its financial aid calculations, you've also just reduced a substantial asset that would normally be considered available to pay for college.

Secret #215
The Two Best Loans You Can Get From the College's Financial Aid Office

If you don't own a home or decide you don't want to put your equity at risk to pay for college (which is what you're doing when you take out a home equity loan), there are several good loans available to students at very attractive rates.

The best loan to try to get is a Federal Perkins Loan (formerly called a National Direct Student Loan). With this loan, no interest accrues while the student is in school, and payment doesn't start until six months after the student graduates. The student typically has 10 years to repay the loan.

If you're offered a Perkins loan, I strongly suggest you take it. It offers the best interest rate and terms of any federally-subsidized loan available today. The student will be able to borrow up to $3,000 a year (the college will determine the amount) without a need for a credit check or parents' cosignature on the loan. As with all federally-subsidized loans, the college allocates the money, but it must be borrowed from a bank.

The second best loan to try to get is a subsidized Stafford loan. As with Perkins loans, interest does not accrue on Stafford loans until six months after the student graduates, and the student does not have to begin repaying until then and can stretch out payments for 10 years. The biggest difference between the Perkins loan and the Stafford loan is the interest rate: Stafford loans are slightly higher.

The maximum amount you can borrow on a Stafford loan is currently $2,625 for the student's freshman year, $3,500 as a sophomore and $5,500 for the junior and senior years.

Secret #216
The Dirty Trick Some Colleges Play With Stafford Loans

The best kind of Stafford loan is a *subsidized* loan that doesn't require repayment to begin until after the student graduates, and interest doesn't accrue until repayment begins. There is also another kind of Stafford loan, an *unsubsidized* loan that requires repayment to begin 60 days after the date of borrowing. This still may be a good deal because you're still getting an attractive interest rate, but the arrangement is very different: Interest begins accruing right away, and repayment starts 60 days after borrowing.

If the colleges you're dealing with offer you a Stafford loan as part of a financial aid package, be sure to find out whether it's subsidized or unsubsidized. The unsubsidized loan may still be worth it because of the low interest rate, but it lacks the major advantage of subsidized student loans: no interest accrual until repayment begins, which is after the student graduates.

Secret #217
Why It Pays to Repay Student Loans on Time

Besides the fact that it's just plain responsible to repay all loans on time, it is especially valuable for student loans, thanks to a new program sponsored by the Student Loan Marketing Association or Sallie Mae.

If your lender is participating in the Sallie Mae Great Rewards program, and you repay the first 48 months of your student loan on time, the interest rate on your loan will be lowered by 2 percent. Now if that's not enough incentive to repay on time, I don't know what is!

Secret #218
What's Wrong With Winning a Scholarship

Ah, the magical scholarship solution. It's every parent's dream. Young Master John becomes an expert bagpipe player and wins the coveted Bagpipers Association scholarship. Or Young Mistress Jane displays expert horseriding prowess and becomes the envy of her peers when she wins the prized Horsewoman's Association scholarship.

Despite the fact that most of these scholarships are a mere pittance compared to what college costs, and the fact that the truly big scholarships only go to one in four trillion high school football players, scholarships have another major pitfall: They could eat into your financial aid.

Say the college of your youngster's dreams determines that you can afford to pay $10,000 toward the $20,000 annual total cost. Of the $10,000 missing, the college will give you a loan for $2,500 (gee, aren't they nice?) and a grant for $7,500. Sounds great. Then junior gets a scholarship for $1,000. Way to go, junior. Now you only have to shell out $9,000 out of your pocket, right? Wrong. Chances are, the college will snatch that $1,000 right away from you and put it toward the $7,500 grant they're giving you. And you still have to come up with $10,000.

It's one of the dirty little truths few people know about scholarships. But that doesn't mean you should never try for a private scholarship. First of all, if you don't qualify for aid at all, anything you can get goes right to your pocket anyway.

Even if you do qualify, it may be worth it. The college may agree to put the scholarship toward your loan, which means you or your child will have less to pay off in the future (not bad). And you can at least try to convince the college to let you keep the scholarship money for your portion of the costs. I'm not saying you'll get it, but you can try, and it beats having nothing.

Secret #219
Another Potential Pitfall of Scholarships

If your child receives a scholarship that requires him to perform a service in return, say teaching or working for the federal government in the future, the money will be treated as compensation and, therefore, will be fully taxable as income.

By contrast, scholarships that are grants with nothing expected in return are income-tax-free as long as the money is used to pay for tuition and course-related fees, books, and supplies.

➤ **Inside Tip:** If your child works as a teaching assistant or research assistant for the college and receives a tuition reduction *in addition to* regular pay, the tuition reduction will be tax-free.

Secret #220
You Can Make Yourself More Attractive for Financial Aid

Colleges give money to students they deem attractive. In most cases, that means students with good academic records, students who are from far away, and students who have unusual talents. Think of it this way, the college wants to brag that 90 perecnt of its students were in the top of their high school class. It wants to claim that it attracts students from all over the country (if you live in Alaska or Hawaii, you've got a great shot at negotiating for more financial aid). And it wants to tout the varied talents of its student body.

One kid I knew got offers from all over the country, including Princeton, because he played the bagpipes! So use your assets to your advantage—not only to help your child get into the college of her choice, but to pay for it too!

Secrets #221-225
Five Ways to Cut the Cost of College

So far, most of this chapter has been devoted to ways to save, borrow, or get financial aid for college. But there are a number of unique ways you can actually *cut* the cost of college, including:

Secret #221
Get College Credit Without Going to College

Many high schools offer advanced placement (AP) classes, which are designed to prepare students for advanced placement exams at the end of the year. If the student passes the advanced placement exam, she can get college credit for that course. Even if the student doesn't take an advanced placement class, she can still take the exam and try to get college credit. I've seen students get credit for an entire semester—even an entire year—just by taking advanced placement exams.

Not all colleges accept advanced placement credits, so check with the colleges your student is interested in before signing up for the test.

Secret #222
Go the Nontraditional Route

Attending classes is only one way to get an education. Literally hundreds of well-known colleges, from Syracuse to the University of London, offer programs where students can take classes by mail, video, television, even electronic mail at a fraction of the cost of traditional courses.

Dr. John Bear is the undisputed authority on the subject. If you're interested, read his *College Degrees by Mail* (Ten Speed Press, 1993) for the inside scoop on the best schools with the cheapest nontraditional programs.

Secret #223
Get Credit for Life Experience

If you're an older student returning to school to finish a degree or going to school for the first time, explore the possibility of getting credit for your life experience. Hundreds of colleges offer life experience credit for skills ranging from fluency in French to magazine writing.

You'll need to match your skills to courses being offered by the school you're attending, then demonstrate proficiency in the subject matter. Requirements differ for each school, but to get a general idea of what you'll have to do and which schools offer credit for life experience, consult John Bear's *Guide to Nontraditional College Degrees* (Ten Speed Press).

Secret #224
Work for the College

Most colleges offer employees, children of employees, and spouses of employees free or partially-free tuition. That goes for secretaries as well as department heads. So if you have any interest at all in joining the faculty or staff of a college, make the move before your children go to college. Not only will tuition cost you next to nothing, but you won't have to pay taxes on the benefit either!

Secret #225
Barter!

Are you in a business that could be useful to colleges? Is there any special talent you have that you could exchange for a cut in tuition costs? If so, then try bartering with the college of your child's choice. As old as the hills, but never out of style, bartering is an excellent way to make college costs more manageable.

Some excellent bartering ideas: If you're a public relations executive, offer to create a public awareness campaign for one of the college's programs. Do you plan conventions, meetings, or parties for a living? Offer to do the planning for an alumni weekend or freshman orientation. Are you an architect? You could draw up the plans for a new addition to the college library.

Colleges are more willing than you might think to trade services for tuition. But one word of caution: If you strike a deal, keep the arrangement to yourself. Most colleges don't like to advertise the fact that they're willing to barter to traditional "paying" students.

9
How to Axe Your Taxes

In 1913, Congress was given the "power to lay and collect taxes on incomes from whatever source derived." Some 82 years and 9,000+ pages of tax code later, taxes are an integral part of every American's life.

Indeed, most of us don't even own our own paychecks until May 3. That's right. If you put every cent of your paycheck toward your annual tax bill starting on January 1, it would take most folks until May 3 to pay the bill in full. That's why people call May 3 Tax Freedom Day. It's the day when you finally start working for yourself.

This chapter is designed to help you find ways to make your own personal Tax Freedom Day come sooner (or at least not later) and help you keep more of what you make in your own hands— not Uncle Sam's.

Secret #226
What's Wrong With Getting a Big Refund

I just love checks. And as long as they have my name on them, the bigger, the better. I'm sure you know the feeling. But there's one time when a big check isn't good for you: when it's coming from the IRS. Look at it this way: A refund is really just a return of your own money—money you've let the IRS use for the past year, interest-free. Banks don't loan money interest-free, why should you?

Now I know it's much nicer to fill in the line that says, "Amount to be Refunded to You" than the line that says, "Amount You Owe" on your tax return. I get a little charge out of getting a refund myself. The trick is to make sure the refund isn't too much. $100, $200, even $500 is okay. But when it starts getting to be more than $500, that's when I say the IRS is taking advantage of you. Then it's time to go back and recalculate your withholding. Get a W-4 form from your employer and use the worksheet on the back to figure out how many exemptions you can take. If you figure it out correctly, you should have more money in your paycheck each month and get less of a refund next year.

Secret #227
Fifteen Expenses You Can Pass on to Uncle Sam

Uncle Sam may not be the most generous guy when it comes to tax breaks, but fortunately there are still a few expenses he'll help you out with. Many come under the "miscellaneous expenses" deduction on your tax return, which means that they must add up to at least 2 percent of your adjusted gross income in order to qualify for the deduction (actually, you can only deduct the amount *over* 2 percent of your adjusted gross income). Among the expenses included in this category are:

1. Union dues
2. Professional and business association dues (but not country club dues)
3. Uniforms for work
4. Cleaning and laundering of work uniforms
5. Subscriptions to publications related to your job
6. Resumé preparation and other expenses associated with looking for a new job (as long as it's in the same field)
7. Tax advice

8. Tax preparation fees (including fees for tax-preparation software)

9. IRA custodial fees

10. Safe deposit box rental fees

11. Fees to investment advisors

12. Subscriptions to investment-related publications

13. Unreimbursed travel expenses for your job, including meals, airfaire, hotels, telephone calls, taxi fares, and the like

14. Other unreimbursed expenses associated with your job, including business publications, telephone calls made for business outside of your employer's offices, certain legal and accounting fees, certain safe deposit box fees, and business equipment, such as a calculator or fax machine, if it's needed for your job and your employer doesn't provide it

15. Educational expenses, including tuition, textbooks, fees, equipment, transportation expenses to school and living expenses while away at school if (a) you are employed; (b) you already meet the minimum requirements of your job, business, or profession, and (c) the educational courses maintain or improve your job skills or you are required by your employer or the law to take courses to keep your current position or salary.

Secret #228
How to Deduct Business Travel, Educational, and
Other Miscellaneous Expenses
Without Meeting the 2 Percent Floor

Do you have a lot of miscellaneous expenses, but can't deduct them because they don't meet the 2 percent floor? If you have a small business, even just a sideline business, you can deduct some of these expenses on your Schedule C (business tax form) without having to meet the 2 percent floor (as long as they are business expenses, of course).

Eligible items include: educational expenses, dues to professional societies, subscriptions to professional journals, tax preparation fees, business travel costs, and business equipment expenses up to $17,500, including a home computer, typewriter, adding machine, calculator, copier, or fax machine.

You can also deduct the cost of a business phone line as long as you have another phone line coming into the home (the IRS won't let you write off the basic charge for your home phone) and all business-related long-distance phone calls.

In some cases, you can even deduct the costs of business trips where you also take some vacation time, as long as the primary purpose of the trip was business. Costs included in the deduction are lodging, transportation, and 50 percent of your meals.

Secrets #229–232
Four More Tax Breaks for the Self-Employed

Self-employed taxpayers can also get a break on other not so "miscellaneous" expenses, including rent, food, electricity, employee salaries, and health insurance. Here are the rules:

Secret #229
Deduct Your Basic Operating Expenses

You can deduct many of your basic operating expenses without having to meet the 2 percent miscellaneous itemized deduction floor, including supplies, rent for office space, salaries of assistants, books, professional instruments, and equipment with a useful life of a year or less.

Secret #230
Deduct Your Home Office

If you work from home, you can deduct costs associated with your home office if (1) the office is used exclusively and on a regular basis to meet with or deal with clients or customers and (2) it is your principal place of business. If you only occasionally use a home office to do paperwork or meet with clients and you have an outside office, you cannot take the deduction.

The IRS has really cracked down on this deduction in recent years because it has been abused so often. That's why many tax advisors believe a home office is a red flag to the IRS, asking for an audit. I say, if the deduction is rightfully yours, by all means, take it. But first be sure it's worth it.

Under the home office rule, you can deduct all mortgage interest, real estate taxes, home insurance premiums, repairs/ maintenance costs, utilities, and depreciation for that portion of the house. However, your home office deductions cannot exceed your net income. So if you don't have a lot of income, the home office deduction is probably not worth it, especially since you can deduct mortgage interest and real estate taxes—probably your biggest expenses—on your personal return.

Secret #231
How to Deduct 100 Percent of
Your Business Meals

Despite what you may have heard, you can deduct 100 percent of certain business meals and entertainment as long as they meet one of the following requirements:

- The meal is provided for employees on the business premises as part of an entertainment activity.
- The meal and/or entertainment is given to employees as part of their compensation and is subject to withholding taxes.
- The meal is a reimbursement to employees.
- The meal is part of a company-wide picnic, Christmas party, or other recreational event and is not geared primarily for highly-paid employees or owners.
- The meal is for an employee, business, or shareholder meeting that is not held for social purposes.
- The food is provided to the public as part of the company's advertising or to promote goodwill.

In all of these cases, you can deduct 100 percent of the cost of food.

Secret #232
Deduct Your Health Insurance Premiums

You may be able to deduct part of your health insurance premiums without having to meet the 7.5 percent floor for medical expenses if you're self-employed. As of this writing, the 25 percent deduction on health insurance premiums for self-employed people has expired. This often happens. Then Congress reenacts the law and makes it retroactive to the time it expired so that the deduction, in effect, was always available. (Kind of makes you wonder why they have expiration dates on these laws in the first place, doesn't it?) But since Congress hasn't reenacted the legislation yet, check with a tax specialist to see whether this deduction is still available to you.

➤ **Special Hint:** Most people think you can only take this deduction if you could not have been covered by an employer plan at any time during the year. That's the way the law worked in the past. But now you can apply the test on a monthly basis, so you can qualify even if for just one month you weren't covered by an employer-sponsored plan.

Secret #233
Give Unto Others and Get a Tax Break Too

There aren't many tax deductions Uncle Sam gives his nod of approval to, but fortunately giving gifts is one of them. You can deduct the full amount of all gifts to charity as long as you haven't received anything in return. Just make sure you get a receipt or written acknowledgment for contributions of $250 or more (a cancelled check won't do).

If you do receive something in return, like dinner at a charity ball, you can still deduct the part of the donation that goes to the charity. Just ask the charity to give you written notification of what portion of your contribution is tax deductible.

And don't forget your cash donations. Cash contributions to the church collection plate, twelve-step programs, and any other nonprofit organization are all acceptable, as long as you can prove you made the contribution. One way to do that is to keep a log of all cash contributions as you make them throughout the year.

➤ **Inside Tip:** Gifts to charities aren't the only deductions you can take just for being generous. You also get a tax break for gifts to coworkers. Deductions are allowed of up to $25 per colleague.

Secret #234
Increase the Value of Your Charitable
Contributions and Give
Yourself a Double Tax Break

One of my favorite tax breaks is the gift of appreciated assets to charity. This little-known technique allows you to:

1. Give more to your favorite charity than you otherwise might have.
2. Give yourself a double tax break.

It's a true "win-win" situation. Here's how it works: You donate an appreciated asset (like stock) to your favorite charity, and you can deduct the full market value of the contribution *and* avoid paying taxes on your capital gains as long as you have owned the asset more than a year.

Say you bought 100 shares of ABC stock at $25 a share (for $2,500) two years ago. Now it's worth $50 a share (or $5,000). If you give the stock to a charity, you can take a deduction for the entire $5,000 *plus* avoid paying taxes on your $2,500 gain. Now that's really spreading your "appreciation" around!

Secret #235
How to Give to Charity and Get a Double
Tax-Break From a Losing Investment

How would you like to get rid of a losing investment, give to charity, and get a double-tax break all at once? It's simple—all you need to do is sell the losing investment, then donate the proceeds from the sale to your favorite charity. You get to deduct both the capital loss from the investment and the charitable contribution!

➤ **Potential Trap:** Just be sure to sell the depreciated asset first, then give the proceeds to charity. If you give the asset directly to the charity, you won't be able to deduct your capital loss.

Secret #236
How to Increase the Value of Your Charitable
Contributions Without Giving Any More

How would you like to increase your gifts to charity without spending one dime more? It's all possible with the Fidelity

Charitable Gift Fund (800/682-4438). This fund, sponsored by the Fidelity family of mutual funds, allows you to invest the money you would have given to a charity, watch it grow, and then, when you're ready, make the contribution. You get an immediate tax deduction for your initial investment, and you can choose to invest in three different pools comprised of Fidelity mutual funds.

Secret #237
How to Take a $22,500-a-Year IRA Deduction

It's true that the maximum allowable contribution to an IRA is $2,000 a year. But self-employed people can get an extra bonus. Whether you run a full-time business with millions in revenue or you freelance occasionally on the side, you can take up to 15 percent of the net profits from your business—up to $22,500 a year—and contribute it to a Simplified Employee Pension plan or SEP-IRA.

A SEP-IRA works just like a regular IRA. You have the same flexibility of choice of investment options (i.e., stocks, bonds, CDs, mutual funds, etc.) and your earnings compound tax-free until you withdraw. What's more, the paperwork required to open a SEP-IRA is simple to fill out—usually just a page or two. And like an IRA, you have until April 15 of the following year to open one for the current tax year (in other words, you can wait until April 15, 1996 to open a SEP-IRA for the 1995 tax year).

Secret #238
The Single Most Important Mistake
to Avoid When Rolling Over a 401(k) or
Other Pension Plan

It used to be that when you left a company to start a new job, you could take the money from your pension plan, 401(k) or 403(b), and you'd have 60 days to invest it somewhere else with no penalty. No more. In January, 1993, a law went into effect that gives Uncle Sam the right to take 20 percent of your money right off the bat—you'll never see it—and never give it back to you *even if you plan to roll over the money to another qualified retirement plan within 60 days.* What's worse, if you do plan to rollover the money, you'll have to come up with that

20 percent yourself. If you don't, the government will treat it as a withdrawal, and you'll owe taxes plus a 10 percent penalty on it.

Say you have $5,000 in a 401(k). You leave your job and decide to take the money with you. You plan to put it into an Individual Retirement Account (IRA), but you want to take a few weeks to decide where. When you leave, you'll get a check for $4,000, not $5,000, and a few weeks later, when you do open your IRA account, you'll have to start it with the full $5,000 (yes, you have to come up with an extra $1,000 on your own). If you don't, the IRS will levy a 10 percent penalty ($100) plus charge you for taxes on the $1,000 as if you had withdrawn the money. You'll owe $280 in taxes (if you're in the 28 percent tax bracket) plus the $100 on money you've never even seen! What's worse, the nest egg you worked so hard to build has just automatically shrunk by 22 percent!

Fortunately, there is a way around this annoying rule. It's called a direct custodian-to-custodian transfer. Instead of taking possession of the money and rolling it over yourself, have your old employer and your new investment company take care of the transaction for you. Here's how it works:

1. Before you leave your job, notify your employer that you want to do a "direct custodian-to-custodian transfer." This means you'll never take physical possession of your pension money, so your employer won't have to withhold 20 percent.

2. Select a new investment. If your new employer offers a 401(k) or 403(b) plan and accepts transfers, you can rollover the money from your old plan to the new employer's plan. If not, you can rollover the money into an existing IRA, or you can open a new IRA. Remember, an IRA is not an investment; it is a tax-deferred retirement account that can hold just about any type of investment you choose, including individual stocks, bonds, certificates of deposit (CDs), money market funds, stock mutual funds, bond mutual funds, etc.

3. Fill out a form with the bank or investment company that is administering your IRA to allow them to contact your old employer and have your pension money transferred into your new account.

4. Send in the form and sit back in your favorite easy chair with your feet up. You deserve to relax; you've just made a very smart move!

Secret #239
How Uncle Sam Can Help Slash
Your Medical Expenses

If rising health care costs are taking a bigger chunk of your pay-check, take heart—at least the IRS will offer you some relief. You can deduct all out-of-pocket medical expenses as long as they exceed 7.5 percent of your adjusted gross income. It's a high floor, but the good news is a lot more expenses qualify than you might think, such as:

- Exams by an optician
- Psychiatric sessions
- Contact lenses
- Acupuncture
- Sterilization
- Whirlpool baths (if for medical reasons)
- Birth control pills
- Vitamins if prescribed by a doctor to treat a specific ailment
- Drug treatment
- Prescription drugs
- Seeing-eye dogs

And don't forget the more basic unreimbursed medical expenses, like check-ups that aren't covered by your health plan, prescriptions, health insurance deductibles, and copayments. But not every medical or health-related expense qualifies. Examples of expenses that *don't* qualify include:

- Diaper service
- Health club dues
- Ear piercing
- Toothpaste
- Weight loss programs
- Maternity clothes

Be sure to keep track of *all* your medical expenses throughout the year. I suggest keeping a folder and just throwing your receipts in it. Don't even worry about whether or not the expenses qualify, just save the receipts. At the end of the year, you can weed out the ones that don't qualify and add up the others. Any amount over 7.5 percent of your adjusted gross income can be deducted.

Secrets #240–243
Four Ways Your Home Can Shelter
You From the IRS

Home is more than where the heart is; it's also the heart of a major tax deduction. But in this age where refinancing, prepayment, and home equity loans are more popular than ever, you must be careful about what you deduct and when you deduct it, for the rules differ dramatically depending on the type of mortgage you have. Here's the rundown:

Secret #240
How to Slash Your Taxes When You Buy a Home

On an initial home purchase, you can deduct all the mortgage interest you pay, including "points." A point is really just interest paid up front. You cannot, however, deduct the expenses associated with getting a mortgage, such as the commission for your real estate agent, recording fees, and other closing costs. Use Form 1098 as your guide. Your mortgage company will send it to you shortly after the end of the year. It will show you how much interest you've paid for the year, including any points you've paid.

➤ **Inside Tip:** Don't assume Form 1098 will include all the interest deductions you're entitled to. If you bought a house or refinanced during the year, check your settlement sheet for possible additional mortgage interest deductions. For example, say you settled on June 15. On a conventional loan, you would have paid 15 days of interest at settlement. Call your lender to find out whether that interest was included on Form 1098. If not, you can add it to the interest deduction you're taking for the interest you paid every month.

Secret #241
How to Slash Your Taxes When You Refinance

On a refinancing, your monthly interest is deductible just as it was for your initial mortgage, but you cannot deduct points you've paid up front. Instead, you have to treat them as interest paid over the life of the loan. So if you paid $3,000 in points in refinancing a 30-year loan, you can deduct $100 a year for the next 30 years. However, if you sell your home before your loan is paid off, you can deduct whatever amount is left in points. In this example, if you sold your home five years after you refinanced, you could deduct the remaining $2,500 you paid in points to refinance ($3,000 − [$100 × 5] = $2,500).

Secret #242
How to Slash Your Taxes on a Home Equity Loan

On a home equity loan, you can deduct all of the interest you pay as long as the loan doesn't exceed $100,000 (or $50,000 if you're married filing separately). Also, the loan can't be for more than the current market value of the house minus the principal balance. So if your home is worth $200,000 and the principal balance of your mortgage is $150,000, you can't get a loan for more than $50,000.

It doesn't matter what you use the home equity loan for—a new car, college tuition, vacation, whatever—the interest is still deductible. That's why a lot of people like using home equity loans as opposed to credit cards to make large purchases, since the interest on credit cards is no longer deductible.

Secret #243
Get a Tax Break When You Prepay Your Mortgage

You can get a tax break if you prepay your mortgage and your lender charges you a penalty. I like prepaying the principal on your mortgage as a way to build equity in your home and boost your net worth, but many lenders try to discourage the practice by charging a prepayment fee (after all, the sooner you pay off your loan principal, the less you'll pay them in interest). So if you've paid any kind of prepayment penalty, take heart, you can deduct it.

Secret #244
How to Get a Tax Break
When You Sell Your Home

Selling a home can be a tax buster too—if you know how to take advantage of the rules. You may know, for example, that when you sell your house, you can defer paying taxes on the gain as long as you buy a new house within two years that costs more and as long as you use the new house as a principal residence. And if you or your spouse is 55 or older, you can avoid paying taxes on your profits up to $125,000 (this is a one-time exclusion). But did you know that there are a number of deductions you can take to reduce your taxable gain? Costs you paid to buy the home, such as closing costs, reduce your gain as do all of the costs that reduce the selling price of your home. These include preparing the deed, the commission for the real estate agent, advertising, and legal services.

You can also subtract fix-up costs you've paid to improve the home before selling it, such as wallpapering, painting, and shampooing the carpets. Finally, if you paid any points for the buyer as an incentive when you sold your home, you can deduct that amount from your profit, which also reduces your tax liability.

Bear in mind, these reductions are worth taking even if you plan to rollover your gain into a new, more expensive house because you'll still eventually owe taxes on that gain. Your gain is merely deferred, it is not erased. So eventually, when you do sell your last home, you'll not only owe taxes on the gain from that home, but on all the gains from all the previous homes you've sold and deferred paying taxes on up to that point.

Secret #245
How to Get a Tax Break for
Expanding Your Cultural Horizons

Have you ever thought about hosting a foreign exchange student in your home? If the idea appeals to you and you haven't yet acted on it, perhaps Uncle Sam can give you an extra incentive. If you host an elementary or high school student for an educational program that is arranged by a charitable organization, you can deduct up to $50 a month for supporting the student. Just make sure you have a written agreement with the organization that spells out your support. And be sure to keep records of the amount of money you spend on the student's food, tuition, books, and recreation.

Secret #246
For Gamblers Only—
How to Make Your Losses Pay Off

If the blackjack dealers in Vegas and Lake Tahoe seem to have gotten more of your money than you had hoped, take heart. At least you can get some relief from the IRS. Yep, that's right, gambling losses are fully tax deductible. The catch? You must deduct them against winnings, which must be reported to the IRS and are fully taxable. But hey, if you win some and lose some, at least you can count on the IRS to ease part of the pain of losing!

Secret #247
Why Your CPA May Know Nothing About
Preparing Taxes

One of the biggest mistakes people make in looking for tax advice is to assume that Certified Public Accountants (CPAs) are better qualified than other tax preparers. Not true! On the national CPA exam, only 20 to 25 percent of *one part* is devoted to income tax questions! Hardly enough to qualify a CPA as a tax expert.

In fact, more than two-thirds of the people currently working as tax preparers are not "regulated agents," meaning they have received no certification, license, or degree that qualifies them to prepare taxes. Kind of scary when you consider that you need a state license to cut hair!

So how do you ensure you're getting a good tax advisor? One way is to go with an "enrolled agent." These are people who have passed a special tax exam administered by the Department of the Treasury. They are regulated by the Treasury Department and can represent you at IRS hearings.

Another way is to ask for personal references. This is the method I prefer. After all, there are thousands of competent tax preparers who have no license or degree, just as there are thousands of

CPAs who are competent in tax preparation despite the lack of required tax training to become a CPA. The only way to truly find a good tax advisor is to find satisfied customers.

Start with friends and relatives who own businesses. Business-owners have to do year-round tax planning and, very often, have complicated returns too. If they're satisfied with a tax advisor, you probably will be too. If you don't know anyone who can give you a reference and you end up calling a preparer cold, no problem. Just ask for references from the tax advisor—but don't stop there. Call the references and ask about their experiences with the advisor. If you get mixed reviews, move on. There's no need to settle for second best when it comes to something as important as tax advice.

Secret #248
Five Questions to Ask a Potential Tax Preparer

When interviewing potential tax advisors, the first question most people ask is: "How much do you charge?" While a reasonable fee is certainly important, it won't tell you a thing about the experience and ethics of the person you're dealing with.

Use the following checklist to determine the competence of potential tax advisors. If a candidate gets even one question wrong, move on. Remember, the IRS has the ability to seize your personal property and freeze your bank accounts if it feels it is warranted; you don't want to be dealing with an amateur.

1. I seem to have lost most of my records. Can we just fudge it?
   Wrong answer: "No problem."
   Right answer: "We have a serious problem."
2. What happens if I'm audited?
   Wrong answer: "Gee, that would be a real bummer."
   Right answer: "I stand behind my work. I'll represent you, and I'll do the talking."
3. If I get audited, how much will I have to pay?
   Wrong answer: "Whatever the IRS says."
   Right answer: "My clients don't generally have to pay penalties because I've got the supporting documents to back up my work. If I did make a mistake, I'd negotiate with the IRS on your behalf to get a lower penalty."

4. Who pays if you make a mistake?
   Wrong answer: "Don't worry about it. That won't happen."
   Right answer: "If it was my mistake, I'll pay. And I'll put that in writing."
5. Can I get an estimate of how much it will cost to prepare my return?
   Wrong answer: "I won't know until I'm finished."
   Right answer: "Absolutely."

Secret #249
What a Tax Preparer's Audit-Free Track Record Really Means

Does your tax advisor boast a track record of never having been audited? If so, don't be impressed. The fact of the matter is your chances of getting audited are about the same as winning a sweepstakes. In 1992, the IRS only audited around 0.9 percent of all returns filed. Self-employed and high-income people were more likely to get audited than others, but even self-employed people with over $100,000 in income had only a 3.95 percent chance of getting audited. With those odds, it's quite likely that your tax preparer—and every other tax preparer in town—won't have experienced an audit.

By the same token, even if your tax advisor has undergone an audit for a client, remember that it isn't a badge of guilt or incompetence. Audits are triggered by a computer that scores returns for a set of specific criteria. If a return meets the criteria (has a high income and a home office deduction, for example), then it is selected. Of course, the criteria for selection are highly confidential, but the point is, being selected for an audit is a routine process and does not mean that you or your tax preparer has necessarily done anything wrong.

Secret #250
How to Audit-Proof Your Tax Return

Want to know what triggers an IRS audit? Sorry, I can't help you there—it's top secret. But there are a few simple tricks that seem to work to lessen the chances of IRS scrutiny.

First, keep your return as boring as possible. Anything that makes your return stand out and anything the IRS feels is difficult to prove could trigger an audit. For example, if your deduction for mortgage interest is twice as much as the average for your income bracket and geographic area, the IRS may take notice. Similarly, if you deduct a home office or a car for business use, the IRS' ears will perk up. These deductions are tempting for taxpayers to take, and the IRS is convinced that this is an area rife with fraud.

Second, if you have an unusual deduction or a strange circumstance, attach a note of explanation to your return. Describe the deduction or circumstance, show your calculations if need be, and mention that you have supporting documentation. The IRS is likely to view this as a good faith effort, and like a burglar who sees a German shepherd on your front lawn, they'll probably go someplace else.

Finally, keep records of everything. I can't stress this enough. The more documentation you have, the more able you'll be to answer questions that may arise.

Secret #251
You May Still Get Audited
After You've Received a Refund

When that Department of Treasury refund check arrives in the mail, most people breathe a sigh of relief. "Whew," they think, "I made it another year without being audited."

Too bad it's not true. The processing of refund checks and payment checks is totally independent of the audit process. When you file your return, it goes to an IRS service center, which basically just checks the accuracy of the calculations. Service center workers then either process a refund check or deposit the remittance check into the IRS' account.

Then a computer record is made of your return, and it's sent to Martinsburg, West Virginia for storage. The IRS has up to three years to raise questions for an audit. If a material error is found, the period is extended to six years and if fraud is suspected, it can be extended indefinitely. So don't assume that if you get a refund or if the IRS accepts your check, you're free and clear. And be sure to keep your returns and detailed records of all supporting material for at least three years.

Secret #252
Never Go to an Audit

Okay, so you're selected as one of the unlucky few to get audited, and you're wondering, "Now what?" There's no need to panic. It could very well be just a routine question or it may be a random audit (which gets pretty detailed). The point is try to find out as much as possible from the IRS before the day of the audit. It could be something as simple as the IRS computers having spit out your name for having larger than average medical or charitable deductions. In that case, all you'd have to do would be to mail in copies of your canceled checks or other documentation.

If the audit is more serious, your best bet is to make yourself scarce. Hire an accountant or attorney who has a solid command of tax law and regulation to represent you. That way, the auditor can't put you on the spot, and you and your tax pro can work out reasonable responses to questions in your own time. If the IRS insists on having you there, go ahead—just be sure you bring your tax advisor with you.

Secret #253
What to Bring to an Audit if You Must Go

If you must go to an audit, make sure you let the IRS agent do most of the talking. The less you say, the better. And don't bring any more materials than the IRS originally requested. If the agent only requested your back-up material for your Schedule C and you bring your whole tax file, the agent may just decide to go over your miscellaneous itemized deductions at the same time. Do you really want that?

Also, let the agent direct the audit. Don't volunteer information that wasn't asked of you, and don't try to take control. Answer completely and concisely, but don't give more than you're asked.

And if you're especially nervous, tape the interview. You have the right to do so (as long as you notify the agent of your plan before the audit begins).

Secret #254
The Best Tax Software

If you choose to brave the tax preparation world alone, consider using Andrew Tobias' TaxCut. I've used this program myself for several years, and I like it because it's powerful, yet user-friendly. You stick the disks in, type a key or two, and you're ready to go. There are no special commands you need to learn or documentation you need to read to be able to use it.

What really makes TaxCut special, though, is its interview format. The program acts like a tax preparer, posing questions to you. You answer, and the program fills out your return accordingly. If you choose, you can do your whole return without ever seeing an IRS form! In addition, the software has nice help features to explain IRS rules and terminology if you get stuck. The program is available in DOS, Windows, and Macintosh editions. Contact Meca Software at 800/820-7462 for current prices.

Secret #255
When It Makes Sense to File Electronically

I love the idea of filing your tax return electronically. It's fast, it's easy, and it's immediate. Unfortunately, right now, banks and tax preparers charge for the service. And since there is a free and perfectly reasonable alternative (the U.S. mail), I just don't think it's worth it.

However, I do believe the price will come down (to free, I hope) in the future, as more competitors get into the act. When that happens and you can find a way to file for free, then it's worth it. And be sure to have your refund check directly deposited into your bank account. That way, you'll gain instant use of the money as soon as it is transmitted.

10
How to Make Sure You're in Good Hands

Insurance is the only product you'll ever buy that you hope you never use. When you buy health insurance, you're certainly not hoping to get sick so you can use it, are you? You're buying the peace of mind that comes with knowing that if you had a major illness, you wouldn't have to sell your house to pay the doctor bills. It's the same with life, disability, car, and homeowner's insurance. So don't look at insurance as something that needs to be used to be worthwhile. In fact, the smartest reason to buy insurance is to give someone else (the insurance company) the burden of worrying about a loss that would be financially devastating.

This is important to remember because several times in this chapter I'll recommend that you avoid or drop some type of coverage. In every case, it is because it violates the basic underlying principle of insurance: to transfer the burden of bearing a potentially disastrous loss to someone else.

Secret #256
The Best Way to Find a Safe Insurer

Safety should be your number one concern in selecting an insurance company. This is especially important with life insurance because you may be locked into a policy for many years to come. But it is also important for other kinds of insurance too. After all, safety ratings are based on financial stability, and if your insurer isn't financially stable, what do you think your chances are of being able to collect on a claim?

There are a number of rating services—A.M. Best, Moody's, Standard & Poor's, Duff & Phelps—but there is only one that stands head and shoulders above the rest: Weiss Research. That's because unlike all the others, Martin Weiss does not get paid by the insurance companies to rate them. That's right, believe it or not, all of the other rating services get paid by the insurance companies they rate. That's how they make their money. So if an insurance company doesn't pay them, the company doesn't get rated!

Now I don't know about you, but that seems screwy to me. If I'm looking for a safety rating, I want it to be done by an objective source, not one that's getting paid by the insurance companies. Weiss is such a source. For a $15 fee, Weiss will give you a rating of one insurance company over the phone. For $25, you can get a one-page "Personal Safety Brief" in writing, and for $45, you can get an in-depth report, including all of the company's financial statements. Contact Weiss Research at 800/289-9222; 2200 N. Florida Mango Rd., West Palm Beach, FL 33409 for details.

Secret #257
The One Type of Insurance They
Won't Try to Sell You
(Even Though You Probably Need It)

You can always tell what the profit margins are on a particular product by how much the insurance company is pushing it. Take life insurance. This is a big money maker for insurance companies and their agents. That's why you're always hearing about the latest universal, variable, or variable universal product. But it's what you *aren't* hearing about that you probably need the most: disability insurance.

Insurance companies and insurance agents don't push disability insurance because it just isn't a big commission-booster. However, it is vital for just about every working adult to own. Consider this: According to a study by the American College of Life Underwriters, one in three people who reaches age 35 will become disabled for at least three months before reaching age 65, and one in ten will be permanently disabled.

What's more, if you become disabled, not only do you lose your source of income, but at the same time, you'll have higher expenses (for health care, rehabilitation, etc.). This is why it's crucial to have some form of disability insurance.

Disability insurance comes in two basic forms: short-term and long-term. Short-term disability insurance provides benefits for a short period, ranging from a few months to two years. Long-term disability insurance can provide benefits for your entire lifetime. Chances are, you may already have some form of disability insurance through your employer. Check to see if you do. If you don't, contact your insurance company *today*. This is too important to ignore.

Secret #258
The Most Important Feature to Have in a Disability Insurance Policy

In evaluating a disability insurance policy, it's critical that you get the right definition of what constitutes a disability. Some policies will only pay benefits if you become disabled and can't "engage in any occupation." This is way too restrictive. After all, if you're a brain surgeon, do you want a policy that will only pay if you can't perform any type of work or do you want it to pay if you can't perform brain surgery?

The best definition of disability is "the inability to engage in *your own occupation*." In fact, this is the only definition I would settle for when buying an individual disability insurance policy.

Secrets #259–262
Four More Things to Consider When Buying Disability Insurance

In addition to the definition of the disability, you'll also want to look for the following provisions in a disability insurance policy:

Secret #259
Select an Appropriate Elimination Period

Basically, the elimination period tells you how long you have to wait after the disability occurs before the company will begin paying benefits. The longer you agree to wait, the lower your premiums will be. Of course, you'll have to weigh choosing a long elimination period against how long you think you can live without your income. I wouldn't go much longer than two or three months.

Secret #260
Get as Much Coverage as Possible

The amount of coverage is how much you'll actually receive if you become disabled. It's generally expressed as a percentage of your income. You will be unable to get a policy that pays 100 percent of your income because insurance companies don't want to give you an incentive not to work! Sixty percent is customary for short-term disabilities, while 75 to 80 percent is typical for long-term disabilities. Obviously, the more coverage you can get, the better.

Secret #261
Keep the Money Coming In

The maximum benefit period is the length of time the insurance company will pay you benefits. I'd go for the longest period you can afford. Since premiums do not increase exactly in line with increases in time (i.e., a 26-week plan doesn't cost twice as much as a 13-week plan), it's worth it to get as much coverage as you can afford.

Secret #262
Make Sure the Renewable Provisions
Are Adequate

Finally, you'll want to buy a policy that the company can't cancel and that prevents the company from jacking up the premiums in an effort to get you to cancel. The terminology to look for is "noncancelable." This means that as long as you pay your premium, the company can't cancel the policy and can't raise your premium for the length of the contract (usually to age 60 or 65).

A reasonable alternative to this provision is "guaranteed renewable." This means that they can't raise the premium unless they are raising it for an entire class of insured people. So they can't just jack up your premiums in an effort to get you to drop the policy. They can only raise your premium if they're raising it for everyone else in your age group and insurance classification.

The renewal provisions to avoid are "renewable at the company's option," which is basically the same as having no provision; or "cancelable," which means that the company can cancel your policy at any time—even during a period for which you've already paid a premium.

Secret #263
The Problem With Long-Term Care Insurance

The good news is we're living longer. The bad news is we'll need more care for longer periods of time, and it's terribly expensive. Enter the latest innovation in insurance: the long-term care policy. Long-term care insurance pays for the cost of extended nursing or custodial care. Benefits are typically paid on a flat per day basis up to a limit of say, $100.

The concept is terrific, but it has several flaws. First, it's new, and insurance companies don't have a lot of claims experience, so virtually all policies provide for premiums to be raised at the insurance company's discretion.

What's more, many policies are so restrictive they never cover anything. The worst offenders are those that require that you be hospitalized immediately before entering a nursing home. Only about 50 percent of people entering nursing homes come directly from hospitals, so if you're one of the other 50 percent, you wouldn't be covered.

Another restrictive requirement is that benefits will only be paid if you need skilled nursing care first. Skilled nursing care is the most expensive and comprehensive type of long-term care, and few people need this at the outset. If you're one of the lucky few who needs 24-hour availability of a registered nurse under a doctor's supervision right off the bat, you'll be covered. If you just need a little help getting around or bathing and dressing, forget it. Not only won't this type of home custodial care be covered, but even if you do eventually require skilled nursing care, that won't be covered either because you didn't need it from the outset.

In short, my advice on long-term care insurance is to purchase it only if you're in or very near retirement and only if it has the liberal provisions outlined in Secret #264.

Secret #264
What to Look for in a Long-Term Care Policy

In addition to having no prior hospitalization requirement and allowing benefits to start at whatever level of care is needed first (see above), a good long-term care policy will:

- Have a reasonable elimination (waiting) period. I recommend no longer than 30 days.
- Offer lifetime benefits.
- Be guaranteed renewable for life (can't be canceled as long as the premium is paid, but can increase as long as it increases for an entire class of insureds and doesn't discriminate against one individual).
- Have no limitation for preexisting conditions.
- Include a waiver of premium clause that allows you to stop paying premiums once the benefits begin.
- Allow you to choose any state-licensed facility, not just those that are Medicare-certified.
- Provide coverage for all organic-based mental illnesses, including Alzheimer's, Parkinson's Disease, and senile dementia.
- Have an inflation rider that will increase coverage as prices rise.

Secret #265
What's Wrong With Using Life Insurance to
Pay for Long-Term Care

Certain permanent life insurance policies (whole life, universal life, variable life, etc.) include a provision that allows you to withdraw or borrow against the death benefit to pay for long-term care. This provision is usually termed a "living benefit" rider.

I don't like this plan because it unnecessarily ties the need for long-term care coverage to the need for life insurance. It assumes that your need for long-term care coverage reduces your need for life insurance (because the long-term care coverage is taking money away from the death benefit). In addition, you must keep your life insurance coverage intact in order to get your long-term care coverage. But in many cases, the need for life insurance diminishes just as the need for long-term care coverage increases. What's more, if the long-term care benefit is based on a percentage of the "death benefit" or "net amount at risk," it will decrease over time as the cash value increases, thus providing you with less coverage as time goes by.

Instead of using your life insurance to pay for long-term care, buy a separate long-term care policy or set up an investment plan on your own to provide for long-term care.

Secrets #266–275
Ten Ways to Slash Your Car Insurance Premiums

Once you've found the right insurance company and you've gotten a premium quote, ask the agent or broker about getting discounts if you agree to:

Secret #266
Raise Your Deductible

Think about what you could afford to pay today if you totaled your car. That should be your deductible. Remember, the higher the deductible, the lower your premiums. According to the National Insurance Consumer Organization, raising a collision deductible from $100 to $250 will slash around 20 percent off your premium. Raising it to $500 will save you 50 percent.

Secret #267
Drop Collision Coverage

Collision coverage tends to be the most expensive part of car insurance. And if your car is over five years old, it probably isn't worth it to pay for collision coverage. If you get into an accident, the most you'll receive is the blue book value of the car, which may even be less than what it will cost you to replace the car. Understand, though, that if you drop collision coverage, you'll be assuming the risk yourself.

And that risk will translate to rental cars too. When you drop collision coverage on your own cars, you are no longer covered for collisions when you rent cars either, which means you may have to buy the collision coverage the rental car company offers.

Secret #268
Get Good Grades

Good students tend to have fewer accidents and are therefore better risks for insurance companies. If you're a student, keep your grades up, and you'll qualify for the good student discount.

Secret #269
Take a Defensive Driving Course

Like good students, defensive drivers have fewer accidents. Completion of a defensive driving course should take another 5 to 15 percent off your premiums.

Secret #270
Install Antitheft Devices

The installation of a burglar alarm, hood lock, or any other anti-theft device will typically shave 5 to 15 percent off your premiums.

Secret #271
Buy a Car With Passive Restraints

Air bags and automatic seat belts can shave 10 to 30 percent off your liability coverage. If your car has them, make sure you ask for the discount.

Secret #272
Carpool to Work

If you use your car only for "pleasure purposes," you can shave up to 25 percent off your premiums, depending on how much you drive. This is also something to take advantage of if you have a child who attends college far from home and is covered on your policy. If the student only drives occasionally, that portion of your premium should be lower.

Secret #273
Give the Insurance Company
More of Your Business

Insurance companies want your business, and the more business you bring them, the more they'll reward you. If you own two or more cars, insure them with the same company, and you'll receive a "multicar discount."

Secret #274
Drop Duplicate Coverage

Many car insurance policies include medical payments coverage to pay for your medical bills if you've been in an accident. But if you already have decent health insurance, there's no need for medical payments coverage. And if you don't have decent health insurance, put your money into getting some—that's where it will work harder for you.

Secret #275
Drop Unnecessary Coverage

Remember the purpose of insurance: to pay for losses that would be financially devastating if you had to incur them yourself. I don't think towing and emergency road service fall into this category. I'd much prefer to see you become a member of AAA or another roadside assistance service for towing and emergency service than to pay for that coverage under your car insurance policy.

Secret #276
The Most Important Decision You Need to Make
When Buying Homeowners Insurance

Nothing is more important when you buy homeowners insurance than correctly calculating how much of your home you want to insure. The figure has nothing to do with the market value of your home; it's based on how much it would cost you to rebuild your home if it were totally destroyed today. So if you could sell your home for $175,000, but it would only cost $130,000 to rebuild it, then that's the most you'd need to insure it for. (Remember, you're just insuring your *home*, not your land.)

I recommend insuring your home for 100 percent of the replacement cost. This is the most expensive type of insurance, but I feel it's worth it. A good alternative is to insure for 80 percent of the replacement cost. You'll still receive the full amount it costs to replace any part of your home that is damaged. And since it's much more likely that part of your home would be damaged as opposed to all of your home being damaged, this is a fine alternative.

What you want to avoid, however, is insuring for anything less than 80 percent of the replacement cost. If you do, you'll only be paid for the "actual cash value" of your loss. That means depreciation is taken into account. So if your 10-year-old carpeting is destroyed in a fire, your insurance company will pay you about what you could get if you sold it in a garage sale (in other words, a pittance). And you'll have to buy brand new carpeting at probably three times what it cost you to buy the original carpeting. If, on the other hand, you had insured the home for at least 80 percent of the replacement cost, you'll receive not what you paid for the original carpeting, but what it would cost to replace the carpeting *today*.

Also, be sure to get replacement coverage on the contents of your home as well. This will guarantee that if the 8-year-old sofa you bought for $300 is damaged, you'll receive enough money to buy a brand new sofa of the same type.

Secret #277
How to Guarantee You Don't Outgrow Your Homeowners Insurance Policy

Once you've determined how much to insure your home for, you need to make sure you continue to have adequate coverage for as long as you live in the home. That means every time you make an improvement, build an addition, or do anything to enhance the value of your home, you add coverage for those improvements to the policy.

Also, it's important that you make sure your coverage is always equal to at least 80 percent of the replacement cost of the home. So if construction costs rise dramatically in your area, you'll have to increase your homeowners insurance coverage as well. If you don't want to have to worry about keeping up with building costs, consider buying an inflation guard endorsement. This is essentially a rider you can add onto your policy that will automatically increase the amount of coverage on your home as inflation increases. The problem with these endorsements is that they're usually tied to the Consumer Price Index, which often has little bearing on construction costs in a particular area. Still, it's worth considering to ensure that you're fully covered.

Finally, make sure you purchase replacement cost endorsements (riders) for jewelry, art work, and other personal property that exceeds the policy's limits. For example, if you own a diamond ring worth $6,000, and your limit for recovery of individual jewelry items is $1,000, you'll probably want to buy a rider to cover the full value of the ring.

Secret #278
Your Homeowners Policy Is Good for a Lot More Than Damage to Your Home

Have you ever had your wallet stolen? Chances are, you probably immediately called your credit card companies to notify them. But what about your insurance company? If you had homeowners insurance, you had no need to worry. Losses from stolen credit cards and stolen checks are covered on most homeowner's policies up to $1,000. And that includes not only cash losses, but also any court and legal costs you may have to pay in bringing the thief to justice.

Indeed, there are oodles of things covered under homeowners insurance that few people know about. Here are just a few:

- The cost of removing debris after a fire
- The cost of protecting property that has been damaged so it doesn't get damaged any more
- The cost of paying a fire department to put out your fire

- Damage to property you tried to remove from a burning building
- Extra assessments from your condominium association, such as unexpected common property damage
- A suitcase stolen from your car
- Theft of your jewelry from a hotel room

When in doubt, call your insurance agent to see if it's covered. You may just find a nice check in your mailbox!

Secret #279
How to Cut Your Homeowners Insurance
Premiums Down to Size

As with car and health insurance, the higher your deductible, the lower your premiums. Again, I'd choose the highest deductible you possibly can that wouldn't put you in serious financial difficulty.

Also, ask about discounts for:

- Burglar alarms
- Deadbolt locks
- A sprinkler system
- Window locks
- A brand new home
- Mature (over 55) owners
- Multiple policies with the same insurance company

Secret #280
Use an Umbrella for the Best Protection

In today's litigious society, civil suits over seemingly trivial matters aren't uncommon. In most cases of individual liability, you would be protected under your homeowners or car insurance. But the limits of those policies are typically $100,000 to $300,000, and awards these days can go into the millions. For the most complete protection possible, buy an umbrella policy.

These policies typically provide coverage for $1 million or more over and above the limits of a basic homeowners or car insurance policy. So if your car insurance liability limit was $100,000 and you were being sued for $300,000, the umbrella would pay the extra $200,000 in damages. I like umbrellas because they're relatively cheap—around $100 a year for a $1 million policy—and they offer extra protection not covered by basic homeowners or car insurance policies, such as protection for automobile liability worldwide (as opposed to just in North America), libel, slander, and violation of privacy. For perils such as these that aren't covered by a basic car or homeowners policy, you'll pay a deductible, typically $5,000 to $10,000, before the coverage kicks in.

➤ **Inside Tip:** To get the maximum protection for the lowest cost, drop the liability limits on your car and homeowners policies to the state minimums and buy a $1 million umbrella policy. You'll lower your car and homeowners insurance premiums and still be able to get $1 million in liability protection. I know a couple that used this strategy and their homeowners and car insurance premiums were so much lower that the extra umbrella coverage only ended up costing them $14 more a year than they were paying before.

Secret #281
The Worst Reason to Buy Life Insurance

Life insurance is designed to replace your income stream should you die, so that your dependents will be able to maintain a normal standard of living. Life insurance is *not*, I repeat, *not* designed to fund your retirement or pay for your child's college education. In fact, the single worst reason to buy life insurance is as an investment.

Now, I know your friendly neighborhood insurance agent will try to convince you otherwise. He'll show you lovely projection tables with lots of zeros to show how your "cash value" will grow. He'll promise you the benefits of protection and savings. He'll sweet talk you into believing it's "really the best thing you can do for yourself and your family."

Don't believe it! First of all, those lovely projections are just that—projections. They are based on assumptions of investment returns—*not guarantees.* And if you look a little closer, you'll see that those beautiful zeros in your cash value account don't start showing up until many years (like 10) after you've been paying premiums. Sure, you may have built up a cash value account worth $190,000 but that's after you've shelled out $156,000 in premiums! That's about a 2 percent average annual return, not even better than a money market fund.

The bottom line is life insurance should be bought for protection, not for savings. There are many good investments out there to build a nest egg; life insurance isn't one of them.

Secret #282
The Second Worst Reason to Buy Life Insurance

The second worst reason to buy life insurance is for the purpose of guaranteeing your insurability. Insurance agents love to use this rationale. "You may not be able to get insurance in the future, you know," they say, "so you better buy a permanent policy now while you still qualify. After all, you could contract a horrible disease that renders you uninsurable."

Well sure, that's true. But you could also become fabulously successful, marry a fully self-supporting spouse, and never have any children, and you wouldn't even need life insurance. The kind of logic the "guarantee your insurability" strategy is based on ranks right up there with reserving a date for your teenage daughter's wedding reception 10 years into the future. Sure the place gets booked months—even years—in advance, but that's no reason to reserve it for an event that may never happen! You wouldn't even think of doing that. Yet it's surprising how many people get talked into buying some type of permanent life insurance based on this same logic (of course, the insurance agent is usually such a good salesperson, the way he presents it makes it seem perfectly logical). I say buy life insurance based on your needs *today.* Worry about the future when it happens.

Secret #283
The Smartest Reason to Buy Life Insurance

Life insurance makes sense when your death would cause a financial hardship to someone else, principally dependent children (under age 18) and spouses. In many cases, a spouse is working and would be able to earn enough to support himself or herself, and the only funds needed are to support the children and pay off outstanding debts. Life insurance can also make sense to provide funds to pay estate taxes (see Secret #358). Life insurance should *not* be bought so that you can leave a big inheritance to your kids. Once the need to support dependents is passed, so should the need for life insurance (unless you're buying it for estate planning purposes, but even then, the amount would change).

Secret #284
How to Decide What Kind of
Life Insurance to Buy

Okay, so you've decided you need life insurance. Now the big question: What kind to buy? First of all, you need to be clear about what your needs are. The biggest mistake most people make in buying life insurance is deciding on the kind of insurance they want before figuring out why they're buying it! It's easy to fall into this trap since insurance companies have come up with so many different innovative kinds of life insurance—universal, variable, variable universal, and so on—but all the snazzy features in the world won't amount to a hill of premiums if you don't need them.

The truth is what you want from a life insurance policy is the most protection at the lowest cost. And for most people, that means term insurance. Now don't expect insurance agents to tell you this; after all, they get higher commissions from permanent (or whole life) insurance. But the fact of the matter is term unquestionably offers you the most protection for your premium dollar. That's because your premium dollars are only being used to pay for death protection (the reason you buy insurance), unlike whole life policies, which also include a "cash value" component. The cash value is the excess of what is needed to provide for the death benefit. You provide this excess by paying higher premiums, which are then invested in a cash value account that accumulates over time. So with whole life insurance, you're paying more so you can accumulate extra money in a savings account.

You're also paying more because whole life policies are designed to be permanent—lasting as long as you live, as opposed to term policies, which expire when the term is up. Since we're all going to die eventually, a permanent policy would naturally cost more because the insurance company would have to pay benefits eventually. Whereas if you only maintain a policy for a term, the insurance company has an opportunity to pocket the premium without ever paying a benefit.

There are a variety of forms of whole life insurance, including straight whole life, limited pay whole life, universal, variable, and variable universal, but they are all derived from the same basic concepts of offering permanent protection and building a cash value account. Since I don't believe in buying life insurance as an investment, you're probably wondering if I ever think whole life is a good idea. The answer is yes—as long as it gives you the most protection at the lowest cost. That usually happens at around age 50 or so.

You see, term insurance grows increasingly more expensive as you get older (obviously the risk that you'll die increases as you get older, so the insurance company wants to be compensated more as that risk increases). By about age 50, whole life insurance generally ends up being less expensive, so that's when I believe it makes the most sense. If you're over 50 and can find a term policy with a safe insurer that is cheaper, by all means, buy that.

Secret #285
The Biggest Trap of Whole Life Insurance

By now you've probably noticed that I'm not particularly fond of whole life insurance. It's more expensive than term, and it offers the unnecessary "savings element," which I feel shouldn't be coupled with life insurance. But let's say you don't agree. Say you don't mind paying the extra premiums because you figure it'll force you to save some extra money, and in a few years, when you no longer need the life insurance protection, you'll let the policy lapse and withdraw the cash value.

Fine. I just want you to make sure that you get all the protection you need. The biggest mistake most people make is letting the type of policy dictate the amount of protection. This can be dangerous. Remember, you want the *most protection for the lowest cost*.

If you need $500,000 to provide adequately for your children, but you can't afford the premiums for a $500,000 whole life policy, don't settle for a $400,000 whole life policy! Buy $500,000 worth of term instead. After all, the reason you're buying life insurance in the first place is to protect your family. Do you really want to cut back on the death benefit just so you can have a cash value account?

Secret #286
The Truth About Cash Values

Most people misunderstand how life insurance policies with cash values work. Most people assume that the cash value account works like a regular savings account and that its value is not linked in any way to the face value of the policy. Not true. If you purchased a $100,000 policy and had built up $10,000 in cash value, your beneficiary would still receive only $100,000 upon your death. What happens to the $10,000 in cash value? It's forfeited.

The only way to get access to the cash value in your life insurance is by "borrowing against it" or relinquishing the policy. You see, you don't actually own the cash value the way you own a savings account. It's part of the death benefit that is paid to your beneficiary. So whether you have $10,000 or $90,000 in cash value, if you have a $100,000 policy and no outstanding loans, your beneficiary still receives a $100,000 death benefit (or whatever the face amount of the policy is).

Why bother building a cash value then? Well, you can choose to borrow against it. The idea here is that you buy the life insurance for death protection when your children are young and living at home. Then when the children are grown and can take care of themselves, you use the cash value for income. In this situation, your death benefit will decrease as you withdraw the cash value, but you won't need it anymore anyway. So if you had a $100,000 policy with $10,000 in cash value, you may borrow the $10,000, and if you died before you paid it back, your beneficiary would receive only $90,000 (the $100,000 face value minus the $10,000 loan).

Another option is to forfeit the entire policy. That way, you receive the $10,000 in cash value, but you have no more death protection at all. Of course, you also have no more premiums, which is why some people take this approach when they no longer need life insurance.

Just be sure you know what you're getting into when you buy cash value insurance. It isn't an investment on top of life insurance protection. If you leave the money in the account, neither you nor your beneficiary will ever see it.

Secret #287
What's Wrong With Return of Cash Value Policies

Some people just can't accept the idea of paying higher premiums to build up a cash value account, but getting the same death benefit as they would if they had no cash value (see Secret #286). To satisfy this desire to get both the face amount of the policy plus the cash value at death, insurance companies came up with the idea of "return of premium" or "return of cash value" policies. In a word, these are a rip-off.

They don't return your premium or your cash value. Period. What they do is charge you higher premiums because you're actually buying two policies. With the return of cash value policy, you're actually buying two whole life insurance policies—one to provide the face amount and one to provide an amount equal to the cash value of the base policy.

In the return of premium form, you're supposedly getting the face amount of the policy plus all the premiums that have been paid (as long as the person insured dies within a certain period of time). In reality, you're buying a basic whole life policy, which will pay the face amount plus an increasing term insurance policy. The term policy has a face value that grows as the amount paid in premiums grows.

As you can see, neither policy really returns the cash value or the amount you've paid in premiums, and as such, both types of policies are worthless.

Secret #288
The Truth About Vanishing Premiums

The "vanishing premium" gimmick is another attempt by insurance companies to reel in consumers with a promise that seems (and is) too good to be true. The idea is you'll pay premiums for a number of years, but eventually, you'll be able to stop paying premiums, yet still keep the insurance policy intact.

Like the return of cash value and return of premium policies, the vanishing premium policy is too good to be true. The concept is based on the premise that the cash value in the policy will earn enough in interest and dividends to pay for future premiums. Of course, there may be enough to pay for *some* future premiums, but the assumption is that you'll have enough to pay for *all* future premiums. This is highly unlikely. It requires that the company meet aggressive investment projections.

If you're considering buying a policy that promises vanishing premiums, be sure to find out what interest rate assumptions the company is using to provide for the vanishing premium. Then compare that rate to the actual interest and dividends the company has paid out over the past 10 years. If the target interest rate is much higher than the actual rate paid, consider the vanishing premiums a vanishing promise.

Secret #289
What's Wrong With Buying Life Insurance on a Child

Selling couples life insurance on a young child has become all the rage lately. Insurance agents claim it's a superb way to finance a college education. After all, they say, it offers tax-free accumulation of earnings, and the child will never have to worry about qualifying for insurance again.

Excuse me? *Qualifying for life insurance?* I haven't met too many children who have any need for life insurance whatsoever, let alone need to worry about qualifying. I mean, how many kids do you know who are supporting their families? Last time I checked, lemonade stands and paper routes weren't paying *that* much.

Remember, the only purpose for life insurance is to replace a breadwinner's income stream. If you have no dependents, you don't need life insurance. And if you are a dependent (like a child), you certainly don't need life insurance.

Secret #290
How to Ensure You're Getting the
Lowest Premiums

With any type of insurance, it is difficult to compare different policies from different companies because each offers different features and options. Enter Select Quotes. For a $50 fee, this price comparison service will search its database of 17 companies to find the five lowest-price term insurance policies that meet your needs. Call 800/343-1985 for more information.

Or try TermQuote at 800/444-8376. They'll compare prices of the six to seven insurance companies they represent for the lowest one. You don't pay TermQuote a fee at all. Both services receive a commission from the insurance company if you buy through them.

Secret #291
Another Way to Slash Your Premiums

Another way to cut your insurance premiums is to buy from companies that don't use agents. When you cut out the agent, you cut out part of the commission, and that savings can be passed on to you. Two such low-commission companies are: Lincoln Benefit (800/525-9287) and USAA (800/531-8000).

Secret #292
Eight Kinds of Insurance Never to Buy

You've got to hand it to them, if nothing else, insurance companies are creative. Who else would come up with the idea of health insurance on your pet? It's a nifty idea—definitely worth a chuckle, but not worth one dollar of your hard-earned cash. Here are some other insurance policies to avoid:

- *Wedding insurance.* You pay around $125 for $3,000 worth of coverage if your wedding dress rips on the big day or there's a fire in the reception hall. Now I ask you, if you're that concerned about something going wrong, will $3,000 really make up for the loss?

- *Rental car insurance.* In most cases, you'll already be covered under your own car insurance policy or under a perk associated with your credit card. And even if you don't have coverage, if you're renting in Illinois and New York, collision coverage is already included in the price of the rental car.

- *Contact lens insurance.* These policies typically cost around $20 a year and pay to replace a lost or damaged contact lens—hardly a catastrophic loss. If you know you tend to lose or tear your contacts often, buy from one of the discount places recommended in Secret #293 instead. It'll cost you about the same as the insurance premium to replace one lens.

- *Mugging insurance.* Talk about specialized and ridiculous! Mugging insurance pays when you're hurt or you die in a mugging. Call me nuts, but if you're concerned about paying for medical bills or protecting your dependents in case of your death, wouldn't you want insurance that would provide health or death benefits no matter what the cause?

- *Limited health or "dread disease" policies.* Like mugging insurance, these policies are ridiculously specialized. They only pay if you contract certain diseases, like cancer or polio—as if you wouldn't need health benefits if you got multiple sclerosis.

- *Air travel insurance.* Like mugging insurance and "dread disease" policies, this kind of insurance provides super specialized benefits—in this case, death benefits only if you die in a plane crash. Again, if you have dependents or have other reasons for buying life insurance, do so. Don't buy coverage for something that is very unlikely to happen and will only pay off in one circumstance.

- *Vacation insurance.* If rainy weather put a damper on your beach vacation, it's a real shame. But it's hardly a catastrophe worth insuring. This goes into the category of "America's Most Unbelievable Insurance Policies."

Yes, you sure can admire them for their creativity. These policies are kind of like commercials, a mild diversion worth a laugh or two. Just make sure you don't *buy* any of them.

11
Live Like a Prince on a Pauper's Paycheck

Saving money has always been somewhat of a sport for me. Whether it's finding a pair of jeans at 50 percent off or snatching a pair of theater tickets for half price, I just love a bargain.

So you can imagine how I felt when wholesale food clubs, like Price Club and B.J.'s Warehouse came into vogue. Four hundred thousand square feet of discounts. Pure heaven.

But lately I've noticed some folks have taken this bargain-hunting thing to extremes. Reusing plastic bags? Shopping for wedding dresses at garage sales? Now I don't know about you, but that kind of takes the fun out of deal-chasing for me. I mean, I like to save money as much as the next guy, but making your own Bisquick? Come on!

If you're like me, and you want to cut costs, but you're not willing to shop for your daughter's prom dress at the Salvation Army, read on. I think you'll find a few ideas that may interest you.

Secret #293
How to Save Up to 70 Percent Off the Cost of Contact Lenses

It's happened to me four or five times in the past three years: A month or two after I get a new pair of contacts, I tear one. Then I have to spend another $40 or $50 to replace it. Since I'm practically blind and I haven't been able to find a pair of glasses comfortable enough for me to wear day in and day out, I guess I'm stuck buying three or four new lenses a year. Fortunately, I've discovered an excellent way to cut the cost: Buy your contact lenses through the mail.

Contact Lens Supply promises to save you up to 65 percent off the cost of your lenses. For example, a pair of Ciba soft lenses at Contact Lens Supply cost just $46 compared to $80 from a full-price retailer. You'll need a doctor's written prescription to order, and there's a $4 shipping charge. Call 800/833-7525 for a brochure. You'll even get a coupon for $5 off on your first order.

Lens Express (800/666-LENS) is another mail order contact lens supplier that gives you discounts. For a $25 fee (good for three years), you can become a member of the service, which offers you up to 50 percent off both contacts and eyeglasses—my Ciba soft lenses were $45 a pair. You can also use Lens Express without joining. You'll just pay an extra $10 to $15 per pair. But if you join, you only pay the $8.95 shipping charge on your first order. After that, shipping is free.

Although I was pleased with the prices, it did seem to be a bit of a hard-sell operation. When I called to place my order, the salesperson tried to talk me into signing up for some automatic replacement program where new lenses are sent every three or four months. I wasn't interested, but it took a few minutes to convince him. If you can overlook that flaw, Lens Express offers good prices and convenience. I was able to do everything over the phone—they even called my doctor for me to get my prescription.

The Ultimate Contact (908/264-1177) is another membership service. But like Lens Express, you can opt not to join and just pay a slightly higher fee per pair. This service promises to save you $8 per pair if you join, plus you get free brand name cleaning products—a nice bonus, considering what contact lens solution and cleaners cost these days.

Secret #294
How to Get China and Crystal at
Up to 65 Percent Off

Like most young couples, when my husband and I got engaged we registered at a department store. We picked many beautiful things,

things we knew we probably wouldn't get, but we selected them because we liked them, and we figured we'd buy them for ourselves some day. As it turned out, our guests were a lot more savvy than we were. We were showered with Gorham crystal bowls, Lenox wine glasses, and Sasaki silverware. Yet our registry showed that people hardly bought us a thing! What our friends and relatives knew that we didn't was that you can buy top-quality china and crystal at up to 65 percent off from your own living room—if you know where to look.

We received a great many presents from Ross-Simons Jewelers (800/556-7376), which offers discounts on china, crystal, flatware, and gifts. This place is a gold-mine of values on names ranging from Baccarat to Wedgewood. And with over 2,737 patterns in stock, chances are, even if something isn't in the catalog, Ross-Simons can get it for you. I was particularly impressed with their service. We had to return something that had gotten damaged in the mail, and the customer service representatives handled the situation quickly and efficiently.

Barrons (800/538-6340), Midas China & Silver (800/368-3153), Nat Schwartz & Co. (800/223-3003), and The China Warehouse (800/321-3212) also offer discounts of 15 to 65 percent on china, crystal, silver, and flatware from names like Lenox, Mikasa, Gorham, Waterford, Royal Doulton, and Christian Dior.

If you aren't hooked on buying the real thing, Irish Crystal Company (804/496-8363) manufactures and sells quality copies of Waterford crystal. Everything originates in Ireland, so you can still feel a bit of Irish magic in every piece.

Secrets #295–299
Five Ways to Cozy Up to 40 to 70 Percent
Savings on Furniture

Furniture is one purchase where quality really counts. Cheap furniture really does tend to wear easily, and more expensive furniture really does last longer. That is not to say, however, that you have to pay "expensive" prices to get expensive furniture. The following secrets will help you find high-quality pieces at bargain basement prices.

Secret #295
Buy From a Furniture Rental Store

You've heard of buying barely-used cars from car rental places, why not use the same technique to get discounts on furniture? In fact, furniture rental places often have clearance centers where you can find stylish pieces at up to 50 percent off, and many places will even deliver. Look in your local yellow pages for furniture rental stores under "Clearance" or "Discount Centers."

Secret #296
Buy the Contents of a Model Home

Ever wonder what builders do with the furniture they have in model homes after they've sold the models? Many cities have model home clearance centers, such as Builders Model Home Furniture Store in Chantilly, Virginia (703/803-1090), where you can find wonderful groupings of brand new furniture and accessories. Check the Home section of your local newspaper or the yellow pages under furniture for a model home clearance center near you.

Secret #297
Buy Directly From the Manufacturer

Most furniture is made in North Carolina, so why not go there and buy it directly from the source? It's really not such a far-fetched idea. In fact, I know people who've spent the weekend in North Carolina just to buy furniture! But you don't have to go that far. You can buy direct from North Carolina without leaving home—simply order by phone. Shop around at local furniture stores, copy down the style numbers, and call one of the following showrooms for prices:

- Mallory's (P.O. Box 1150, Jacksonville, NC 28541; 910/353-1828) has been in business over 40 years and has two 30,000-square-foot showrooms of furniture in styles ranging from contemporary to country French and everything in between. If you can't find what you want at a local retailer, call and describe what you're looking for and Mallory's will send you brochures and catalogs. To order, send a 25 percent deposit (payable by Visa,

MasterCard, or check), and you'll get a receipt, itemizing each piece. The balance is due on delivery by cashier's check, certified check, or money order.

- House Dressing Furniture (2212 Battleground, Greensboro, NC 27408; 800/322-5850) promises to save you 40 to 50 percent on more than 200 different manufacturers. Call for a free brochure.

- Village Furniture House (146 West Ave., Kannapolis, NC 28081; 704/938-9171) advertises savings of up to 70 percent off retail on 300 brand name manufacturers. Plus, Village Furniture House offers worldwide delivery.

Secret #298
Buy Good Quality Reproductions

The Bombay Company (800/829-7789) makes eighteenth and nineteenth century reproductions at affordable prices. Although the quality is not quite up to Ethan Allen standards, I was pleasantly surprised by the features and detail work on a desk and filing cabinet I bought there. The desk had a pull-out drawer for a computer keyboard, and the filing cabinets came with decorative keyhole locks and easy-glide drawers. Besides, you've got to love a store whose motto is, "Good taste doesn't have to be expensive."

The Bombay Company's sister company, Alex & Ivy, offers similar deals on country furniture. Call 800/359-2539 for a catalogue.

Secret #299
Buy From a Kit

Yield House is a catalog company that offers both finished and ready-to-assemble furniture in country, Shaker, and Mission styles. The prices for the ready-to-assemble furniture run about one-third less. Call 800/258-4720 for a catalog.

Secret #300
Two Ways to Slash Your Prescription Drug Costs

You can get thousands of prescription drugs at savings of up to 50 percent off through Family Pharmaceuticals of America, a mail-order pharmacy. All you need to do is send in a written prescription with your check or credit card or have your doctor call (quantities must be in hundreds). Your prescription will be delivered by first class mail, complete with invoice copies for your insurance company. The charge for shipping and handling is $1.50. Call Family Pharmaceuticals at 800/922-3444 for a price quote.

Action Pharmacy (800/452-1976; 207/873-6226) works much the same way, but Action charges less for shipping and handling (postage is free up to 3 pounds, and handling is just 75 cents). Action also sells over-the-counter drugs, from antacids to vitamins, at a discount. And when you ask for a catalog, Action will send you a coupon good for $5 off your first order.

Secret #301
Where to Buy Vitamins at a Discount

For discounts on vitamins and other natural therapies, try Nutrition Warehouse Inc. Nutrition Warehouse sells its own line of discounted vitamins as well as Solgar and Twin Labs brands at 20 percent off. Shipping and handling is $3. Call Nutrition Warehouse Inc. at 800/645-2929 or 516/741-2929 for more information.

Secret #302
Where to Find Huge Savings on Cookbooks

Like to cook and try out new recipes? Find yourself drawn to big cookbooks with glossy pictures whenever you're in a bookstore? Then you'll love Jessica's Biscuit. Jessica's Biscuit is a discounted mail-order firm specializing in cookbooks of all types. From barbecuing to biscuits, chili to cheesecake, macrobiotic to microwave, they've got them all—and at huge savings too. Call 617/965-0530 for a free catalog.

Secrets #303-314
Twelve Ways to Sleep Cheap While on Vacation

Lodging can really eat into a vacation budget—often it's the single most expensive cost of a vacation. Doesn't it make sense, then, to find out how to cut that cost? The first step is to understand the hotel business from the hotel's perspective. Hotel rooms are perishable items. They must be booked in order for the hotel to make money. So every night a hotel room isn't booked, it's essentially costing the hotel money. Hence, the prevalence of discounts.

Of course, hotels won't advertise all the discounts they offer. After all, they want to get the highest price possible. It's up to you to take the initiative. The following tips and tricks will help you slash your lodging costs by 30, 40, even 50 percent or more. Now that's something to give you a good night's sleep!

Secret #303
Call the Hotel Directly

What most people don't realize is that the way you make your reservation can save you money right off the bat. If you use the 800 number, for example, you'll only hear about published discounts. That's because the folks at central reservations aren't located anywhere near the site you're going to and therefore, have no sense of how desperate the location you're interested in is to book rooms. If, on the other hand, you call the hotel directly, the reservations clerk will know about any specials the hotel is offering at the time to fill rooms.

What if the hotel doesn't have any published specials, but you suspect they could be desperate for your business? Simply ask the reservations clerk, "Is that the best you can do?" If the hotel is underbooked, the clerk will most likely come back with a lower rate. Even if the hotel isn't underbooked, the clerk may offer a cheaper rate. After all, it's better for the hotel to be booked at 80 percent capacity, with a little less profit, than to be booked at only 70 percent capacity.

And if you don't get any satisfaction with the reservations clerk, ask for the hotel manager. The hotel manager is the person with the greatest power to save you big bucks. So put on your negotiating shoes and start talking. Let the hotel manager know how frequently you travel to that location. Mention that you'd like to find a nice place to stay and to come to back again and again. Then ask if there's any way the hotel manager can cut the rate for frequent travelers. You'd be amazed at how well this works. Remember, few hotels are ever booked at 100 percent capacity. There's stiff competition out there, and most will do whatever they can to get your business.

Secret #304
Ask for Weekend, Seasonal, or Holiday Rates

Hotels depend on business travelers for their bread-and-butter business, which means Friday and Saturday nights can be dead in many hotels. To stimulate vacation business, many hotels offer special rates for weekend and holiday travel. Even if there aren't special weekend or seasonal rates, hotels often slash their rates just to attract your business. The trick is to act like you expect there to be a special rate. That way, if there is one, the reservations clerk will assume you know about it.

Secret #305
Ask for Affiliation Discounts

Lots of hotels offer discounts for AAA members, government employees, airline frequent flyer club members, and AARP members, to name a few. When you get on the phone, have a list of all of your affiliations. Run down each one with the clerk, asking for discounts. Be sure to go through your whole list, since some affiliations offer better discounts than others.

Secret #306
Be Flexible

In the hotel business, value is all in the timing. A hotel in a resort area that may command $300 a night in the summer would likely go for half as much in the winter. But even if you can't change the month or season of your travel plans, you still may be able to cut the price of the hotel room by being flexible about your travel dates. Ask the reservations clerk if you could cut the price by changing either your date of arrival or departure. Sometimes one night either way can shave as much as 20 percent off the bill.

Secret #307
Be on the Lookout for Special Promotions

Hotels run ads for special promotions all the time. If you see a special rate in an ad, be sure to mention the ad when you book. But even after you've already booked a room, keep an eye out for promotions. Most hotels will give you the promotional rate even after you've booked at another rate. Once again, all you have to do is ask.

Secret #308
Offer to Pay Up Front

Paying in advance is unheard of in the hotel business, which is exactly why offering to do so can command steep discounts. Marriott has adopted a formal prepayment plan that gives you discounts of up to 50 percent off on many Marriott properties if you pay 14 to 21 days in advance. Ask for Marriott's Advance Purchase Rate when you call to make your reservation.

Secret #309
Use a Discount Booking Service

Buying in volume can lead to big discounts no matter what you're purchasing, and hotels are no different. That's how the following booking services can offer discounted hotel rates.

Quikbook (800/789-9887) offers discounted hotel rooms in 22 U.S. cities. For hotels just in and around Washington, D.C., call Capitol Reservations (202/452-1270) or Washington, D.C. Accommodations (800/554-2220; 202/289-2220). Express Hotel Reservations (800/356-1123; 303/440-8481) offers discounts in New York and Los Angeles. For hotels in Miami, Orlando, New York, and San Francisco, try Central Reservation Service (800/950-0232; 305/274-6832). And in San Francisco, call San Francisco Reservations (800/677-1550; 415/227-1500). And if you're going to London or Paris, try Hotel Reservations Network (800/964-6835). Hotel Reservations Network also books rooms in major U.S. cities.

Secret #310
Ask About Packages

It used to be that vacation packages offered a lot of extras that nobody ever wanted, like free tote bags. Today, packages can be real money savers, especially if your trip includes air travel. To ensure that you're getting a good deal, first calculate the cost of each individual item in the package. Then consider whether you would have used each item if it weren't included in the package. If, for example, you don't exercise, it doesn't matter how much a free trip to the hotel spa saves you. But if combining three nights at the hotel with dinner and a show slashes the nightly room rate by 20 percent, then a package is a great deal.

Secret #311
Swap Houses

Hotels aren't the only lodging around. In fact, there are numerous unique lodging options available to the knowledgeable and adventurous traveler. Take house-swapping. Not an idea most people would consider, but it has a number of unique advantages, like it's *free!* You contact a home exchange agency, such as Intervac Home Exchange (800/756-4663), to find someone who lives in the place you want to visit and who wants to visit your hometown. The exchange agency arranges the swap. Other exchange agencies and home swapping services include: Vacation Exchange Club (800/638-3841), Loan-a-Home (914/664-7640), Worldwide Home Exchange Club (301/680-8950), Trading Homes International (800/877-8723), and The Invented City (800/788-2489).

➤ **Inside Tip:** Before you consider a home swap, make sure your homeowners insurance policy doesn't preclude you from leasing to or housing nonfamily members. If it does, you'll have to absorb any property damage by the swap family yourself. Or consider buying a rider that will cover the home exchange. Call your insurance agent for details.

Secret #312
Stay in a Hostel

If you're willing to rough it, consider staying in a hostel. You'll pay around $8 to $20 a night. And although you may be required to do some chores, some hostels can be quite nice. Contact Hostelling International-American Youth Hostels (P.O. Box 37613, Washington, DC 20013; 202/783-6161) for more information.

Secret #313
Stay in a College Dorm

Wish you could go back to your college days? Why not relive the experience on your next vacation and save a bundle to boot? Lots of colleges open their dorms to travelers in the summer. Rates generally range from $15 to $30 per night. Contact The Campus Travel Service (P.O. Box 5486, Fullerton, California 92635; 714/525-6625 or 800/525-6633) for its annual "University Residence Guide." The guide costs $12.95 and lists more than 700 participating campuses all over the world, including universities in Australia, New Zealand, Great Britain, France, Germany, Austria, and Spain.

Secret #314
Stay at a YMCA

YMCAs aren't just for community activities. Twenty-seven Y's in the United States and 13 Y's abroad provide cheap lodging to travelers. Contact *The Y's Way* (224 East 47th St., New York, NY 10017; 212/308-2899) for more information.

Secret #315
Join a Discount Travel Service and Cut All Your Travel Bills by Up to 50 Percent

If you travel frequently, consider joining a discount travel service. For around $50, you'll get discounts on hotels, car rentals, meals, entertainment, and air fares. The trick is to find the service that best fits your needs. For example, America at 50 Percent (800/248-2783; 410/825-3463) publishes a travel book that lists 1400 hotels across the country (mostly Holiday Inns, Best Westerns, and Ramada Inns). Each hotel offers members a 50 percent discount off the rack rate. In addition, members can get car rental discounts and a 5 percent rebate on certain air fares. The cost to join is $49.95 for the first year and $24.95 after that.

Quest International (800/325-2400) also offers a 50 percent discount on hotels, but the participating hotels are more along the lines of Sheratons, Hiltons, and Marriotts. The fee to join is $99 per year.

The International Airline Passengers Association (800/527-5888) is a bit more expensive to join ($99 per year) but it provides members with discounts of 10 to 40 percent off more than 4,500 hotels worldwide.

Encore (800/638-8976; 301/459-8020) offers 50 percent discounts on more than 4,000 hotels in the United States, Canada, and Europe as well as 25 to 50 percent off on small inns and bed & breakfasts. Plus, Encore members receive a 20 percent discount on meals at about 300 restaurants as well as car rental discounts. And if you make your airline reservations through Encore, you're guaranteed to get the lowest fare at the time you book. The membership fee is $49 per year.

The Privilege Card (404/262-0222) provides half-price rates at more than 1,000 independent hotels for your $49.95 membership fee and offers a reservation service for an additional fee.

If you prefer to stay at resorts, check out World Hotel Express (800/482-7847), which offers 50 percent discounts at 3,000 hotels and resorts worldwide in addition to discounted air fares and cruise reservations. Membership fee is $49.95 per year.

And for the total entertainment experience, check out Entertainment Books by Entertainment Publications (800/477-3234). These books, which are sold for specific cities around the country, offer 50 percent discounts on 2,500 hotels in the United States and 1000 hotels in Europe as well as discounts on car rentals, amusement parks, movies, sports, theater events, and meals (see Secret #333).

Secret #316
Shop Around for Great Travel Deals
(Or Let Someone Do It for You)

If you have the time to shop around for bargains, there are literally hundreds of great travel deals available at any given time. Problem is, most of us don't have the time. Enter Travelers Advantage (800/548-1116). For a $49 annual fee, Travelers Advantage acts as your discount travel agency, finding and booking great deals for you on hotels, car rentals, trains, cruises, and air fares. Travelers Advantage guarantees you the lowest travel rates and even sweetens the deal with an extra 5 percent off every booking you make through the service. You can try the service for free for three months, and if you aren't satisfied, cancel and receive a full refund.

Discount Travel International (800/359-0212) offers a similar service for $45 a year, including discounted air fares, cruises, vacation packages, and 50 percent off hotel rooms at over 900 Sheratons, Hiltons, Westins, Holiday Inns, Quality Inns, Best Westerns, and Radissons. Discount Travel International specializes in selling unsold trips and vacation packages all over the world. Plus, every time you book a charter, tour, or cruise through DTI, you get an extra 7 percent off, and every time you book a flight through DTI, you get an extra 5 percent off. DTI is so convinced you'll save money with the service, it promises a free trip to Paris if you don't save at least double your membership fee every time you book a week-long trip for two.

➤ **Bonus Secret:** When you join Discount Travel International with a credit card, you automatically become a member of The Buying Network, a discount shopping service that promises to save you up to 50 percent on over 275,000 brand name consumer products. You can call The Buying Network's toll-free number 24-hours a day to get price quotes. Now that's what I call added value!

Secret #317
The Easiest Way to Find the Cheapest Air Fare

Have you ever called an airline and asked for the price of a particular trip, then called back the next day and gotten a completely different price? If this scenario sounds familiar, take heart. You're not alone. The airline computer systems are so complex, and fares change so frequently, it's common for even airline employees to be in the dark as to certain fare changes.

But there is a way you can be assured of getting the lowest possible fare: Go to an agency that specializes in low fares, like Traveltron. Traveltron is a division of California-based Associated Travel, the fifteenth largest travel agency in the United States. Unlike most travel agencies, which simply use their computer systems to search for fares before they book flights, Traveltron has its own specialized software program that will continually search for the lowest possible fare, 24-hours a day, even after you book your flight.

First, you give the Traveltron agent your dates of travel, destination, and preferred times. Then Aqua, Traveltron's proprietary computer system, goes to work. It ranks all the available flights on your route according to lowest fare. Then it checks to see if that is the lowest fare available; if not, it puts you on a waiting list and continues to monitor the airlines to see if a lower fare comes up.

"So when management puts a new fare on the market at midnight, we get it first," explains Marilyn Voss, manager of Traveltron. Voss estimates this system allows Traveltron to offer fares around 8 to 10 percent lower than other travel agencies.

To reach Traveltron, call 714/545-3335. If you end up booking your ticket through the agency, send in a copy of your phone bill, and Traveltron will reimburse you for the phone call.

Secrets #318–321
Four More Ways to Cut Air Fares

There are so many different ways to cut air fares, it's gotten to the point that virtually no one pays full price anymore. The following secrets will ensure that you always get a good air fare.

Secret #318
Book Through a Consolidator

Consolidators buy large blocks of unsold seats from airlines to sell to individuals and travel agencies. Because they buy in bulk, they get deep discounts, which they pass onto you. For example, TFI Tours International (800/745-8000) flies to 177 cities worldwide from 227 cities in the United States, promising "scheduled service at charter rates." Other consolidators include Travel Bargains (800/872-8385), Euram Tours (800/848-6789; 202/789-2255), Travac Tours and Charters (800/872-8800), and Unitravel Corp. (800/325-2222). Unitravel even promises to beat any consolidator's fare. Now that's what I call a deal!

Secret #319
Buy From a Rebater

The way travel agencies make money is through commissions from airlines, hotels, and other travel providers. In order to attract business, some travel agencies rebate part of their commissions. Travel Agency of Chicago is one of the best-known rebaters. Call 800/333-3335 to see what kind of deal they can get for you.

Secret #320
Fly a Small Airline

A number of small airlines offer rates that can be as much as 60 percent off regular rates. The catch: They tend to serve limited areas. For example, Kiwi International (800/538-5494) currently only flies out of Newark, Chicago, Atlanta, and several cities in Florida. Likewise, Morris Air (800/466-7747) only serves the western half of the United States. But if you can meet the requirements, these airlines can offer good deals.

Secret #321
Take Advantage of a Fare War Even If You've
Already Booked Your Ticket

It's tough to know when it makes sense to buy a ticket early and when to wait, since you never know when fare wars are going to start. But what most people don't know is that airlines will allow you to exchange a ticket you've already purchased for one at a cheaper price as long as you qualify for the lower fare. Simply call the airline and ask to have your ticket reissued. The airline may charge a $25 to $35 fee, but in most cases, you'll still come out ahead.

Secret #322
Barter for Travel Deals

Bartering is making a comeback, and fortunately, you don't have to be selling rugs in an Arabian bazaar to take advantage of it! All you have to do is book your travel plans through a barter travel agency. Here's how it works: When airlines, hotels, restaurants, and car rental companies want to advertise, they sometimes offer the advertising agency credit for their services instead of payment. The advertising agency then sells the vendor chits to a barter travel agency, which sells them to you.

For example, Reciprocal Merchandising Services is a barter travel club that provides discounts of 25 to 40 percent on air fares, 25 percent on cruises, 25 to 50 percent on hotels, and 30 percent on dinners at over 250 restaurants in New York City, Chicago, Los Angeles, Miami, Philadelphia, and San Francisco. Dues are $50 per year. Call 212/244-3562 for information about joining.

Secret #323
Book Your Trip at the Last Minute

Sometimes the cheapest way to travel is to pick up and go at the last minute. There are numerous clubs that specialize in booking last-minute travel vacations at a discount. Take Worldwide Discount Travel Club (800/446-9938), which offers up to 50 percent off on last minute flights, hotels, motels, and condominiums and up to 40 percent off on cruises and car rentals. Moment's Notice (212/486-0500) offers a similar service for $25 per year. Moment's Notice acts as a broker between cruise lines, airlines, and other travel wholesalers, enabling you to get discounts of up to 60 percent.

If you're interested in package trips, try the Short Notice Vacation Savings Card, available from Encore (800/444-9800). For a $36 annual membership fee, you can have access to the Short Notice Vacation Hotline, which describes last-minute cruise and land packages at deeply discounted rates. A similar service is offered by Baltimore Travel Center (800/752-5299; 410/837-3400), but you can call the Baltimore Travel Center hotline (800/548-8546) without paying a membership fee. Most of the trips on this hotline depart from the Baltimore/Washington metropolitan area.

Secrets #324–330
Seven Ways to Take a Luxury Cruise for
50 Percent Less

In the cruise business, sometimes it seems as though there are as many different prices for a single cruise as there are passengers on the ship. The trick is to make sure you're one of the passengers who gets a good deal. Following are my seven favorite strategies for cutting cruise prices down to size:

Secret #324
Sail at Off-Season Times

The first two weeks in January, the week after Easter through May, and Labor Day through the first two weeks in December are the off-season periods for most American cruise lines. This is when you'll get your best deals. In Europe, the off-season is early spring and fall.

Secret #325
Book Early or Book Late

The very worst time to book a cruise is about two months before you plan to sail. That's when you'll pay the absolute highest price. Book earlier (like six to nine months in advance) or book later, but never book with two months' lead time.

If you book early, you'll save hundreds off the published price. When you book late, ask for a "Sea Saver Fare." These fares are available when a cruise line has a large number of unsold cabins. They're typically made available about four weeks before the sailing date. Call that day to get the best fare.

Or, if you really want to go at the last minute, call the cruise line the night before a sailing. If they have any unsold cabins (very likely during off-season), you should be able to get a hefty discount.

Secret #326
Go to a Cruise Consolidator

Cruise consolidators work much like airline consolidators, selling unsold cabins at deep discounts. Try WorldWide Cruises (800/882-9000), South Florida Cruises (800/327-7447), Cruise Line of Miami (800/777-0707), or Spur of the Moment Tours & Cruises (800/343-1991).

Secret #327
Use a Discount Clearinghouse

Vacations to Go (800/338-4962; 800/446-6258) is a discount clearinghouse for the major cruise lines, offering travelers big savings on cruises, as well as airline travel and car rental discounts. For a $19.95 annual fee, you receive four issues of *Vacations* magazine and postcard notifications of short-notice specials.

Secret #328
Go to a Specialist

Some travel agencies specialize in cruises. And because they book in large quantities, they're able to get discounts. National Discount Cruise Company (800/788-8108) is one such agency. A representative of American Express, National Discount Cruise Company claims to "deal with every cruise line available." They promise expert knowledge of the cruise business and good deals too.

Secret #329
Go With Friends and Travel Free!

If travel agencies can get discounts by booking in volume, why shouldn't you? Most cruise lines will offer you a free trip if you book a cruise for 10 friends. Sometimes travel agencies do the same thing. National Discount Cruise Company, for example, will give you a free cruise when you book eight cabins. Call National Discount Cruise Company (800/788-8108) or your favorite cruise line for details.

Secret #330
Sail Standby on the QE2

If you've ever dreamed of sailing on the QE2 but couldn't afford the fare, you may get your chance. Call 800/528-6273 or 800/221-4770 and ask for QE2 standby fares. You'll be put on a waiting list, then, within three weeks of departure, you'll be notified of whether or not you can get on the cruise. Of course, you have to be flexible to do this, but we're talking about huge savings.

For example, the lowest price regular fare on a ship from New York to Southampton when I called was $2,340. The standby rate was $1,099, and that was in an *upgraded* room. Bon voyage!

Secret #331
For 60+ Readers Only: How to Cut Air Fares by More Than 50 Percent

Just about every major airline offers coupon books for senior citizens for deeply discounted air fares. For example, TWA (800/221-2000) recently offered a deal for travelers over age 62: a book of four one-way air travel coupons good for travel anywhere in the continental United States for $496. American, America West, Continental, Delta, Northwest, United, and USAir offer similar programs. All of the programs have certain restrictions and blackout dates, so be sure to plan your travel times well in advance to be sure you can use the coupons.

Secret #332
How to Slash Hundreds Off a Club Med Vacation

The secret to enjoying all the luxury of a Club Med vacation at hundreds less than the regular price is to take advantage of Club Med's Wild Card vacations. As with a regular Club Med vacation, you'll enjoy sun and fun at an all-inclusive resort; the only difference is Club Med picks the location for you. Call 800/CLUB-MED for details.

Secret #333
How to Dine Out All the Time for Half Price

Entertainment Publications (800/477-3234) publishes entertainment books that offer discounts at hundreds of local restaurants for 120 cities throughout the United States. Sold through charities, nonprofit organizations, bookstores, and department stores, the books retail for $35 to $40 and feature hundreds of half price coupons for restaurants of every style and price range. In addition, the books include discounts on hotels, car rentals, video rentals, dry cleaning, car repairs, flowers, balloons, and clothing.

The entertainment books are limited to one city or one region, however. If you want to branch out, consider joining Premiere Dining (800/346-3241). For $49 a year, you can enjoy two meals for the price of one at over 7,000 independent restaurants and 15,000 restaurant chains nationwide.

Secrets #334–335
Where to Buy Gorgeous Flowers at Bargain Prices

Sending flowers is a great way to brighten anyone's day, but starting at $35 for a bare-bones bouquet, flowers aren't a cheap gift. The following secrets are two little-known ways to get high-quality flowers at low, low prices.

Secret #334
Buy Directly From the Growers

Beauty, freshness, and bargain prices all rolled into one are what you can expect from Calyx & Corolla, a San Francisco-based mail-order firm that sells gorgeous flowers at discount prices. Because Calyx & Corolla ships directly from the growers, they're able to cut out the middleman. This not only cuts the cost to you, but it also ensures you're getting the absolute freshest flowers possible. You'll find deals like a dozen long-stemmed roses for $59 or a basket of spring orchids for $39.50. Call 800/800-7788 for a catalog—it's so beautiful it'll make you want to send flowers to everyone you know!

Secret #335
Buy From American Wholesale Floral

American Wholesale Floral is a chain that sells flowers and plants for dirt-cheap prices. I'm talking really cheap, like $10 for a dozen long-stemmed roses! American Wholesale Floral also does weddings and parties. Look in your local yellow pages for a store near you.

Secret #336
How to Negotiate for Better Prices on Clothes

Retailers are much more willing to negotiate their prices than most consumers realize. This is especially true of small stores when you can speak directly with the owner. To get the best deal, shop at off-peak hours when business is slow, and you won't have to worry about other customers. Try to find some flaw in the merchandise and ask for a discount. If there is no flaw, offer to pay cash. Since retailers must pay their banks a percentage of every credit card transaction, they're saving money when you pay in cash. So why not ask to share in the savings?

If you can't pay in cash, offer to buy in quantity. The more you buy, the more profit the retailer makes, so why not ask for a price break for your loyalty?

Finally, don't be intimidated by elegant stores. I once saw a beautiful designer suit in Frugal Fannies (one of those bargain-basement stores where you have to try on clothes in a group dressing room), but it wasn't in my size. The next day, I was passing by Nordstrom's and lo and behold, they had the same suit—in my size! Only it was hanging in the designer fashion department, and it was selling for *double* the price. Before I could lift my chin off the floor, I saw an elegantly-dressed saleswoman sashaying toward me.

"May I help you?" she asked.

Without thinking, I blurted out, "Yes. I saw this same suit yesterday at Frugal Fannies for half the price. Will you match it?" My heart was pounding; I had never uttered anything so crass before in a store where the dressing rooms had plush sofas and magazines in them.

But without missing a beat, the saleswoman replied, "Absolutely. I'll just have to confirm the price."

And confirm she did. Not only did I get a gorgeous Christian Dior suit for half price, but I got to try it on in the luxury of soft lighting, three-way mirrors, and a sofa more plush than anything I have in my own home.

Secrets #337–340
Four Ways to Shave 20 to 80 Percent Off the
Cost of a Wedding Gown

When I planned my wedding, I felt a little like Alice in Wonderland. Everything you would normally do in shopping and pricing goods and services seemed to get thrown out the window. I got so swept up into the romance of it all, suddenly I'd find myself thinking $450 sounded darned reasonable for a pair of shoes I'd only wear once. Before you get carried away like I did, consider the following secrets for cutting the price of one of the biggest single purchases for your wedding: the dress.

Secret #337
Rent It

Have your eye on a $2,000 designer wedding gown, but can't stomach the price? No problem, rent it! Rental shops for bridal attire are located all over the country. Just look in your yellow pages under "Bridal Shops." In Washington, D.C., for example, Just One Affair (202/686-7255) rents wedding gowns for $100 to $300, including alterations and cleaning. And many rental shops also have mother of the bride and bridesmaids dresses too.

Secret #338
Buy the Gown From a Consignment Shop

I didn't rent my wedding dress, but the price I paid to buy it was almost as low because I bought it at a consignment shop specializing in bridal gowns. It was a fabulous dress, unique and stylish, and I paid just $400 for it. But the price wasn't the only good thing about buying from a consignment shop; the selection was terrific. I never saw anything like my wedding dress in any of the traditional bridal shops or even in any bridal magazines. What's more, the experience of buying it was just as special and personalized as if I had bought it in a fancy boutique. Look for bridal consignment shops in your yellow pages or the classified ads of your local newspaper.

Secret #339
Shop the Classifieds

It's a sad, but true, fact that weddings are canceled every day, oftentimes long after the dress is bought, the flowers are ordered, and the reception site is booked. While flower orders and reception site bookings can be canceled, not much can be done with an already-altered wedding dress—except sell it. Check the Sunday classifieds of your local paper for deals. You'll find never-worn wedding dresses as well as used dresses. It can be a gold-mine of bargains!

Secret #340
Buy Your Dress Wholesale

As they say in the discount biz, "why pay retail?" Why indeed. Especially when you can buy a designer gown for 20 to 40 percent off the advertised price from Discount Bridal Service (800/441-0102; 800/874-8794). Once you find the dress you like, simply call Discount Bridal Service and ask for a price quote. If the price is right, you can place your order and have the gown shipped directly to your home. But make sure you call well in advance. Some gowns are shipped directly from the manufacturer, but others are ordered through buyers and may take longer.

Also, you'll need to arrange for your own alterations, but Discount Bridal Service representatives can often refer you to good local seamstresses. And don't forget your bridesmaids. You can also order bridesmaids dresses, flower girl dresses, and mother of the bride dresses through Discount Bridal Service.

For more tips on slashing wedding costs, consult Denise and Alan Fields' *Bridal Bargains: Secrets to Throwing a Fantastic Wedding on a Realistic Budget.* It gives some of the best secrets I've heard of for cutting the cost of everything from invitations to photography.

Secret #341
How to Buy Diamonds at a Discount

If a custom-made engagement ring excites you, but the price makes your head spin, have I got a deal for you! Diamonds by Rennie

Ellen sells diamonds of every shape and size set to order at up to 75 percent off retail. It may be hard to imagine buying ruby earrings or a sapphire pendant through the mail, but Rennie Ellen includes a detailed invoice with each purchase and accepts returns within five working days. For a catalog, call 212/869-5525 or send $2 to Diamonds by Rennie Ellen, 15 West 47th Street, Room 401, New York, NY 10036.

12

You Can't Take It With You But You Can Decide Who Gets It: *Estate Planning Basics*

"Estate planning? Who me? I thought that was only for people with names like Rockefeller, Trump, and Kennedy."

Au contraire, my friend. The fact is all of us are going to die sometime. And all of us have accumulated assets—a home, furniture, treasured photographs, or paintings that have been in the family for generations. Of course, to us they aren't assets. They're memories, mementos of our lives. And we certainly don't want them put up for sale at a Sunday afternoon flea market!

Enter the estate plan. Whether you have a complex estate valued in the millions or just a simple home with 2.4 cars and a dog, it's vital that you make provisions for your death or disability when you're capable of doing so. For if you don't, someone else will do it for you.

Secret #342
Eight Good Reasons for Estate Planning—Even If You Think You Aren't Wealthy

Despite the formality of the name, an estate plan in its most basic form is merely a will. And everyone—single, married, divorced, with kids, without kids, with a lover, without a lover—should have a will. Here are eight good reasons why you need a will and why you may need to do some extra estate planning beyond that:

1. *You'd rather not have your prized thimble collection on display at the local county fair six months after you die.* It may not be that bad, but you can be sure that without a will, the state will dispose of your property as it sees fit. And state laws don't take into account who will most appreciate what you have. So your prized thimble collection could be given to your husband who's allergic to thimbles or your great grandmother's antique armoire could be given to your daughter who thinks anything older than Macauley Caulkin belongs at the Goodwill. If you want any say whatsoever in who gets what, write a will.

2. *You have children who are minors.* Without a will, the court will decide who acts as guardian of your children.

3. *You've remarried and have children from a previous marriage.* Without a specific trust, your new spouse would likely get everything, which may be exactly as you wish. But when she dies, your children from your first marriage could be left out in the cold. Secret #361 gives details on how to ensure they are provided for.

4. *You're single and have a lover.* Without a will or a trust, everything will go to your parents.

5. *You have a lot of property, but little cash.* The IRS values property on a fair market value basis for tax purposes. Never mind that your heirs may not have a prayer of getting that price if they sold it today. The IRS doesn't care. It wants the estate taxes (up to 55 percent of the value of the property) in *cash* and quick (within nine months after death). That leaves your heirs in a tough bind: They either have to sell the property at sacrificial prices or borrow in order to raise the money to pay the taxes.

Proper planning can reduce or even eliminate the estate tax burden on your heirs. See Secrets #349 and #358 for details.

6. *You don't have much—except for your spouse and children.* Without a will, the state may divide your assets equally between your spouse and children. If you don't have much, your spouse may not have enough to live on and won't be able to tap the children's share (except to provide for their support).

7. *You have children with a tendency to spend frivolously.* If the state or even your will, names your children heirs, they'll have

access to all your money when you die—even though that may be at a time when they aren't yet capable of handling it properly. With proper planning you can ensure your children still receive their inheritance, but not until they can handle it intelligently.

8. *You don't want everything you own announced on prime time television after your death.* If you're an ordinary citizen with a relatively small estate, it's unlikely that anyone but your heirs will be interested in what you own. But be aware that wills are public documents. If you have any kind of celebrity status or any interest in protecting your privacy, find ways other than a will to dispose of your assets (see Secrets #346, #347, and #348).

Secret #343
What to Include in a Will

I hope by now I've sold you on the importance of writing a will. If not, go back and read Secret #342. A will not only ensures that you've clearly stated your wishes, but it can also speed the process of transferring your assets to your heirs and relieve your relatives of the difficult task of trying to figure out what you would have wanted.

Make sure you hire a lawyer to draw up your will. Lawyers are experienced at drafting wills and can ensure your wishes are stated explicitly in language that won't be misunderstood by the courts. Lawyers are paid to be familiar with little-known state inheritance laws that could prevent your wishes from being carried out. And lawyers can advise you on special techniques to dispose of your property outside of a will.

When you prepare your will, be sure to include:

- A statement revoking any prior wills you may have written
- Provisions for payment of your debts
- Provisions for payment of your funeral expenses
- Any special wishes you have regarding burial
- Provisions for disposal of your property
- Specific provisions for disposal of other assets

- Bequests to charitable or religious organizations
- The name of your executor
- Names of guardians for your children if they are minors
- A simultaneous death clause that dictates how you want your property transferred if both you and your spouse die simultaneously in a common disaster

Once the will is drafted, be sure to update it as needed. For example, as you have more children, you'll want to name them in the will. Likewise, as your children have children, you'll want to include them in the will too. Also, if you move out of state, be sure to update your will. If your will has to be probated in a state different from the one you wrote it in, it could take longer.

Secret #344
How to Choose an Executor for Your Will

If you think it's an honor to be named executor of someone's will, think again. It's a thankless, time-consuming job, requiring assets and property to be assembled and appraised, creditors to be notified, bills to be paid, life insurance to be claimed, investments to be managed, and taxes to be paid. Of course, the executor doesn't have to be a financial expert, she can work with a lawyer to help her. But the executor does have to be responsible, organized, detail-oriented, and tactful (to be able to deal with your heirs).

Before you name a loved one executor, consider how well she'd be able to manage the job. If she has the right qualities, then by all means, ask her. Just be sure she knows about it before you make it official. Naming someone executor without her permission doesn't do her or your heirs any good.

Secret #345
Why It Could Take Years to Settle Your Estate

Okay, you've drafted a will, named a responsible friend executor, and everything should pass to your heirs according to your wishes immediately upon your death, right? Guess again.

There's a little thing called probate that can make passage of property rather time-consuming. Probate is the legal system for proving that your will is valid and ensuring that your property passes to the people whom you intended to get it.

Even if you have a fairly simple estate and a specific will, it can take six months to a year for your estate to go through probate (and that's after states passed simplification laws, which have considerably shortened the process). And if you have any complications whatsoever, the process could literally take years.

That's why it makes sense to consider options other than a will for bequeathing at least some of your property. These include: joint ownership, naming specific beneficiaries, and setting up trusts. See Secrets #346, #347, and #353 for the best ways to use these strategies.

Secret #346
When Joint Ownership Makes Sense—
And When It Could Cost You Big

Joint ownership, or more precisely, joint tenancy, allows everything that's held in two people's names to pass to one owner upon the other owner's death without going through probate. It makes perfect sense for married couples as long as the value of their assets is less than $600,000.

But if their assets are worth more than $600,000, joint ownership could eventually trigger an estate tax when the second spouse dies.

The reason: Each of us gets a one-time $600,000 lifetime exemption from estate taxes. That means you can leave up to $600,000 to anyone you choose, and the money will not be subject to estate taxes (but it may be subject to other taxes). Anything above $600,000 is taxed at an exorbitant rate—up to 55 percent— with one exception: You can leave an unlimited amount to your spouse without triggering any estate tax.

So if you die and all of your property is held jointly with your spouse, your spouse inherits everything and pays no estate tax. But guess what happens when *she* dies? Anything over $600,000 is subject to estate taxes.

"Now wait a minute," you may be saying. "What happened to the $600,000 exemption for me?" Aye, there's the rub.

By holding property jointly, everything passed to your spouse, and your $600,000 exemption was lost. This could have been avoided if the property was held in such a way as to allow your heirs to claim your $600,000 exemption.

How to do this? Set up a family trust that allows the surviving spouse to gain all the income from marital assets during his or her lifetime, but protects both spouses' $600,000 exemptions upon death (see Secret #356 for details).

Estate taxes are also a key reason why assets shouldn't be held jointly between two people who aren't married. That's because half the value of the jointly-owned assets will be subject to estate taxes upon the first owner's death (remember, the unlimited exemption is only for spouses). What's more, the IRS treats the property as a gift to the survivor if the other person owned it first. And that means it could be subject to back gift taxes and penalties as well.

Besides estate taxes, joint ownership could be a potential trap for nonmarrieds who have special concerns about who inherits their property. Say, for example, that you own a beach house with a friend. Upon your death, you want her to have it and upon her death, she wants you to have it. Since that's how joint ownership works, you have no problem. But after you both die, you want the property to be donated to charity for use as a camp for disabled children. Both of your families understand your wishes.

But what happens if you die first? She now has full ownership of the property. But say her long lost, 'neer-do-well son blows into town shortly after you die and wins over your friend's heart. He spends a few weeks with her and then she dies. He goes to court, waxes poetic about reuniting with his mother, and boom! Young James Dean has turned your camp for disabled kids into *Animal House.*

To avoid this situation, own property as tenancy in common rather than joint tenancy. That way, each person owns 50 percent of the property and maintains that ownership stake even after the first person dies. Upon each owner's death, his 50 percent passes to his heirs according to his wishes. So special considerations can be taken into account, like providing for children from a first marriage or ensuring that unwanted heirs do not get access to the property.

Secret #347
How to Name Beneficiaries for
Maximum Advantage

When you name a beneficiary of a particular asset, like an IRA or a life insurance policy, that asset is transferred directly to whomever you named without going through probate. It will still be part of your estate and, therefore, subject to estate taxes, but you'll save your heirs time and money by avoiding probate.

Unfortunately, naming beneficiaries is often done once with little thought, and then forgotten. This can be a big mistake. What happens if you get divorced and then remarried? If you don't update your beneficiaries, your ex-wife and her new mate could end up inheriting the pension plan you worked 30 years to build.

Or what if you have two children, one who lives close by and one who lives across the country? You're filling out some forms for an annuity and your daughter just happened to stop by. Since she's there and can give you her Social Security number on the spot, you name her the beneficiary of your annuity. Then what happens when you die? Your daughter inherits your life savings the day after your death and your son has to wait two years while the house and rental properties go through probate.

Save your family a fight. Update your beneficiary designations regularly—especially whenever there is a major change in your life, like marriage, death, or birth of a child.

Secret #348
The One Tragic Possibility Everyone Should Be
Prepared for, Yet So Few Are

When people think about estate planning, death is usually the first thing that comes to mind. You write a will, name your heirs, plan for your assets and property to be disbursed. But what happens if you become disabled or mentally incapacitated? Who will handle your affairs then?

"That won't happen to me," you claim, "I have disability insurance."

Of course you do. And who is the beneficiary of your policy? You are? That's the common practice, but how do you plan to apply for the benefits and sign the checks you receive if you are in a coma? You see, most people think of "disability" as losing a limb. But more often than not, it's having a stroke or losing memory.

"Okay," you say, "but what if I own everything jointly with my spouse? She can take care of me if I become mentally incapacitated."

Yes, she can—maybe. But the courts can also freeze all of your joint assets if you are declared legally incapacitated. And even if your assets aren't frozen, what if your wife needed to sell your home in order to pay for your care? She wouldn't be able to do that without your signature since you own the property jointly. She would still have to go to court to petition to be able to sell your property.

It's vital that you plan for situations like this. One of the best ways is to set up a living trust and name a spouse or trusted loved one as a co-trustee. With such a trust, you can spell out exactly how you would like to be taken care of, should you become unable to do so yourself. (See Secrets #350 to #354 for details on what a living trust can and can't do for you.)

Secret #349
The Greatest Myth About Living Trusts

Living trusts are touted as the greatest invention since cappuccino, but much of the hype is just plain false.

The biggest lie of all: Trusts enable you to avoid estate taxes. Sorry to say, it's just not true. Most trusts are revocable living trusts, and they do not avoid estate taxes.

Only an *irrevocable trust* avoids estate taxes. But an irrevocable trust is just that, irrevocable. Once you put assets in an irrevocable trust, you can't take them back. Essentially, you are revoking all ownership rights. So if you decide to set up an irrevocable trust, make sure that whatever you put in it belongs there, because there's no going back! See Secret #358 for the smartest way to fund an irrevocable living trust.

Secrets #350-354
Five Good Reasons to Set Up a Living Trust

Even without the ability to avoid estate taxes, living trusts are a great estate-planning tool. They allow you to maintain control over your assets while you are alive, but still position your assets in a way that makes transfer after your death as smooth as possible.

But living trusts are not for everyone. They can be expensive to set up and require an enormous amount of paperwork to maintain. The following secrets give the best reasons for setting up a living trust:

Secret #350
Living Trusts Allow Your Heirs to Take Possession of Your Assets Immediately

All property that is not jointly held, does not have a named beneficiary, or is not in a trust must go through probate. Probate is a lengthy process that can cost thousands of dollars and take years to settle—especially if there are complications. Avoidance of this process is one of the main reasons people set up trusts. Property in a trust passes directly to your heirs immediately upon your death.

And although trusts are three to five times more expensive to set up than wills, they are much more difficult to contest. If you think there is any reason that your family would contest your will (e.g., because you've left everything to your cat), then a trust makes sense for you. Not only will the trust make it harder for your family to contest your wishes, but it also gives your designated heirs immediate access to your property. With a will, all assets are frozen until probate is finished, which means the only people getting rich off your money could be the lawyers.

Secret #351
Living Trusts Make Your Estate Cheaper to Settle

Since assets in a trust don't have to go through probate, trusts make it cheaper to settle your estate. With a will, 3 to 5 percent of your assets will be eaten up in probate costs. With a trust, it should cost less than 1 percent to settle your estate.

Secret #352
Living Trusts Give You Complete Control

While you're alive, you can live off the income in the trust, manage the assets in the trust, even destroy the trust at your whim.

The trust is fully revocable and can be changed or managed at your discretion.

What's more, a living trust allows you to appoint a successor trustee to take care of your assets should you become unable to do it yourself. Without a trust, if you become incapacitated, the court would name someone to manage your affairs. But how could you be sure the court would make the right choice? A trust saves you this heartache by allowing you to name whomever *you* choose to manage your affairs if you become unable to do it yourself.

Secret #353
Living Trusts Are Private Documents

Probate is a public process. Therefore, any assets that go through probate become a matter of public record. Do you really want your neighbors, friends, or anyone on the street to know everything there is to know about your finances? Do you want people to know how much your heirs have inherited?

For the security aspect alone, I like trusts. But I especially like them for people who are public figures, active in the community, or celebrities.

Secret #354
Living Trusts Make It Easy to Transfer Wealth
Across State Lines

If you own property in more than one state or if you live in one state and own property in another, your estate will have to go through probate in *two* states if the property is not held in a trust. That's double the paperwork, double the time, double the expense—but certainly *not* double the fun. Avoid this hassle by putting your assets in a living trust.

One word of caution, though: Be very careful how you set up the trust. If it's done carelessly, it could trigger a hefty transfer tax.

For more information on trusts and estate planning, read Robert A. Esperti and Renno L. Peterson's *Loving Trust: The Right Way to Provide for Yourself and Guarantee the Future of Your Loved Ones* (Penguin Books, 1991). This is one of the best books on the subject around.

Secret #355
The Biggest Mistake People Make
After Setting Up a Trust

As unbelievable as it may seem, countless people go to all the trouble of setting up a trust and then forget to put anything in it. To make a trust useful in protecting your assets, it has to have assets to protect!

That means not only when you initially set up the trust, but on a regular basis, you must put assets that you want sheltered in the trust. This can be a real hassle. You'll have two to three times the paperwork to fill out when you open new accounts and acquire new assets. But it's important. After all, if you don't put anything in the trust, why have it in the first place?

Secret #356
How to Keep the IRS From Stealing Your
$600,000 Estate Tax Exemption

Everyone gets a $600,000 exemption from estate taxes, and everyone can pass an unlimited amount of money to a spouse tax-free. But if you have a sizeable estate (more than $600,000), and you leave everything to your spouse, when he dies, he'll only get his $600,000 exemption. Yours will be lost forever.

Fortunately, there is a way to remedy the situation with a special trust called a family trust. The *family trust* (also called an A/B trust, credit-sheltered trust, marital deduction trust, or bypass trust) is designed to preserve both the husband's and wife's $600,000 exemptions.

Here's how it works. Say Tom and Jane are married and have an estate worth $1,100,000. Tom dies. Upon his death, $600,000 of the couple's estate goes into a trust for Jane. This is the "A" trust. The remainder of the money, $500,000, goes into another trust. This is the "B" trust. Jane can use all of the money in the "A" trust as she pleases. It belongs to her. Technically, the "B" trust belongs to the children, but while she is alive, Jane can also use all of the income from the assets in the "B" trust too.

When Jane dies, the "A" trust goes directly to the children. And since it's only worth $600,000 (or less), it is transferred free of estate taxes. But guess what happens to the "B" trust? It also goes to the children—in fact, they technically owned it when Tom died. And since there is only $500,000 (or less) in the "B" trust, that too, is transferred free of estate taxes.

In this way, both spouses' $600,000 exemptions were preserved, and the children were able to inherit $1,100,000 without owing any federal estate taxes.

➤ **Potential Trap:** If all of the couple's assets are jointly owned, the family trust won't work. Each spouse must own enough of the couple's assets separately to fund his or her trust. That's why it makes sense in this case to own property as tenants in common. See a trust attorney for details.

Secrets #357-358
The Hidden Tax on Life Insurance
and How You Can Avoid It

When used properly, life insurance is an important estate-planning tool. But when bought without proper planning, it won't serve its purpose. The following secrets will show you the smartest way to use life insurance in your estate plan.

Secret #357
The Hidden Tax on Life Insurance

Everyone knows life insurance proceeds are tax-free, right? Right—sort of. The proceeds are *income* tax-free to your beneficiary. But if you have a policy that's in force when you die, the policy becomes part of your estate, and it is subject to *estate taxes*. In fact, the value of the policy itself could even trigger estate taxes (if it causes the value of the estate to exceed $600,000).

Secret #358
The Smartest Way to Use Life Insurance
in an Estate Plan

So then, does it make sense to get rid of all life insurance policies? No. In fact, savvy people often buy life insurance for the sole purpose of helping their heirs pay estate taxes. But if the proceeds are subject to estate taxes, that doesn't help much, does it?

The best way to use life insurance in your estate plan is to establish an irrevocable life insurance trust. This will allow you to leave your heirs a substantial amount of cash (from the life insurance policy), shelter it in a trust, and upon your death, have the proceeds paid to your children free of estate taxes. It's especially useful for people who have a lot of property, but little cash.

What's more, since the proceeds are in an irrevocable trust, they will be free from creditors' claims. That means your kids get the money before any debts have to be paid—a nice bonus.

The key to making this work is ensuring that you don't own the policy. If you do, it will be considered part of your estate and taxed accordingly. Moreover, it's not enough that you don't own the policy at death, you must not have owned it or had any control over it for the three years prior to your death (difficult for most of us to plan).

That's why it's best to have a policy purchased on your life without your ever owning it. So set up the trust first. Then give money to the trust. It's important that you do this right. The money must be gifted to the trust. You can no longer own or have control over that money. And since it's a gift, you can't give more than $10,000 a year per beneficiary or you'll have to pay gift taxes. Next, have the trust buy the life insurance. That way, you've never owned the policy, so from day one, the proceeds will be free from estate taxes.

Be sure to have an experienced lawyer prepare the documents. This area of law is very complicated, and if done improperly could result in thousands of dollars in losses to you and your family.

What if you already have a life insurance policy now? Transfer it into the trust as soon as possible. You'll still have to wait three years before it will be considered to be out of your estate, so the sooner you move it, the better.

Secret #359
Another Way to Buy Life Insurance
for Estate Taxes

If you don't want to go through the trouble of setting up an irrevocable life insurance trust, simply have your children or grandchildren buy a policy on your life. As long as you aren't the owner, the proceeds won't be included in your estate and won't be subject to estate taxes.

Secret #360
The Best Kind of Life Insurance to Buy in an Irrevocable Life Insurance Trust

Okay, so you've decided to set up an irrevocable life insurance trust to pay estate taxes upon your death. Now you must decide what kind of life insurance to buy in the trust. Without question, the answer should be joint and last survivor (also called second to die) insurance.

This kind of life insurance only pays after the second spouse has died, which is fine, since you won't need the policy until the second spouse has died. And since this kind of policy is significantly cheaper than life insurance on a single person, you'll be able to get more insurance for your premium dollar.

Secret #361
How to Ensure Your Children From a Previous Marriage Are Taken Care Of

If you've remarried and have children from your first marriage that you want to take care of, consider setting up a Q-TIP trust. The Q-TIP or Qualified Terminable Interest Property trust is designed to allow you to provide income for your spouse when you die, while maintaining control over how your remaining assets are distributed after your spouse dies.

Here's how it works: Upon your death, all the income from the trust goes to your spouse. The income is tax-free since property transferred between spouses is not taxable. When your spouse dies, the remaining assets are given to the beneficiaries you named when you set up the trust.

➤ **Potential Trap:** If you decide to set up a Q-TIP, don't overfund it. When your spouse dies, the remaining assets in the trust will be taxed, so you want to keep the amount left in the trust under $600,000.

Secret #362
What's Wrong With Giving Your Home to
Your Children Before You Die

A lot of people like the idea of giving their home to their children before they die in order to protect their assets. The problem is if you give your home to your kids before you die, they'll face a hefty tax bill when they go to sell it—a tax bill that could easily have been avoided.

Here's why: If your kids inherit your home *after* you die, their cost basis is "stepped up" to what the current market value of the home is. So if you bought the home for $20,000, but it's worth $100,000 now, your kids' cost basis will be $100,000. When they go to sell, they'll only pay taxes on anything they get over $100,000.

But if you give them your home *before* you die, their cost basis will be the $20,000 you initially paid for the house. That means when they go to sell, they'll have to pay income taxes on $80,000 worth of gains! Not such a nice gift, after all, is it?

Secret #363
How to Give Your Home to Your Children
the Smart Way

If you'd like to ensure your children get your home after you die without having to wait for it to go through probate, consider setting up a life estate. A life estate allows you to give your home to whomever you choose while you're alive without causing them to incur a huge tax bite.

Here's how it works. You hire a real estate attorney to set up the life estate (it shouldn't cost more than a couple hundred dollars). The life estate allows you to continue living in your home for the rest of your life, but it gives your children (or whomever you designate) a remainder interest in the home.

That means that when you die, they inherit your home immediately (without having to wait for it to go through probate) at a stepped up cost basis. The stepped up cost basis means all of your capital gains in the home are wiped out. It's as if your kids bought the home today. And if they choose to sell the home after you die, the only taxes they'll owe are on the gains *above the current market value.*

Let's take an example. Say you bought your home for $30,000, and it's worth $130,000 today. If the kids inherited it at your cost basis ($30,000), they'd have to pay taxes on any gains over that if they wanted to sell—that's taxes on $100,000 at current prices! But since they inherit it at a stepped up cost basis, they owe no taxes if they sell it today. And if they wait to sell it in the future, their cost basis is $130,000, so they'll only owe taxes on the difference between the sale price and $130,000.

➤ **Potential Trap:** The value of your home will still be included in your estate, so it's best to use this technique only if your estate, including your home, will be worth $600,000 or less when you die. Otherwise, you will incur estate taxes.

Secret #364
How to Give Assets to Charity and Gain a Tax Break for Life

Would you like to leave some of your property to charity after you die? If it's a substantial gift, rather than stipulating the contribution in your will, why not make it while you're alive through a special trust called a Charitable Remainder Trust? Here are the wonderful benefits of a Charitable Remainder Trust:

1. *You gain an immediate tax deduction.* You can deduct a portion of whatever you give to the trust from your taxes. And if you don't need that big of a credit in the year you make the gift, you can carry forward the deduction to future years.

2. *You gain a source of income.* While you're alive, you can use the income generated from the assets in the trust to live on.

3. *You get to leave money to your favorite charity without fear of needing it in case of emergency.* You never know when a catastrophic illness or event will require a huge amount of cash. If you make the gift while you're alive, it's gone. You have no further use of the money. With a Charitable Remainder Trust, the charity doesn't get the asset until you die. And in the meantime, you gain full use of the income generated from the asset.

4. *You can get a tremendous tax break on appreciated assets.* You can put a stock, bond, or piece of property that has appreciated sig-

nificantly since you bought it in the trust, have the trust sell it, and avoid paying the capital gains tax on it.

Since you didn't own the asset when it was sold (the trust owned it), you won't have to pay capital gains tax on it. But you still can enjoy the income from the sale of the asset since you can withdraw money from the trust while you're alive.

Secret #365
How to Give Assets to Charity Now and Still Retain Control of the Assets

If you like the idea of a Charitable Remainder Trust, but want to keep the assets in your family, try a Charitable Lead Trust. A Charitable Lead Trust is sort of the reverse of a Charitable Remainder Trust. It allows you to give the *income* from an asset to charity for a specified period of time (or your lifetime). When that time is up, the asset reverts back to the owner.

Let's take an example. Say you put $100,000 in a trust and gift the interest made on that money to charity for the next ten years. You'll get an immediate tax deduction for the full ten years' worth of "charitable contributions," and at the end of the tenth year, the $100,000 will revert back to you. The amount of your charitable contribution deduction will be based on IRS tables that determine what the value of your future contributions are worth in today's dollars. For example, assuming an 8 percent annual interest rate and a 3 percent annual inflation rate, you might get a charitable contribution deduction of $59,400.

If you decide you want to leave the principal amount to charity upon your death, you'll get an estate tax deduction too if the property remains in the trust.

For more information about setting up a Charitable Lead Trust or any other trust, contact an estate-planning specialist.

Afterword

I began investing when I was 6. That's when I started getting an allowance. I think I got 50 cents a week, and my parents made me put half of it away for my college fund.

That was the beginning of my interest in personal finance. I knew saving for college was the right thing to do—in fact, I never really thought twice about it. But if half my income was going to remain untouchable to me, I decided I better not waste the other half. So whenever I wanted something, I saved for it. Then I shopped carefully until I found exactly what I wanted. I never deprived myself—I just learned to be conscious of managing my money.

The funny thing is my parents certainly could have put the money away for me. It would have had the same effect. But that wouldn't have meant the same thing to me. I enjoyed the feeling of contributing to my own future.

This book was designed to help you manage your own finances smarter. By now you've learned ways to conquer your debt, buy a home, negotiate for a car and a raise, cut your tax burden, assess your insurance needs, invest wisely, snag a cornucopia of bargains, and plan your estate.

I hope you will share these lessons with your children. Give them the privilege of becoming financially responsible at an early age. All you have to do is model financial responsibility yourself. Set up an automatic savings plan. Pay your bills on time. Balance your checkbook. Pay off debt. Invest regularly. Give to your favorite charities. Experts say modeling is the best way to teach children behavior, so why not model financial responsibility? It's good for your kids and it's good for you too!